AF323742

DENATIONALISATION OF DEFENCE

Denationalisation of Defence
Convergence and Diversity

JANNE HAALAND MATLARY and ØYVIND ØSTERUD
The University of Oslo, Norway

ASHGATE

Published by
Ashgate Publishing Limited
Gower House
Croft Road
Aldershot
Hampshire GU11 3HR
England

Ashgate Publishing Company
Suite 420
101 Cherry Street
Burlington, VT 05401-4405
USA

Ashgate website: http://www.ashgate.com

British Library Cataloguing in Publication Data
Denationalisation of defence : convergence and diversity
  1. National security - Scandinavia 2. Security,
  International - Scandinavia 3. Privatization - Scandinavia
  4. National security - Great Britain 5. Security,
  International - Europe 6. Scandinavia - Military policy
  7. Great Britain - Military policy
  I. Matlary, Janne Haaland II. Osterud, Oyvind
  355'.033048

Library of Congress Cataloging-in-Publication Data
Matlary, Janne Haaland.
  Denationalisation of defence : convergence and diversity / Edited by Janne Haaland Matlary and Oyvind Osterud.
     p. cm.
  Includes index.
  ISBN 978-0-7546-7119-0
  1. Europe--Armed Forces. 2. Europe--Military policy. 3. Civil-military relations--Europe--History. I. Xsterud, Xyvind, 1944- II. Title.

  UA646.M28 2007
  355'.03354--dc22

2007020225

ISBN: 978-0-7546-7119-0

Printed and bound in Great Britain by MPG Books Ltd, Bodmin, Cornwall.

Contents

Contributors

Jan Joel Andersson is Research Fellow and Programme Director at the Swedish Institute of International Affairs. His research focuses on European and transatlantic security and defence policy.

Alyson J. K. Bailes has been Director of the Stockholm International Peace Research Institute (SIPRI) since July 2002. She earlier spent more than 30 years in the British Diplomatic Service. Her current research interests include European defence issues and Nordic affairs.

Bertel Heurlin. Jean Monnet Professor of European Security and Integration, University of Copenhagen since 1990, Chairman of Danish Institute of Military Studies, Co-director of Copenhagen Middle East Research Project.

Janne Haaland Matlary is Professor of International Politics, Department of Political Science, University of Oslo. She was deputy foreign minister for Norway, 1997–2000.

Anu Sallinen (M. Pol. Sc.) is a researcher at the Planning Department of the Finnish Defence Command in Helsinki. She has been an adviser at the Ministry of Defence and a researcher at the Finnish Institute of International Affairs.

Ragnvald H. Solstrand is Head of Strategy and Plans at the Norwegian Defence Research Establishment where he was previously Head of the Systems Analysis Division.

Ståle Ulriksen is the Director of the Department of International Politics at the Norwegian Institute of Foreign Affairs (NUPI) in Oslo as well as a fellow at the Norwegian Naval College in Bergen. He studies war and military issues.

Øyvind Østerud is Professor in International Conflict Studies, Department of Political Science, University of Oslo. He was chairman of the Norwegian Power and Democracy Study 1998–2003.

Preface

Military defence has been radically transformed in nearly all Western countries after the end of the cold war. The Clausewitzian trinity of people, state and army is disintegrating. Major indicators of the new era are the dual processes of internationalisation of force projection and privatisation of military support.

Still, these processes are non-uniform and unsynchronised, even if there might be causal linkages between them. The Nordic region is a testing ground for these non-uniform processes of change. The Nordic countries differ among themselves, and they diverge from the pattern in dominant states like the UK and the USA. Nordic trajectories thus illuminate the mechanisms of military transformation. They bear witness to the resilience of strong state traditions on the one hand and geopolitical positions on the other. The comparative analyses in this volume brings out the basic mechanisms at work.

The editors are grateful for financial support from the Norwegian Research Council, the Department of Political Science at the University of Oslo, and the Norwegian Ministry of Defence. The Political Science Department has also provided a generous research environment within an overall program for studies of neo-liberal reform processes.

We would like to thank Audun Halvorsen for extensive research assistance and for editorial support. Thanks are also due to John Taylor for competent editorial assistance. We are grateful to the authors who have contributed so enthusiastically to the project.

Spring 2007
Janne Haaland Matlary and Øyvind Østerud

List of Abbreviations

ACE	Allied Command Europe
ACO	Allied Command Operation
ACT	Allied Command Transformation
ALTHEA	EU military operation in Bosnia and Herzegovina
ARRC	Allied Command Europe Rapid Reaction Corps
ASEAN	Association of South East Asian Nations
ASTOR	Airborne Stand-Off Radar
AU	African Union
AWACS	Airborne (Early) Warning and Control System
BALTBAT	Baltic Peacekeeping Battalion
C4IRS	Command, Control, Computers, Communication and Intelligence, Reconnaissance and Surveillance
CBRN	Chemical, Biological, Radiological and Nuclear
CFSP	Common Foreign and Security Policy
CIMIC	Civil–Military Cooperation
COCOM	Coordinating Committee for Multilateral Export Controls
CPA	Concerted Planning Action
CPG	Comprehensive Political Guidance
CSR	Corporate Social Responsibility
CTR	Cooperative Threat Reduction
CV	Combat Vehicle
CW	Chemical weapon(s)
EAPC	Euro-Atlantic Partnership Council
EDA	European Defence Agency
ESDP	European Security and Defence Policy
ESS	European Security Council
EU	European Union
EUBG	European Union Battle Group(s)
EUFOR RD	EU military operation in support of UN mission in DR Congo
FAC	Fast attack craft
FFV	Försvarets Fabriksverk (armaments establishment)
FLO	Forsvarets logistikkorganisasjon [Norwegian Defence Logistics Organisation]
FMLOG	Försvarsmaktens Logistik [Swedish Armed Forces Logistics Organisation]
FMV	Försvarsets Materielverk [Swedish Defence Material Administration]
G8	Group of Eight Industrialised Nations
GP	Global Partnership
GPS	Global Positioning System

GROM	Grupa Reagowania Operacyjno-Manewrowego [Operational Mobile Reaction Group], Polish Special Forces unit.
HCOC	The Hague Code of Conduct
HEU	Highly enriched uranium
HKV	Högkvarteret [Swedish Armed Forces Headquarters]
HQ	Headquarters
HRF	High Readiness Force
HRF-L	High Readiness Force – Land
IAEA	International Atomic Energy Authority
ICRC	International Committee of the Red Cross
IFOR	Implementation force (NATO) in Bosnia
IO	International Organisation
IO/PG	Interoperability/Partnership Goals
ISAF	International Security Assistance Force in Afghanistan
ISTAR	Intelligence, Surveillance, Target Acquisition and Reconnaissance
IT	Information technology
JSF	Joint Strike Fighter
J-STAR	Joint Surveillance and Reconnaissance aircraft
KFOR	NATO's Kosovo Force
LANDJUT	Allied Land Forces Schleswig-Holstein and Jutland
LPD	Landing Platform Dock
MANPADS	Man-portable air defence systems
MNC-NE	Multinational Corps North-east
MoD	Ministry of Defence
MSIAC	NATO Munitions Safety Information Analysis Centre
MTCR	Missile Technology Control Regime
NAC	North Atlantic Council
NATO	North Atlantic Treaty Organisation
NBG	Nordic Battlegroup
NCO	Network-centric operations
NCW	Network-centric warfare
NGO	Non-governmental Organisation
NH-90	Helicopter model (NH-90 programme)
NMSA	NATO Maintenance and Supply Agency
NORDAC	Nordic Defence Materiel Cooperation
NORDCAPS	Nordic Coordinated Arrangement for Peace Support
NORTRASHIP	Norwegian Shipping and Trade Mission
NRF	NATO Response Force
OCC	Operational Capabilities Concept
OECD	Organisation for Economic Co-operation and Development
OEF	Operation Enduring Freedom
OHQ	Operational Head Quarters
OSCE	Organization for Security and Co-Operation in Europe
PARP	Planning and Review Process
PFP	Partnership for Peace

PGM	Precision Guided Munitions
PNG	Papua New Guinea
PPC	Public–Private Cooperation
PPP	Public–Private Partnership
PSI	Proliferation Security Initiative
PSO	Peace Support Operation
RAF	Royal Air Force
RMA	Revolution in Military Affairs
RRF	Rapid Response Force
SFOR	Stabilisation Force (NATO) in Bosnia
SFOR	NATO's Stabilisation Force in Bosnia
SHAPE	Supreme Headquarters Allied Powers Europe
SHIRBRIG	(UN) Standing High Readiness Brigade
SPI	Strategic Partnership Initiative
UAV	Unmanned Aerial Vehicles
UN	United Nations
UNIFIL	United Nations Interim Force in Lebanon
UNITA	União Nacional para a Independencia Total de Angola
UNSC	United Nations Security Council
UNSCR	United Nations Security Council resolution
WA	Wassenaar Agreement
WEU	Western European Union
WMD	Weapon(s) of Mass Destruction
WTO	World Trade Organisation

PART 1
The Forces of Privatisation and Internationalisation

Chapter 1

Introduction: Towards the Post-national Military

Øyvind Østerud and Janne Haaland Matlary

After the cold war, accelerating during the last decade, Western countries have undertaken a swift and radical transformation of their military forces. Preparedness for defence against invading tank divisions is lower on the list of priorities. In Europe, the *peace dividend,* together with new defence objectives, has implied a downsizing of standing armies. The long-term implications for security, warfare and state sovereignty are far from clear. Internationalisation and privatisation of defence capabilities are the most spectacular features of this development, although parallel national processes are far from uniform.

In this volume, we are intrigued by the non-uniform character of the general trend towards internationalisation and privatisation as the manifest expressions of a post-national military. How are state traditions and geopolitical factors serving as prisms to the process? With the Nordic countries as our testing ground, we explore the variable character of the drive towards a post-national military. We even question the inevitability of the drive, contingent as it is on the peculiar character of national and global politics in the early 21st century.

The Nordic countries constitute an ideal test site for comparative analysis, with a wide range of similarities, but also with striking differences in defence postures. The role of the state has traditionally been quite strong in the Nordic region, with an extensive public sector, and with the military establishment as part of a broad popular mediation of civil society and the state. These countries may therefore be more robust than most against a facile market orientation and internationalisation of the military. On the other hand, their security environment and geopolitical positions are rather dissimilar, with Finland squeezed along the western fringe of the former Soviet Union, Sweden with a long tradition of formal neutrality, and Norway and Denmark as somewhat uneasy NATO countries from the late 1940s. This Nordic pattern makes for intra-Nordic comparisons of the new revolution in defence policy and military structures.

Simultaneously, the Nordic countries are closely linked, with features that constitute a regional states system. The overall ambition with the regional and comparative focus employed here is to enhance our general understanding of the contemporary military transformation.

The major argument for delving into the military transformation of traditionally strong states like the Nordic countries are the implications for state power as such. By privatisation of military services and internationalisation of force deployment, the public monopoly of force is at stake. The driving forces, as well as the constraints on these developments, are showing peculiar modes in the Nordic area. We will demonstrate to what extent privatisation and internationalisation are different trends, although there are linkages between them.

Throughout the Western world, there has been an extensive downsizing of the military forces, with revised objectives for the national defence. The defence of national territory is perceived as less precarious in times of crisis, less prone to full-scale occupation, while well equipped and highly mobile forces are seen as more suitable in deterring and fighting political-military provocations at home and abroad. The capacity for limited international operations is generally more prevalent in military planning after the end of the cold war. The capacity for territorial defence is scaled down, while the readiness for participation in crisis situations outside the collective defence area is enhanced.

In the Nordic countries since the end of the cold war, military expenditures in per cent of GNP have declined from 2 to 1.5 per cent in Denmark, from 1.6 to 1.2 per cent in Finland, from 3 to 2 per cent in Norway, and from 2.6 to 1.6 per cent in Sweden (SIPRI Military Expenditure Database). While Finland has retained a substantial part of her active forces during the ten years after the mid-1990s, the three Scandinavian countries have reduced their total forces radically during the same period. Norway had commenced force reductions already in the first half of the 1990s. The reduction of military volume is most pronounced in Sweden, down to 42 per cent of the forces of the mid-1990s, while Finland seems to be least subject to radical downscaling and reform.[1]

At the most general level, the military transformation is a challenge to the Weberian notion of the state as a monopoly of the legitimate use of force (van Creveld, 1999). This monopoly – and thereby the core of modern statehood – might disintegrate as a sequel to the change of the military institution. If this is really the case, there are epochal dimensions to the transformation, even if the range of change is uncertain, the process uneven and the long-term consequences opaque. The Weberian state, however, should not be seen as fixed entity. There is a continuum in the public control of legitimate force, with the complete monopoly as an ideal type (Avant, 2005). There seems to be a general movement along the control-of-force continuum, although the pace and localisation of individual countries differ even within Northern Europe.

Modern defence, as it emerged in the Western world throughout the 19th and substantial parts of the 20th centuries, was intrinsically connected to the development of the nation-state. Mass armies based on general conscription were led by a gradually more professionalised national officer corps. The task of the citizen-soldiery was to deny occupation of the national territory, to re-conquer occupied land, to deter or pre-empt aggression from other states. Military forces were adapted to warfare. The military was a world apart from civilian society, but it was also a national institution with a high degree of participation and legitimacy.

---

1   Comparisons based on numbers from The International Institute of Strategic Studies, *The Military Balance*, from 1990–1991; 1995–1996; 2000–2001 and 2005–2006.

The citizen-soldier replaced the mercenary as the national state emerged, based on popular legitimisation, in the wake of the revolution in France. The revolutionary wars in defence of the Republic represented a breakthrough for the national popular army fighting for the collective interest. This military order – including a professionalised and democratised officer class – gradually became generalised throughout Europe, concomitant with popular nation-building (Howard, 1976; Bond, 1984; Jones, 1987).

It seems reasonable to argue that this military order culminated with the cold war. The idea of national defence was deeply entrenched in the decades after the Second World War – territorially oriented and based on broad mobilisation, combined within tight defence alliances and ultimately tied to nuclear deterrence. The threat perception was one-dimensional and stable, with the Soviet Union as the unifying foe of the West. In the Nordic region, Norway, Denmark and Iceland constituted the Northern Flank of NATO. Finland was formally neutral within the sphere of influence of the USSR, while Sweden also stayed neutral, though a *de facto* Western ally. All the Nordic countries had a broad, territorial defence structure. For the NATO members, territorial defence against aggression was based on the idea of *time of denial*, until major allied forces were in place.

This model is the backdrop to the substantial changes after the end of the cold war. The notion of territorial defence is radically redefined throughout the Western world, with Israel as an exception. Defence is less conceived as denial of occupation – a concept regarded as increasingly less relevant by defence establishments and military planners. Conscription is abolished in many countries, while reduced in duration, range and importance in the Nordic area.

There are paradoxical developments here. While the general political consensus around defence postures is reduced, the practical and operative connections between the military and civilian life make the military system less autonomous. The armed forces are subject to a *civilizing process*, with norms of gender equality, working conditions and terms of employment more harmonised with society in general. The versatility of military tasks is wider, while the national entrenchment of these tasks is weaker. The Nordic militaries are also increasingly integrated in international units where militarily stronger states, such as the UK, normally hold the commanding positions.

Multiplied and Diffuse Threats

After the cold war, the risk of traditional inter-state war seems reduced, while civil wars in former colonial and imperial areas, floating alliances across borders, and violent disorder in failed states are increasing. Post cold war defence and security policy has been redefined accordingly, although threats are more unpredictable and the separation of internal from external challenges less clear-cut.

International terrorism might bring a proliferation of weapons of mass destruction to state leaders and to non-state groups which are deeply entrenched in Western countries. In such scenarios, the defence postures of the cold war – containment and deterrence – are substantially less valid. Fighting terrorism requires a wide spectrum of methods, with international police cooperation and intelligence at the core. Armed forces are primarily useful in multilateral allied action against regimes which support terror groups with a physical infrastructure, like the Taliban in Afghanistan.

A second set of security issues is connected to ethnic turmoil, civil war and collapsed states. These issues arise with waves of migration, organised crime and a regional proliferation of conflict. This was the situation in the Balkans after the dissolution of the federation of Yugoslavia in the early 1990s. NATO forces intervened in both the acute stage of the wars in Bosnia and Kosovo, as well as in the prolonged attempt at peace-building and stabilisation afterwards. Neither in Bosnia nor in Kosovo are the basic tensions between national and social groups solved – more than a decade after the disintegration of Yugoslavia. Without the presence of intervention forces, hostilities on some level could quickly resume.

A third set of issues arose with geopolitical instability after the cold war – an arc of turmoil along the southern and south-eastern peripheries of Europe, from North Africa and the Middle East, across the Gulf area to Afghanistan and the Islamic republics of the former Soviet Union. Territorial contest and resource rivalry still characterise an unstable state system in the wake of the dissolution of the Turkish, French, British and Soviet empires. Several military interventions have been made in these areas after the end of the cold war, including forces from the UK and the Nordic NATO and Partnership for Peace members.

A fourth set of issues originates from humanitarian crises in the developing world, with environmental deterioration, flooding and droughts, intensified by ethnic rivalry. Humanitarian aid is increasingly inseparable from the political conflicts; it might turn the tide of the local power struggle one way or the other, and often requires military backup from UN forces or private security contractors – linking previously unrelated fields of policy and increasing the Western engagement in these regions.

This complex pattern of security risks – with unpredictable ramifications also in more stable parts of the world – has entailed new ways of deploying military forces.

A Defence Agenda Beyond Warfare

Following the new pattern of conflict, the Western military has expanded its range of objectives in addition to the ability to fight. Forces are deployed in peacekeeping operations during periods of ceasefire, with blue UN helmets or under allied command. Soldiers from different countries do humanitarian work in crisis situations, or they serve as escorts and guards for NGOs. Military units construct refugee camps, undertake mine clearing, assist in reconstruction of the infrastructure, and pursue tasks of pacification that border upon, or even imply, police work. It is a general characteristic of international operations that the borderline between military and police work dissipates after the more acute stage of war-fighting. This applies to the multinational forces in Bosnia Herzegovina and Kosovo as well as in Afghanistan and Iraq. The armed forces participate in a low intensity war where warfare, anti-terrorism, peacekeeping and the struggle against crime blend into each other. The role of the military is far less well defined than during the cold war era.

International operations have varying degrees of connection to homeland defence – from pre-emptive strikes, to the quest for international stability, and to the more humanitarian arguments for intervention. Several states may participate in a joint effort, but from quite different or composite national motivations, be they alliance construction, diplomatic visibility and domestic considerations, or the effort to reduce migration and the spread of crime. Therefore, the development of national niche capabilities might be a new military motive, even pure military specialties with little or no relevance for territorial defence. Small countries like the Nordic states will be subordinate partners in international operations, even if they might try to excel in specialised tasks that are primarily developed to acquire goodwill and relevance within the different alliances and international organisations.

The capacity for national mobilisation of the military defence has decreased rapidly within this new and complex environment. The defence policy debate in many Western countries circles around the question of whether the need for territorial mobilisation is relevant at all, or if the ability to defend the territory against occupation belongs to a bygone age. On the other hand, the new and broader military objectives have led to closer contact with the civilian sector, like aid and development agencies, NGOs, commercial companies and diplomatic institutions – both nationally and internationally. Due to operations abroad, the national defence is also integrated in multinational force deployments, often under the command of foreign officers. NATO, the UN, and to some degree the EU, have moved in this direction, even if there is an even tighter integration between subgroups of likeminded countries. Norway and Denmark, for instance, have particularly close ties to military forces in Holland, Germany and the UK.

There is already an element of denationalisation implicit in the structure of security challenges after the cold war, with territorial defence lower down on the scale of priorities. There is also an argument for privatisation of military services in this structure, even if the force of that argument has been recognised quite differently in the Nordic countries.

The Peace Dividend and Rising Cost of Technology

Downscaling the heavy territorial defence is also influenced by a combination of technological and economic considerations. The composition of military forces is conditioned by the new information technology. Weapons systems and command and control networks are computer-based. Force impact, precision, time of reaction and flexibility are improved. The post-cold war *revolution in military affairs* (RMA) is strongly dominated by the United States, but has radical consequences for force composition and military organisation in all Western countries. The downscaling of standing troops has been necessary for the ability to finance the new and increasingly more expensive technology.

Simultaneously, all Western countries have collected the so-called *peace dividend* by reducing defence budgets after the end of the demanding arms race in the cold war. Hence there evolved an acute contradiction between the heavy territorial defence, with high costs of maintenance and salaries, and increasingly expensive technological weapons systems, including the platforms at sea, air and land. The new threat perception and the change of priorities indicated a way out of this contradiction. It provided a *rationale* for downscaling military manpower, reducing the use of conscript troops, and the closing of local bases and defence infrastructure through geographic concentration.

The driving forces in the radical military reforms in the Western world are found in the interaction between the new patterns of conflict, technological modernisation and reduced budgets. The new Western military is generally more slender, more technological and mobile. It is also geographically more concentrated, and with a less autonomous corporate culture. Generally, the military is less exclusively oriented towards warfare. Women are more numerous in the military forces in most countries. The more complex and changing political environment requires officers with analytical skill and international knowledge. The result is a wider market for *soldier-academics*, often with a university degree in addition to military training (Moskos et al., 2000: 8, 86).

These new force structures and technological improvements have proved extremely effective in the initial stages of high-intensity warfare in international operations. The United States attained far better precision bombing in the war against Iraq in 2003 compared to the Gulf war a decade earlier. In 1999, Serbian troops could be bombed out of Kosovo with a minimal deployment of ground forces. On the other hand, protracted stabilisation and peace-building still seem to require a larger deployment of ground troops. This is the acute US dilemma in Iraq, where long term objectives only seem to be attainable, if at all, with manpower beyond present US capabilities. International operations face a severe problem if the acute stage of warfare and the stage of stabilisation afterwards require quite different capabilities for intervention.

The move towards a more post-national military implies that the popular identification with the armed forces is weaker, even if the gap between military and civilian culture is less pronounced. Also, the distance between the military strategic debate and the views of defence policy among non-experts is wider since the military objectives are more complex. Budgetary means might decrease still further under the post-national condition, with the reform policy accelerating downwards in terms of military volume.

The Non-Linear Transformation

The notion of a post-modern or post-national defence is tied to specific organisational trends. They include closer ties between military and civilian spheres, an obliteration of the difference between support services and combat forces, an expanded range of military objectives beyond warfare, a multinational integration of troops in international operations, and an extended role for international defence organisations (Moskos et al., 2000).

In summary, a general trend towards denationalisation can be found in these concrete elements:

- privatisation of military functions, indicating that defence as a public institution around a public good is weaker
- partial dissolution of the state monopoly on legitimate force by national and international market orientation of military services
- abolition or reduction of general conscription
- the military forces as a diplomatic and alliance building institution rather than a tool for maintaining national sovereignty
- closer integration of multinational forces in permanent organisations as well as in ad-hoc coalitions in acute crisis situations beyond the homeland.

Some of these elements are central to the Nordic military reforms, but not in a standardised way or to the same extent. Some of them are more much more profound in countries like the UK than they are for the Nordic countries. Some of the changes are also launched with an official interpretation that anchors them firmly to national defence requirements. Indeed, they may serve national purposes. Alliance building and multinational participation is explicitly intended to serve the military needs of the Nordic countries in a more efficient way than a small country can manage alone. Neither is conscription abolished in the Nordic countries, even if it comprises a steadily shrinking proportion of the male cohorts and has relatively reduced importance compared to professional forces.

In the following chapters, two of the most direct measures of denationalised defence will be analysed in depth – internationalisation and privatisation. Internationalisation of Nordic military forces is well advanced and developing fast in the UN, NATO, EU and in bilateral or multinational force compositions within the organisations. Privatisation is far less pronounced in the Nordic countries compared to, for instance, the UK and the USA, but there is still a tendency towards privatising or outsourcing logistics and support services. Nordic troops also interact directly with private military companies in the international operations in which they take part.

The contemporary trend towards a post-national military imply a form of military organisation that is radically different from the institutional trinity between state, people and defence that has characterised the last two hundred years in the West. We do not know how far these trends will go, or whether they will provoke counter-reactions leading to re-nationalisation or to other and more unpredictable models. The current trend might neither be unfulfilled nor inevitable. The two-level comparison of the following chapters aims at a more nuanced understanding of the current processes of military change.

The Contents of the Volume

The chapters of Part One – *Forces of Privatisation and Internationalisation* – analyse the broad background factors and consequences of the processes of change in modern armed forces, using the two dimensions of privatisation and international military and security integration as an explanatory framework. The privatisation of armed forces generally, on a global and European level, is spelled out by Øyvind Østerud.

Military integration in practical and political terms is analysed by Ståle Ulriksen and Janne Haaland Matlary respectively. Alyson Bailes's chapter focuses on the shifting nature of the boundary between the market and state control, illustrating the ways in which the private sector can decisively influence important aspects of security.

In the comparative and empirical part of the book – *National Defence Beyond the State* – the authors analyse how, and to what extent, the process of denationalisation has manifested itself in the Nordic countries and the UK during the last decade. The country-specific case-studies focus on contemporary reforms and changes in the armed forces and wider defence sectors of the countries in question, analysing whether and how these developments confirm the thesis of denationalisation along the two dimensions.

Privatisation of defence assets comes in different shapes. There is outsourcing of support functions, logistics and the use of contractor services at home and on deployed operations; there are also public-private partnerships and private financing of acquisition and procurement. Defence cooperation and alliance requirements affect the shape of privatisation, as do the national approaches to reform of the public sector.

Ragnvald Solstrand gives a close-up analysis of force deployment and the various types of public-private cooperation in Norway. The analysis is an assessment of the possibilities for securing a core of military activities for public control, while preserving the dynamics of partnership in designed areas. Bertel Heurlin and Jan Joel Andersson analyse the processes of reform in military capabilities and strategic postures in Denmark and Sweden respectively. Both countries have transformed their defence forces quite radically after the end of the cold war. Finland, on the other hand, has retained more of the former military volume as a measure against potential territorial aggression. Anu Sallinen provides an account of the degree of military reform in Finland.

The mechanisms of denationalisation of defence are non-uniform in the Western world. State traditions and position in the international system interact to affect the dual processes of internationalisation and privatisation.

References

Avant, Deborah. (2005), *The Market for Force* (Cambridge: Cambridge University Press).

Bond, Brian. (1984), *War and Society in Europe* (Bungay, Fontana).

Howard, Michael. (1976), *War in European History* (Oxford: Oxford University Press).

The International Institute for Strategic Studies, *The Military Balance 1990–1991; The Military Balance 1995–1996; The Military Balance 2000–2001; The Military Balance 2005–2006* (London: IISS).

Jones, Archer. (1987), *The Art of War in the Western World* (Oxford: Oxford University Press).

Moskos, C. et al. (eds) (2000) *The Postmodern Military. Armed Forces after the Cold War* (Oxford: Oxford University Press).

Stockholm International Peace Research Institute (SIPRI), *Military Expenditure Database.* Available at http://www.sipri.org/contents/milap/milex/mex_ database1.html (Accessed August 2006).

Van Creveld, Martin. (1999), *The Rise and Decline of the State* (Cambridge: Cambridge University Press).

Chapter 2

The New Military Revolution – From Mercenaries to Outsourcing

Øyvind Østerud

In many states, the military is no longer a public monopoly. Military services is a growing industry. Private companies have expanded into the traditional areas of the national defence establishment, like logistics, maintenance, guard duties, training, support services and intelligence. Private contractors have been fighting in civil wars and interstate conflicts. Similar to the present situation in Iraq, where private military companies (PMCs) have been booming, there are diffuse boundaries between armed struggle, guard duties and instruction.[1] Private contractors are working for governments, combatant groups, international organisations, NGOs, and a wide range of private enterprises, both legal and illegal. There is certainly also a wide range of private firms, from security companies to more war-fighting units, and from small agencies based on subcontracting to large, diversified business companies.

In the Western world, PMCs became prominent in the Balkans after the dissolution of Yugoslavia, in particular US firms on government contract. In Africa, PMCs were decisive in the power struggles in Liberia, Sierra Leone and Congo in the 1990s. They have also played a crucial role in the Pacific, in Asia and in South America.

During the first Gulf war, the ratio between ordinary troops and private contractors was approximately 50:1, while it was close to 10:1 in Iraq after the American intervention in 2003. During 2003–2004 there were about 20,000 private contractors in Iraq doing guard duties, transport and escort, support services and even interrogation of prisoners. Some of these services such as guard and escort duties have involved private contractors in armed struggle against Sunni activists in Najaf and Falluja. Iraq is the breakthrough for private contractors in Western warfare after the initial experiences in the Balkans (Isenberg, 2004; Avant, 2005).

Private companies operate on the full scale from defence industry to armed involvement. Western countries have generally drawn a line at actual war-fighting, while most countries have been outsourcing – at least in part – transport, maintenance, catering and other support services. Guard duties, logistics, intelligence and repair of

---

1   Private military companies, or firms, are organised contractors, in contrast to individual mercenaries. They also undertake a broader field of services than the traditional mercenary, and in most military operations they do not engage in direct war-fighting. Since many of these firms also operate in the civilian sector, they are often referred to as private security companies.

weapons systems and platforms are strategically vital. The development has probably outpaced the formulation of well-argued principles and regulations.

There is no standard mode of privatisation of defence, not even among Western countries. The United States and Great Britain have gone quite far, while Germany, France and the Nordic countries, among others, are more reluctant. Nevertheless, the global trend is towards increasing privatisation along the full scale, with extensive outsourcing of support services which are crucial for effective warfare. How, then, does military commercialisation work after the cold war, and what are the political implications?

The Return of the Condottieri

During the age of nation-building, mercenary troops, prominent throughout history, were relegated to the shadows. From the late 18th century they were increasingly replaced by conscript armies with the *citizen-soldier* as an embodiment of the Clausewitzian trinity between state, people and military. Machiavelli`s critique of the hired *condottieri* (after *la condotta* or the contract which they signed) as unreliable in defence of the city state, gained general acceptance in a new national context. Throughout the 19th and 20th centuries, the Western military was predominantly public and national. Participation by civilian specialists and the supply of support services from the private sector was not unknown: the French had their *Foreign Legion* and the British their *Gurkhas*. The backbone of the defence was still conceived as a public institution. Territorial defence by conscript mass armies was the core of defence as a popular project throughout the cold war.

This core did not extend to the cold war in the periphery – the zones of combat in the Third World. Decolonisation, colonial war and imperial dissolution led to states where the trinity of state, people and defence did not take hold. One line of evolution towards the present privatisation of military power originates in the turmoil of decolonisation in the 1950s and 60s.

The modern renaissance for mercenaries in war erupted in the former Belgian Congo with the decolonisation of 1960. Adventurers with experience from the French Foreign Legion or from various special forces, entered the centre stage of world politics as contractors in the secessionist struggle of the province of Katanga. Veterans from this struggle later fought a series of African wars – in secessionist battles in Biafra and South Sudan, and in attempted *coups* in the Comores and the Seychelles (Mockler, 1986; Thomas, 1984; Péan, 1983).

The market for mercenaries willing to fight for or against decolonisation was not well organised. The interested parties on the market were political leaders with a weak power-base in what are now called 'failing states', rebel movements fighting for secession or state control, or economic interests with a basis in the former colonial power, like the Belgian mining company *Union Minière* in Katanga. There were often close connections between military and economic interests, concentrated in rivalry for the control of resources like minerals and oil. The *resource curse* – whereby an abundance of natural resources became a source of conflict and malfunction rather than a blessing – was an early fate of many of the new states.

These features indicate some of the stable conditions for the military market in former colonies, even if there are great differences in size and form of the mercenary contract business in the 1960s compared to the present. First and foremost, the contemporary market is globally connected. After the cold war, the development in Africa is linked up with changes in the industrialised world. From the early 1990s there has been a growing world marked for military services. While mercenaries in the colonial wars of independence had little international legitimacy, modern PMCs are part of a globalised business network and of regular support services in war. There are parallels to the trading companies which operated overseas in the 17th and 18th centuries. These were also private contractors with privileges given by treaties with the states, and with hired military forces to protect them.

During the cold war, there was a sharp separation between the bands of mercenaries in the colonial wars on the one hand, and the development of a private defence industry in Western countries on the other. They were worlds apart. Today there is complex network of strings between local and global markets for privatised military capabilities. The mercenaries in poor and failing states may be organised in firms that are sub-companies within widely differentiated business enterprises. Public–private partnership in the industrialised world may diversify into services that border upon – and go into – the combat zone. How should we explain these developments?

The Post-Cold War Dynamics

The end of the cold war as such was a causal factor in the Western world as well as in the former colonial areas. First, the reduction of defence budgets and downscaling of military forces supplied the market with a surplus of professional soldiers. This was the case in Europe and the United States, and to an even greater extent in the former Soviet Union. These cutbacks created a major recruitment pool for the PMCs. In the Republic of South Africa, the end of apartheid and the solution of the Namibia problem implied a downscaling of the public security forces. Veterans from these forces were ready for new assignments.

Second, the demand for military expertise in the private market expanded swiftly. This applied to poor as well as rich countries, and to the former Eastern Bloc as well as to the NATO area. The demand side has a plethora of important aspects. Authoritarian regimes in many poor countries became precariously weaker when they lost protection and support from their allied superpowers. The end of superpower rivalry in the Third World led to this termination of interest not only from the Eastern Bloc, but also from the United States. In Africa in particular, many states became more vulnerable to rebel mobilisation and potential collapse. Somalia is a case in point where the regime of Siad Barre disintegrated with the decline in US military and economic support. Somalia dissolved into anarchy and factional strife. A similar fate hit large countries like Zaire/Congo and Angola, and smaller states like Liberia and Sierra Leone. State authority failed and the struggle for natural resources and territorial control intensified and became more violent. Contested inter-state borders also were destabilised as the superpower interests of the cold war evaporated. The conflicts between Eritrea and Ethiopia and between Zaire/Congo and the neighbouring countries flared up with superpower withdrawal.

The governments in many of these weak states did not control effective armies, but some could mobilise resources to hire private contractors. During the Angolan civil war, the South African company *Executive Outcomes* (EO) supplied the government with weapons, training and direct combat support. Composed of veteran troops from the SA special forces, with experience from the Namibian wars, the company was instrumental in the defeat of their old allies in UNITA. Inspired by EO's success in Angola, the government of Sierra Leone hired the company during the struggle against rebel forces in 1995 – rapidly defeating the insurgents. When the contract with EO was terminated as part of the resulting peace agreement and the firm withdrew, the government fell after just a few months. From exile it then employed a British military company, *Sandline International*, to support its reinstatement. This contract resulted in the so-called 'Arms to Africa affair', embarrassing the British government, and in the end distending public attention to the role of private companies in modern conflicts.

Private military companies as well as forces resembling more traditional mercenaries were also hired to fight for different parties in the insurgencies against Mobutu Sese Seko in Zaire/Congo, in the civil wars in Liberia, and in the conflict between Ethiopia and Eritrea. In the latter case it has been argued that Ethiopia gained the upper hand on the ground due to private instructors, as well as the wholesale leasing of Russian fighter planes, complete with pilots and maintenance crews (Singer, 2003).

The violent fault lines after the cold war – failed states, factional strife, resource rivalry and terrorism – led to increased demand for private military services. The fault lines indicate that ordinary defence forces have dissolved due to budget crises and factionalism within the military. Non-state actors, like rebel movements, business enterprises and international organisations, have increasingly engaged armed protection in the private market. The power vacuum that emerged in some African countries after the cold war was filled by local warlords from within or from outside the public offices, often with the support of PMCs. In Colombia, all sides in the narcotics war have engaged private contractors (Somme Hammer, 2006).

The modern PMCs are quite different from the archetypical mercenaries of the 1960s. They are organised as legal businesses, have a wider scope of activities and a more varied group of customers, and they can mobilise more advanced military expertise and greater firepower. They are often merged within wider business conglomerates and financial institutions, and they often regroup under a new name and within changing economic alliances. Firms like *Executive Outcomes* and *Sandline* are both officially dissolved, but with an afterlife in a new shape and with different names. There is an informal division of labour between the companies: some specialise in military instruction, some in support services, while others are prepared for combat (Singer, 2003: 73–148).

Even in parts of the former Soviet Union, the public monopoly of violence has dissolved, parallel to the availability of veterans from the Soviet security forces on the private market. The war in Chechnya is a growth enterprise for PMCs on contract with the Russian government. More generally, the vast increase in organised crime has stimulated a corresponding increase in private security services. In the former Soviet Union, the Western distinction between PMCs and traditional mercenaries is unclear. In many post-Soviet conflict zones, instability is lucrative and violence is a business enterprise. Crime prepares the market for forced offers of protection, resulting in financial benefits for organised crime and spiralling growth in the protection industry. The dynamics is partly driven by the merger of crime and protection, and partly by the opportunity for different criminal syndicates to offer protection against each other. This type of *violence as enterprise* has characterised the development in parts of the former Soviet Union, in the Balkans, in the factional strife and civil wars in Africa, and in the contest between government forces, narcotics cartels and guerrilla movements in south-American countries like Colombia (Chabal and Daloz, 1999; Mehlum, Moene and Torvik, 2002).

A Post-National Constellation in the West?

The new conflict configurations after the cold war work differently in the Western world. Military commercialisation takes hold also here, but through other mechanisms. PMCs benefit from the reduction in territorial defence based on conscription, to force deployment to crisis areas abroad. The USA and Great Britain have repeatedly led international operations with expeditionary forces from their national military, but with a wide range of support services supplied by private contractors, including training, maintenance and intelligence. One reason is the need to scale down standing armies and reduce the number of reservists by flexible outsourcing. After the stage of intensive war-fighting, with the need for re-stabilisation, there is a phase of undefined limits between military engagement and police work. Here, with the intervention in Iraq as the paramount case, came the opportunity for PMCs to perform guard duties, transport and training of local forces.

NGOs have also employed private contractors for guard duties and logistics in international operations. There have been contours of debate within the UN about the extent to which PMCs should be engaged in peacekeeping, as national contingents have often been slow to mobilise, as well as inefficient and difficult to coordinate (Holmqvist, 2005: 45 ff; Singer, 2003: 182–188).

The major trend in some conflicts in poor and failing states after the cold war is engagement of PMCs directly into combatant roles, closer to traditional mercenary engagement. In international operations led by rich powers, private contractors have primarily performed support services, although approaching the battlefield. Further, outsourcing is increasingly a system of organisation that transforms the military in peacetime.

This picture, however, is not unambiguous. Both the US and Great Britain have sent private contractors to battle zones abroad or into covert operations (Avant, 2005: 143 ff). The advantage is partly to divert political criticism in case of casualties and partly to avoid political interference. Public visibility is reduced and the political costs may decrease, although at a risk.

Ordinary national troops may be provocative in the vicinity of crises, like the repercussions of US bases in Saudi Arabia after the first Gulf War. The allied presence close to the sacred places led to increased Islamic mobilisation against the West. American forces were withdrawn, but the greater part of Saudi defence is virtually staffed by the private American company *Vinnell* and other contractors. With the deep involvement of private contractors, the political costs of a heavy presence of foreign troops are reduced. The benefits for the US are relatively stronger geopolitical control by indirect means, relative to countries without a policy of outsourcing overseas (Avant, 2005: 136).

The massive employment of private contractors after the initial battles in Iraq in the spring of 2003 illustrates the extensive and complicated structure of the military market. The business corporation *Halliburton* has been engaged in oil-drilling technology since the aftermath of World War I, and it is developing and safeguarding Iraqi oil installations on contract. Their sub-company, the engineering firm *Kellogg, Brown & Root* went into military logistics and planning in the early 1990s within an umbrella contract with the US government, gaining experience in Bosnia and Kosovo before becoming a major contractor in Iraq. The American security company *Blackwater* has performed armed guard services in Iraq and became engaged in battle when the offices of the provisional administration were attacked in 2004. Vice president and former defence secretary Richard Cheney was president of Halliburton from 1995, but he has kept a formal distance to the contracting between the companies and the US defence. Still, the personal networks illustrate the community of interest and the revolving doors between the new military market and the political leadership. The close personal links may be nourishing the fast and extensive commercialisation of military services in the US (Shearer, 1998: 35).

The revolution in military affairs has also stimulated the privatisation of the ways and means of warfare. Three elements have defined this technological revolution since the early 1990s. One is improved sensor technology in satellites, manned and unmanned aircraft, with improved capabilities in surveillance and intelligence. Another is improved command and control capacities by new computer technology. The third is wider range and better precision in missile attacks and bombing. This technological revolution, with complicated guidance systems and maintenance work, has made the national defence more dependent upon private–public cooperation (Sloan, 2002; Spearin, 2004). It is time-consuming and expensive to educate and pay military personnel with the adequate technological competence. Private contractors have therefore expanded their role in the guidance of the high-tech military systems. Private companies on the inside of the revolution in military affairs are more than equal to the defence authorities in the qualitative aspects of modern warfare.

The development of military technology reverses the transformation from the Napoleonic wars when new and simple firearms made conscript mass armies militarily more effective. The new technology again requires prolonged and highly specialised training. The US defence, which is technologically hegemonic, has prioritised special services and advanced information and weapons technology at the expense of standing troops. On the other hand, the downscaling of personnel has led to manpower shortage after the initial military campaigns, like the situation in Iraq as early as the summer of 2003. The way international operations has developed, private contractors have become more crucial *both* in the high technological warfare and in the subsequent attempts at political stabilisation which requires numerous personnel.

More generally, privatisation of the military is the transformation of one of the last bastions against the wave of privatisation and market orientation of the public sector in the Western world (Goldsmith and Eggers, 2004). Outsourcing and stock exchange listing of former state companies and public services acquired an ideological breakthrough from the late 1970s. The background was the oil crisis, economic recession and fiscal overload of the state, followed by a liberalistic turn in public policy in the US, Great Britain, Australia, New Zealand and eventually the entire OECD area. Neo-liberal solutions were the general response to the need for relieving and improving public activities within health, communications and education. *The new state*, reformed by the principles of 'New Public Management', was open to private contractors and public–private partnership (Christensen and Lægreid, 2001).

There was a counterpart to this development in the non-Western world. In many developing countries, institutions like the IMF demanded a more slender and partly privatised public sector as a condition for financial support. The former Communist Bloc also became a paradise for private enterprise after the dismantling of the Soviet economy. Privatisation of security and defence was an intrinsic part of the transformation of the former communist regimes. Thus, the global demand for PMCs grew after the end of the cold war, even if different mechanisms were operative in various parts of the world.

The privatisation of the defence sector came later and was less comprehensive compared to many other public activities. Objections against commercialisation remain stronger in this area, since the military – and generally the control of the legitimate use of force – is at the core of the notion of a sovereign state. The new models of governance and the ideological climate for radical change were better adapted to non-military activities. The end of the cold war abruptly implied new horizons and needs, with improved conditions for letting the neo-liberal solutions affect the military forces. The economic programs for improved efficiency fortified the changes in threat perceptions, fiscal constraints and new technology. Economic globalisation synchronised these tendencies across borders, and expanded the framework for reform of the private companies. Still, and somewhat amazingly, national traditions and different modes of action made the transformation non-uniform.

Military Market and Political Dislocation

The global market for military power may increase the instability and unpredictability of violent conflicts. Local balances of power may change over night. It becomes harder to estimate the military capabilities of adversaries. Militarily weak parties may be able to hire an efficient fighting force and tilt the outcome. By contracting a private company with helicopter capacity, the government of Sierra Leone managed to halt the advance of the rebel guerrillas towards the capital in 1995. The corruption and lack of professionalism within the government had undermined the national defence forces.

Traditionally, there have been two interrelated processes in the formation of national defence – the gradual establishment of capable military forces on the one hand, and the building of credible alliances on the other. The importance of these traditional factors has decreased with the evolution of PMCs, especially in poor regions of the world where the military institutions are initially weaker.

The privatisation of military capacity also increases the potential power of non-state actors – humanitarian organisations and legal business enterprises, but also rebel groups, terrorist movements, narcotics cartels, and other criminal associations. Countries like Colombia are characterised by a complex network of government agencies, organised crime, rebel forces and foreign interests – each with a different and changing element of military contractors of some sort.

The military market may also enable small states to gain relative independence from allied great powers. The relationship between Australia and Papua New Guinea (PNG) has economically and militarily been a patron-client relationship, long after the formal independence of PNG. The major Australian motive for supporting the government in Port Moresby was to sustain a dominant position in the South Pacific. When local rebels made an attempt to control the rich copper mines on the island of Bougainville, protesting against environmental deterioration and the favouring of external companies, Australia refused to support military action against the islanders. The government in Port Moresby responded by a move towards independence. Fortified by helicopters and commando forces from the British firm *Sandline* – who turned out to be subcontracted by the South African company *Executive Outcomes* – PNG could eventually operate independently of Australia (May and Regan, 1997; Singer, 2003: 176 ff).

In the next round, this privatisation of the military force was decisive for the domestic civil-military balance in PNG. The option of private force projection may, in some circumstances, fortify the civilian government relative to the military. In PNG it could be argued that the consequence was the opposite. The humiliated and displeased army commanders orchestrated a *coup* in which the government was overthrown before the contract obligations to *Sandline* were fulfilled. The new military regime broke the contract with the company and provoked it to sue the new authorities for outstanding claims. This subsequently led to a strained diplomatic relationship between Canberra and London since the Australian government was displeased by interventions from a British military company within their traditional sphere of influence (Singer, 2003: 194 ff). The outcome increased the leeway for negotiations between the parties and a potentially deadly escalation of the Bougainville conflict was diverted.

The presence of private military contractors has tilted the domestic balance of power in capital cities like Monrovia and Port Moresby. PMCs also played a crucial role in the upheavals in the former Yugoslavia. The American company *Military Professional Resources Incorporated (MPRI)* served to fortify the power base of President Tudjman in disfavour of Parliament and the Croatian opposition (Avant, 2005: 110).

Private contractors may serve the strategic and economic interests of great powers in areas of turmoil. Presence by proxy on contract may serve the interests of outside powers and influence the outcome of conflicts. The military firm, *Vinnell*, is this kind of American proxy in Saudi Arabia. Correspondingly, the US drug enforcement authorities employed the firm *Dyncorp* to operate on contract against the narcotics cartels in Colombia (Spearin, 2004: 251, 254; Somme Hammer, 2006).

In grand strategy, the consequences of privatised military force surpass the local horizons. The American *war on terror* after 9/11 had two paradoxical implications for the system of states. The importance of national security (called *homeland defence*) increased immediately. Nevertheless, the anti-terror efforts led to more numerous and more comprehensive contracts with private security and military companies both domestically, and in the international operations in Afghanistan and Iraq. The international defence alliances from the cold war were no longer seen as adequate expressions of a common interest against the new kinds of threat. The international alliance pattern was strained by fragmentation and internal disagreement among allies. Private contractors became relatively more important as a resource base for US dominance.

US military superiority has increased rather than decreased after the cold war: the technological revolution in military affairs was led by the US. European countries have reduced their defence budgets parallel to the decline in financial support to investments from NATO. In international operations like in the Balkans and Afghanistan, there is also a functional divide within NATO. The US is mainly responsible for force deployment in the stage of acute war-fighting, while European powers assume more responsibility for the subsequent peace-building effort. On the American side, private contractors are increasingly numerous during both these stages (Spearin, 2004: 251).

The domestic implications of the privatisation of security and means of warfare – *outsourcing* to private companies of services that used to be part of the state – are that the divisions between the military, civilian and economic sectors have become blurred. Defence forces are less well-defined, with a seamless web between the military and other economic enterprises. *Governance* or *governing by network* is the modern euphemism for this opaque dislocation of public authority structures (Goldsmith and Eggers, 2004).

Security as a Private Good

The new multitude of threats and security concerns is less collectively cohesive than territorial defence. The traditional defence posture was to protect the national population as a whole against invasion and occupation. It is less obvious that participation in international operations is existentially vital to the national community. Security policy after the cold war is more complex and less obviously mandatory. Whether it serves a collective national good is more contested. On the other hand, it is better suited for being dissected and offered on the market.

Pure collective goods are goods that are available to the whole community, whether they choose to pay for it or not. Such goods are also equally useful to everybody independent of individual consumption. Environmental quality, traffic lights, national defence and national police may be examples of collective goods (Shaw, 2002; Krahmann, 2005). The new defence policy may be seen as a less pure collective good. The foundation in common interests that are immediately understandable is less convincing. As a consequence, the state monopoly on the legitimate use of force – the core of the Weberian notion of the state – is more vulnerable and contested, even in rich Western countries.

Several new threats after the cold war, such as terrorism or organised crime, are relatively better suited for individual protection (and thus for market solutions) than traditional territorial defence. More numerous and more high profile security risks expand *within* national borders, or they float across borders in a way that is beyond national control. This means that the market for individualised security solutions is growing. Private security firms started as a supplement to the police but have gradually expanded as part of the military system which is already oriented towards a variety of objectives in addition to interstate war and territorial defence.

In principle, most Western governments would almost certainly argue that PMCs should be subject to public authority and control. The increasingly obscure boundaries between public and private, and between military and civilian, pose a challenge to the maintenance of principles. It is becoming less obvious whether there are military core functions which cannot be privatised without unforeseeable problems. It is equally less obvious where the critical delineation of such boundaries should be drawn. There is no uniform solution nor agreement between Western governments in these matters, if they have been considering the challenge at all.

Military Entrepreneurs – The Dilemmas Defined

As commercial enterprises, PMCs are primarily responsible to their stockholders. When they are given strategically important tasks in the military forces, the direct public control of power projection is reduced. PMC employees are not subject to military command, and beyond the contract they are not politically responsible to the public authorities. The reason for engaging them is based on practicality, capacity and economic considerations. A dominant motive is to introduce competition for contracts and relieve public budgets from the constant cost of support functions and services.

One challenge presented by the PMCs themselves is their unstable and ever-changing structure. Due to business mutations, mergers, acquisitions and change of firm labels, ownership is often unclear. Subcontractors are often used for a variety of services. Thus, the continuity of market relations may be obstructed. The consequence may not only be lack of operational continuity, but also an increased security risk due to the opaque flow of sensitive information and changing access to critical insight.

The running of weapons systems and field maintenance require reliability and unambiguous lines of command. Logistics and security are also strategically vital. These operations have increasingly been left to private contractors in the international interventions since the mid-1990s. All Western countries have drawn a line around armed battle as such, but beyond that line there are vastly different practices from one country to another. Since international operations are conceived as multinational and collective enterprises, all participating countries are confronted with the challenge of PMCs within the new theatres of war, whether they have hired them themselves or not.

The general trend is towards a defence that is inoperable without private services. Defence and war-fighting capability is thus shared with private contractors operating under business rules. Private participation within or bordering upon the battle zones also complicates responsibility in relation to the Geneva Convention and other parts of international humanitarian law. On the other hand, the obliteration of the difference between operative forces and non-combatants has been a driving force towards privatisation because of the need to avoid public scrutiny and political repercussions from a controversial intervention. The unintended consequence may be, however, that private contractors pursue their business interests and compromise the political authorities. This was the experience of the British government when *Sandline* allegedly broke a UN weapons embargo and delivered arms to the exiled government of Sierra Leone, and equally so when the company sued the new regime for breach of contract after the military *coup* in PNG.

The swift growth of PMCs is also a challenge because the state is deprived of military competence. Public vulnerability may increase as the expertise and capacity for logistics, maintenance and intelligence goes elsewhere. The special forces that are vital to international operations are equally vulnerable. While the state covers expenses for education and training of elite personnel, PMCs might profit from the employment of competent forces by offering several times the public salary. Thus, the long-term capacity for developing advanced military expertise might deteriorate.

The dilemmas of military contracting have all been exposed in Iraq (Avant, 2005b; Percy, 2006). The contractors are flexible, with the ability to recruit personnel swiftly; they have a variety of specialised skills, and they may entail lower political costs compared to the employment of national troops. On the other hand, economic costs have been out of control because of insufficient contract specification. Unclear rules of engagement and the unregulated flow of military information in theatre have jeopardised missions; and, above all, public accountability for actions – including the interrogation of prisoners – has lead to political repercussions.

It is unlikely that the system of private contractors in the military forces will be dismantled or even reversed in the short or medium term, despite the problem of public accountability. The neo-liberal drive for a more slender public sector has been quite strong. Perhaps even more important, the new objectives of armed forces – international operations far from home – do not command the broad political legitimacy of the traditional territorial defence. In the long term, any trend might turn.

It has been argued that the more acute problems of privatisation could be managed with rules of licensing nationally and internationally, with more careful contract specification and a better system of legal sanctions, and potentially with shared public-private ownership of the companies (Holmqvist, 2005; Percy, 2006). In those parts of the world where the privatisation of the military has advanced furthest, as in many African countries, the counterpart to the PMCs is not states in the Weberian sense with an accomplished monopoly of legitimate violence. In this context, the question of public accountability is irrelevant.

Conclusion

The privatisation of military capabilities and services – as has developed swiftly during the last decade – raises fundamental questions of public control and state sovereignty. The challenge is posed in the most radical way in countries where substantial parts of the armed forces are staffed by private contractors as in parts of Africa and certain oil rich Arab countries. In the Western world, the extent of privatisation in the military is non-uniform. Some countries hire PMCs for a wide variety of tasks next to armed battle. Others, like the Nordic countries, have only recently started to outsource support functions to private firms. Here, the development has been prepared by public–private partnership in the defence industry while it has accelerated with the general adoption of neo-liberal principles and *new public management*. The barrier towards transformation of the core functions of state sovereignty is lower due to the new conflict pattern, to the changing supply-demand relations, and to the altered threat perception after the cold war.

Privatisation is a challenge to principles of accountability, lines of command, and control of sensitive information. The emerging military revolution is altering a basic form of political organisation in Europe. The military used to be a national and public institution. Internationalisation of force composition, command and deployment is changing this basic form externally, while privatisation transforms it internally. Taken together, the external and internal transformations jointly dissolve the trinity of state, people and defence.

References

Avant, D. (2005), *The Market for Force* (Cambridge: University Press).

Chabal, P. and Daloz J-P. (1999), *Africa Works. Disorder as Political Instrument* (Oxford: James Currey).

Christensen, T. and Lægreid P. (eds) (2001), *New Public Management. The Transformation of Ideas and Practice* (Aldershot: Ashgate).

Goldsmith, S. and Eggers W. D. (2004), *Governing by Network. The New Shape of the Public Sector* (Washington: The Brookings Institution).

Hammer, A. S. (2006), *The Control of Private Security Companies. A Study of the Relationship between the United States and Private Actors in Plan Colombia*, Masters thesis (Oslo: Department of Political Science, University of Oslo).

Holmqvist, C. (2005), *Private Security Companies. The Case for Regulation*, SIPRI Policy Paper No. 9, January 2005.

Isenberg, D. (2004), *A Fistful of Contractors: The Case for a Pragmatic Assessment of Private Military Companies in Iraq*, British-American Security Information Council, Research Report 2004: 4.

Krahmann, E. (2005), 'Post-national Security in Europe: Collective Good or Commodity?' Conference paper, Stiftung Wissenschaft und Politik, June 3–4.

May, R. and Regan A. J. (eds) (1997), *Challenging the State: The Sandline Affair in Papua New Guinea* (Canberra: Australian National University).

Mehlum, H. et al. (2002), 'Plunder & Protection Inc.' *Journal of Peace Research*, **39**(4) 447–459.

Mockler, A. (1986), *The New Mercenaries* (London: Corgi Books).

Péan, P. (1983), *Affaires Africaines* (Paris: Fayard).

Percy, S. (2006), *Regulating the Private Security Industry*, Adelphi Paper 384. (London: IISS).

Shaw, J. S. (2002), 'Public Choice Theory', in David H. Henderson (ed.), *The Concise Encyclopedia of Economics* (New York: Warner Books).

Shearer, D. (1998), *Private Armies and Military Intervention*, Adelphi Paper 316. (London: IISS).

Singer, P. W. (2003), *Corporate Warriors* (Ithaca and London: Cornell University Press).

Sloan, E. (2002), 'Terrorism and the transformation of US military forces', *Canadian Military Journal*, Summer, 19–24.

Spearin, C. (2004), 'The Emperor's Leased Clothes: Military Contractors and their Implications in Combating Terrorism', *International Politics*, **41**, 243–264.

Thomas, G. S. (1984), *Mercenary Troops in Modern Africa* (Boulder: Westview Press).

Chapter 3

A 'New Deal' between State and Market

Alyson J. K. Bailes

Introduction: Triumph of the Market?

The dramatic shift in geopolitics that took place in 1989–90 is most commonly referred to as the end of the cold war or – by those allowing themselves a little more partisanship – the victory of the Western democratic model over Communism (at least in the Euro-Atlantic region). It is much less likely to be described as the victory of capitalism, unless by those of an ideological disposition on the losing side. Nevertheless, a case could be more that one of the more pervasive effects of the Soviet bloc collapse has been to remove from the contemporary world scene any widely accepted or widely practised economic philosophy that does not base itself on the free market to a greater or lesser degree. The largest remaining state to call itself 'Communist', the People's Republic of China, has moved far towards exploiting market dynamics and incentives both externally and internally. Ironically enough it is now more frequently blamed by Washington for insufficient state intervention to adjust the trading value of its currency.[1] Former Communist states in South-East Asia are converging with the politically paternalistic but economically laissez-faire ways of their neighbours, within the loosely harmonizing framework of ASEAN.[2] Twelve nations of Central and the Mediterranean (including Romania and Bulgaria)[3] have not only learned the capitalist catechism well enough to qualify for entry to the European Union (EU), but are raising concerns in older member states because of the competitive edge they have acquired through applying it extra-zealously.[4]

This change in what might be called geo-economics could hardly fail to have repercussions in all important areas of public administration, including the field of defence and security. The free-market vitality of the Western side, and the way it allowed the USA and others to constantly extend their technological superiority over the East while still maintaining a buoyant civil economy, was credited by many with

---

1   The USA would prefer the renminbi yuan to be up-valued or allowed to float freely as one means of curbing its own bilateral trade deficit with China (Lau, L. and Stiglitz, J. 2005).

2   The Association of South East Asian Nations, established in 1967, now includes Vietnam, Cambodia, Laos and Myanmar as members.

3   The reference is to Estonia, Cyprus, the Czech Republic, Hungary, Latvia, Lithuania, Malta, Poland, Slovakia and Slovenia who joined the EU in 2004, while Bulgaria and Romania did so on 1 January 2007.

4   For example, by seeking to attract business through 'flat tax' rates and more flexible labour markets.

assuring the outcome of the cold war itself. True, the defence industry suffered from the subsequent cut-back in NATO and former Warsaw Pact defence expenditures. At the same time, however, it gained new freedoms for sales and collaboration with other world regions no longer starkly divided on East–West lines. The dynamics of change in private sector roles was boosted by other trends unconnected or less directly connected to the end of the cold war. This included the progressive merging of the defence-related and civil brands of high technology (where increasingly significant breakthroughs now originate in commercially owned, including privatized, laboratories) (Hagelin, 2004). The rise of concern about 'homeland security' stimulated demand for a wider range of products and skills suited to civil protection, border defence and domestic law and order. These were all fields where the *chasse gardée* of purely government expertise is likely to be even smaller than for the arms industry proper. The shift away from territorial defence goals towards overseas intervention, largely in the form of multilateral (and 'coalition') peace missions, has been accompanied by a pressure for 'professionalization' of the military career itself. In addition, there were multiple inducements for governments to 'outsource' one-off and permanent, rearguard and front-line services from commercial suppliers. Several of the world's most militarily active and interventionist states now use private-sector assets for everything from resource supply and transport to in-theatre combat support services and post-conflict policing, training and reconstructions. When this is added to the role long played by non-state combatants in 'weak-state' or chaotic environments,[5] it is hard to avoid concluding that a significant shift of authority and control has been taking place in favour of business and thus, of the free-market sphere in general. This is so, irrespective of whether it is viewed as a private-sector incursion or a public-sector alienation of competence.

Other chapters look at traditional defence activities more particularly; the aim here is to place the observations made above in a somewhat broader perspective in the interests both of analysis and of better-informed policy prescription. This approach could be made from several standpoints. Only one – the historical – will be briefly considered in this introductory section. It would lead us to recognize that the notion of the nation-state's exclusive prerogative of war-making and punishment ('monopoly of force') is based on assumptions that have dominated in the Western world for just a few centuries, and may never have gained the ascendancy in some other parts of the world. Diffused, intra-societal violence has always typified tribal societies and their relations with neighbours. Echoes of this survive even in some of the most advanced Western states in the shape of gang warfare, mafias, vendettas and so forth. The notion that it is the state that selects fighting personnel – conscripts or recruits, and that the state alone can endow them with the related special tasks and equipment alien to their normal existence. But this would meet with little understanding among the gun-carrying menfolk of Afghanistan, Pakistan's North-

---

5 Non-state players operate in and usually aggravate the chaotic environments typical of intra-state conflict in various capacities, as combatant factions, brigands and criminal groups, traffickers of war supplies, terrorists, and 'mercenaries' consciously hired by the government, by anti-government groups or by outside interests. For a discussion of the use of private services by 'weak' and 'strong' actors respectively, see Holmqvist, 2005.

West provinces, or even as close to home as parts of the Balkans. In these cases, it is *society* as a theatre of warfare (or of war-like behaviour and possessions) that offers the antithesis to the modern notion of state monopoly. In other historical contexts the *commercial* provision of warlike services has also been the rule more so than the exception. Examples range from the Italian *condottieri* of the late Renaissance, through the Swiss and German mercenaries of the 16th and 17th centuries, and the whole notion of armies 'living off the land' rather than from the government purse, which lasted into the 20th century. History also offers cases of 'multinationalization' of provision, as when nationals of country A were recruited by government B to guard or attack country C. In fact, any given army in the field up to the early 18th century, including the armies taken to the continent by Sweden's warrior kings of that period, was likely to include as many nationalities as any 'coalition' operation today, or more. Particularly strong parallels to 21st century 'de-nationalization' of the military function may be found in historical Western empires, from ancient Rome to the late 19th century Austro-Hungarian regime. Here, the men of ethnic groups considered to be especially good at fighting or at enforcing internal order might be deployed to the opposite end of the territory from their own birthplaces and might settle elsewhere again upon retirement, while the central authority making such dispositions arguably had 'multi-national' or at least non-national characteristics of its own.

The point of this type of perspective-stretching is to show that the normative concerns which most analysts bring to the contemporary question of 'privatizing' (or perhaps better, 'marketizing') defence and security functions are themselves historically determined, and in that sense relativistic. This remark in no way belittles, or should belittle, the concerns themselves. On the contrary, the historical approach can help to underline the reality of the problems faced when actors enter a sphere of activity whose rules, norms, disciplines, rewards and punishments have not been tailored to fit this type of actor *for a significant and habit-forming period of historical time*. It is not the intrinsic 'newness' of the private sector and (in this case) trans-national actors that explains the difficulty; rather, it is the fact that they are *different from the recently dominant players* (nation-states and public sector authorities). In short, the basic challenge is one of change management. Recalling that mankind may have been round this historical loop on various occasions before can, however, help us to formulate more clearly – and, ideally, to confront more dispassionately – the question of whether successful management this time round would lie in adapting present norms and/or practical controls as *little* as possible, or as *smoothly* as possible, to the private intrusion.

The bulk of this chapter attempts to illuminate this last-mentioned, and crucial, question by showing that the issues defined as security and defence-related 'privatization' or 'de-nationalization' not only arise in the realm of military activity *stricto sensu*, including conflict transactions. It will also show that such issues arise in relation to the so-called 'new' fields of high security concern: terrorism, proliferation, and organized international crime. This extension of the agenda may have value not only in adding further substantive evidence for the 'privatization' thesis, but also in drawing more widely the stage upon which appropriate public governance solutions will need to be found. For the kind of conjoined policy-making that today's compound security challenges demand, any prescription or set of prescriptions to regulate and optimize the new public–private sector relationship will need to follow coherent guiding principles across all the fields analysed here, and indeed over several others such as the handling of environmental, health, infrastructure-related and energy-related security challenges. The third and final section below will return to the generic issue of what those principles should be.

The Private Sector and 'New Threats'

It is by now almost a cliché to note that the driving security preoccupations of the early twenty-first century all increasingly involve non-state actors, both as part of the problem and as targets and instruments of corrective policy-making. The example of contemporary intra-state conflict has already been noted above and elsewhere in this volume. It can easily be shown that the same remark is true of terrorism and the proliferation of mass destruction technologies, the two 'new' or 'asymmetrical' threats that have dominated the USA's strategic analysis (and hence inevitably, much of the rest of the world) since the horrendous terrorist attacks of 11 September 2001. The USA's new National Security Strategy of September 2002 captured the shift from the traditional landscape of threat analysis in a striking phrase when it identified the single largest current threat to the nation as lying 'at the crossroads of radicalism and technology' (The National Security Strategy of the United States of America 2002). Terrorists of the supremely transnational Al-Qaeda type, or even those who operate in a more confined setting for more concretely definable causes, move in the sphere of *society* rather than in the formal inter-governmental space of traditional warfare, but they also move *par excellence* within the private, civilian economy. Their funds may come from private wealth, from donations channelled through private banks, illicit trading, theft, or from proceeds of other criminal activity. Their equipment – weapons, explosives, electronics – may also be obtained through illicit state and non-style transfers, or by simple purchase on the market given that bombs (for instance) can be put together from many everyday ingredients. The environment of normal present-day economic activity with its massive and varied flows of human travel, goods circulation and communications, provides an ideal setting for terrorists to prepare their attacks, and often the targets for executing them – given the importance of kidnapping wealthy victims as a method for many terrorist groups, and the explicit commercial targets of many 'eco-terrorists'. Last and not least, the global IT networks that help terrorists harvest and exchange information, and the media establishments that they rely on to publicize their exploits, are today commercially owned if they are owned by anyone.

The problem of destructive technologies intersects with that of terrorism not just in the sense that terrorists may be able to acquire and wish to use such extreme weapons (Allison, 2004), but also because many of the same features of the globalized economy tend to foster both plagues. The Secretary-General of the International Atomic Energy Authority (IAEA), Mohamed El Baradei, was right to talk about a 'Wal-mart' of nuclear smuggling following the revelation of how Pakistani scientist

A.Q. Khan had spread his assets and knowledge abroad,[6] not just in the sense that a shop had been opened where almost anyone could buy, but also inasmuch as the motives and transactions involved had a strong *commercial* streak. Even if Khan himself was not motivated by profit, the middle-men whose involvement has been traced in this instance to such varied locations as Dubai, South Africa and Malaysia – and those uncovered in parallel cases such as the post-mortem on Libya's nuclear ambitions[7] – were part of a shady establishment liable to be involved in many other kinds of illicit goods and money transfers. The same may be said of the milieux in which various attempts to trade nuclear materials originating from programmes in the former Soviet Union have been unmasked (Bunn, 2000; Lee, 2000; Statens kärnkraftinspektion, 2000).

This connection with the 'black' or 'grey' market is, however, only the narrower and arguably more easily managed end of private sector involvement with Weapons of Mass Destruction (WMD)-related assets and technologies. A far greater challenge is that all the techniques involved – the harnessing of the atom, synthetic chemical production and the human creation and use of biologically active organisms or substances – have their primary, major and quite legitimate use in the sphere of the civilian economy. In the nuclear case it is true that the processes creating nuclear weapons and civil nuclear power diverge markedly in their later stages. But the whole conundrum of nuclear non-proliferation (as illustrated in the current Iranian and North Korean cases) is that they involve the same materials and share many of the same prerequisites and initial processes (Blix et al., 2006). Moreover, terrorists could use 'innocent' nuclear products including medical isotopes to set off so-called 'dirty bombs' (radiological weapons) involving extremely disruptive releases of radioactivity in a social setting. In the fields of chemical and biological weapons the challenge is even greater, to the point where it is hard to be sure what a 'weapon' is. Certain limited combinations of chemicals have been favoured by governments which built up stocks of chemical weapons munitions and delivery systems from the early twentieth century towards, and these substances are among those that terrorists might try to reproduce or to acquire through the black market.[8] Nevertheless, many everyday chemicals have explosive, corrosive, poisonous or otherwise incapacitating effects that terrorists might equally well exploit with generally less danger to themselves. (The scale of human damage done by the industrial chemical accidents at Seveso in Italy and Bhopal in India, or by accidental industrial releases of mercury in parts of Japan, is eloquent enough.) Similarly, governmental experiments to develop biological weapons and ways of delivering them are believed to have

---

6   A. Q. Khan, the 'father of Pakistan's bomb', had been suspended from work since 2002, but the first clear evidence of his proliferation efforts came with an Iranian confession in October 2003 to having received centrifuge components from Pakistan. For his story see Powell, B. and McGirk, T (2005). El Baradei's 'Wal-mart' remark was made to the *New York Times* (2004).

7   Under a agreement with the USA and UK in 2004 Libya agreed to stop all efforts to acquire Weapons of Mass Destruction (WMD) technologies, and surrendered information on its related programmes. See Hart, J. and Kile, S.N. (2005).

8   Thus, the attacks launched by Aum Shinrikyo in the Tokyo underground in 1995 made use of the well-known CW gas Sarin.

focussed on relatively few, historically well-defined diseases. These include anthrax, smallpox and varieties of plague; but the range of bio-substances that could cause massive human damage through intentional (including terrorist) use is as wide as or wider than those that can harm humans 'naturally' or by accident – any kind of disease organism, any organic poison or contaminant, any pest affecting animals and crops or making water undrinkable, and so on. Even antidotes, cures and protection techniques could be misused for offensive purposes if attackers used them to protect their own people while releasing the corresponding bio-hazards into the environment (Roffey, 2004). Neither should we overlook chemical and bio-agents developed for other purposes that could be misused by terrorists (e.g. internal security and riot control), or the mass destruction potential of techniques still in the early stages of commercial development such as genetic manipulation and nanotechnology.

The point here is not just to emphasize how far the substance of society's nightmares today is created and circulates within society itself, but to emphasise that the environment where these risks arise and must be detected, tackled and suppressed is overwhelmingly a private sector, free-market one. Privately owned companies not only produce and operate nuclear, chemical and bio-industrial equipment, but presently carry out by far the greatest share of the basic scientific research and development that powers the evolution of the relevant technologies, goods, and methods of application. Even university research is often commercially funded or carried out within a commercial partnership, while the tendency of Western governments to explore various forms of 'public–private partnership', even for explicitly defence-related research, has been noted above. Companies produce nuclear power as well as radiation monitoring equipment and iodine tablets, gases as well as gas-masks; they isolate disease strains, and produce the pharmaceuticals or bio-active cures to counter these. When these WMD-relevant dimensions are added to the private sector's massive grip upon the process of conventional arms production, which also helps to create and define the degree of threat from terrorists and other non-traditional users,[9] the point about commercial ascendancy would seem to be more than proven. But it is still necessary to note the relevance of *delivery techniques* for which the illegal as much as the traditional agents of violence must look to private sources of missile technology, guidance and target acquisition techniques, methods of pre-use containment and transport, and other delivery and dispersal methods such as air-spraying or aerosolization.

Controlling the 'market' of terrorism and proliferation

As mentioned at the beginning of this section, none of these developments has been hidden from modern security analysis and governments have had both reason and time since 9/11 to reflect on ways of tackling the inherent dangers. The most

---

9   Terrorists, criminals and saboteurs do not, of course, commonly use the more elaborate types of weaponry: civil airliners served the cause of the 9/11 attackers far better than fighter aircraft would have done. However, there is growing international awareness of the need to curb illicit access to some smaller commercially produced items, notably shoulder-launched anti-aircraft weapons (MANPADS).

dramatic and debated measures have been those taken under the USA's leadership to interrupt the circulation of WMD-related goods to unreliable participants, starting with the Proliferation Security Initiative (PSI) which includes – but is not limited to – cooperative measures to inspect and confiscate suspect cargoes on the high seas.[10] The PSI has been controversial partly because it has not led to many effective 'catches', and partly because of doubts over its compatibility with the existing legal framework, especially the Law of the Sea (Ahlström, 2005). It is nevertheless fair to note that when inaugurated in July 2003 it also had the merit of drawing countries like France back into anti-terrorist cooperation with Washington, and demonstrating a not wholly inept way of applying military resources for the purpose. In fact, the PSI also entails wider exchanges of information and cooperation among its members in the field of maritime security, and here complements the new regime of container transport security and enhanced standards of port and harbour security introduced by the USA from 2002. Initially, Washington sent its own customs agents to major centres of maritime traffic to check on containers before delivery, leading to protests about the costs and delays involved. But over time, other partners have seen the advantages in better security so that the International Maritime Organization is now working on universally applicable measures to the same effect. The economic burden on legitimate sea traffic is detectable, but appears to be relatively small (Lenain 2004), and is somewhat offset by the fact that the new measures have helped to catch smugglers, people traffickers and other criminals as often, or even more often than terrorists. In fact, the main problems now cited are those arising for ports too small to be included in the US scheme and which are subject to even longer security screening of their exports as a result (ibid.).[11]

Other aspects of the problem have been tackled from the outset by more cooperative methods of international negotiation and regulation. The USA inspired the adoption by the United Nations in September 2001 of Security Council Resolution No. 1373,[12] which creates a universally valid prohibition on the handling and holding of funds owned by or destined for terrorists It further requires all governments to take measures in their own jurisdiction to ensure that corporations and individuals as well as state agencies act accordingly. The UNSCR was backed by the creation of a special implementing committee at the UN and by provisions for monitoring states' performance and channelling practical assistance to any who asked for it. Although of limited effectiveness as measured by the funds actually frozen,[13] UNSCR 1373 has rightly been seen as a milestone both in the exercise of something like a universal legislative power by the UN (although not all analysts view this as a good thing), and in the attempt to design security instruments for challenges arising in the fields of private economy and individual behaviour. It was followed in April 2004 by UNSCR 1540, which in a similar spirit outlawed the ownership, trading

---

10　The official PSI website is at http://www.state.gov/t/np/c10390.htm.

11　The equivalent tightening of security for air freight deliveries, as well as air passenger transport, is too obvious and well reported to need special reference here.

12　The text of this and other UNSCRs referred to is at http://www.un.org/Docs/sc.

13　By October 2003 just $134 million of assets were reported to have been frozen, about one quarter of them by the USA alone (Biersteker, T., 2004).

and transfer of WMD materials and technologies by non-authorized actors of all kinds including companies and individuals. It also called on governments to take the necessary measures, especially in terms of export control regimes and ensuring the prosecutability of offences. This measure was a direct and logical response to the 'Wal-Mart' challenge mentioned above, even if its implementing machinery was initially somewhat more flimsy than for UNSCR 1373. It was also of interest as a relatively rare attempt to define standards and targets of export control at a truly global level (Anthony, 2006). In the cold war, groups of Western-aligned countries were created to set up common standards and networks for blocking the leakage of dangerous goods to enemy powers. COCOM and its successor, the Wassenaar Agreement,[14] dealt with conventional military equipment, but the majority of specific sub-groups had a WMD-related focus. After 1990, a number of previous Warsaw Pact and developing-world countries of interest were admitted to these groups, but none of them yet has more than 44 members and they have been cautious in their approach to powers with a different strategic orientation, such as China. Since 9/11, the USA and like-minded states have been working in all the specific export control groups to focus their roles better on the objects now seen as most dangerous, on the most risky state users or categories of users, and on potential non-state users including terrorists. UNSCR 1540, however, offers a possible starting-point for conducting the same attempt with the involvement of all UN member states and under a relatively impartial institutional authority – something of great value in principle, even if the challenges of agreeing on and enforcing standards in such a diverse community are clear.[15]

Returning to the main theme of this chapter, it should be clear that even the most internationally inclusive and well-designed export control systems will not work unless they are made to bite upon firms operating in the real market. Most national control regimes make use of licensing systems, and in these cases it is necessary as a minimum that (a) companies should know which exports require a licence (b) applications should be wisely handled, (c) the judgements handed down to the company should be respected, and (d) customs and other executive agencies should be able to catch any exports that are attempted without a licence or that do not conform with the terms of the licence. It is obvious how hard it must be to operate such disciplines in chaotic, conflict-ridden or corrupt settings. Further difficulties arise in modern conditions where the producing and exporting entity is multinational and/or where the transfer entails intangibles ('dangerous knowledge'). (The USA has developed the notion of a 'deemed export' for the transfer of information within, say, a multinational cooperative research group where the recipient comes from a

---

14 The WA was created in 1996 to cover exports of conventional arms and dual-use goods and technologies. It now has 40 members including Russia and the Ukraine.

15 Some lessons may be drawn from the attempt to supplement Missile Technology Control Regime (MTCR) with a more 'inclusive' control regime, the International Code of Conduct (now known as The Hague Code of Conduct, HCOC). Although its terms are relatively loose, HCOC did not manage to gain the adhesion of important producer nations like China, Israel, Iran, India and Pakistan who dissented on issues ranging from missile definitions to 'excessive' transparency (Ahlström, 2003).

licensable destination, even if the person concerned is US-employed and on US soil at the time.) Good international cooperation can help considerably in blocking gaps, and the EU in particular is devoting great effort to improving coordination and monitoring among its members, making use i.e. of the value of transparency measures to allow more public and parliamentary control (Bauer and Bromley, 2004). However, effectiveness can be, and is also, greatly improved when governments work directly with business interests, using especially designed dialogue mechanisms, existing institutions (employers' federations, chambers of commerce) or sectoral organizations. Not only is this the best way ensure that producers and exporters get to know of changes in the 'control lists' of prohibited or licensable goods, but business itself can help to refine the systems. This is done both by drawing attention to new items of concern that governments may not be aware of, and by helping to remove over-burdensome and inefficient features and to correct weaknesses in the actual process of implementation.[16]

The need to invoke help and partnership from within the business sector is even plainer when it comes to the earlier stages of invention and development, and to security and safety issues arising during the production process. There is growing interest in establishing general and specific 'codes of conduct' for scientists and technicians in commercial as well as public employment, sensitizing them to the possible security impact of their discoveries, and 'codes of practice' both for individuals and for workplaces that remind of the many precautions needed to avoid dangerous leakage of the objects and technologies involved (Roffey and Kuhlau, 2006). To take the example of potentially 'weaponizable' bio-organisms and technologies, such codes and practices can and should be designed both to cover the considerations of *bio-safety*. This includes the protection of the workers themselves, decontamination, containment etc., and *bio-security* which focuses more on the risks of theft, leakage and improper transfer including of intangible knowledge. In the case of the civil nuclear industry and nuclear research, the corresponding challenges start with the familiar – if by no means successfully mastered – discipline of *nuclear safety.* – They also include, however, numerous demands and tasks for industry flowing from the imperative of nuclear *non-proliferation.* Ways must be found to ensure (and verify) that civil power plants are not themselves embarking on a weapons cycle. Commercial producers must refrain or be prevented from transferring potentially weapons-producing systems and knowledge to others, and controls are needed on the trade in nuclear fuels (including spent fuel) that may be implicated in illicit efforts to produce highly enriched uranium (HEU) or plutonium.

In recent years there has been intense international interest in new ways of managing the fuel cycle, including waste disposal, that would facilitate legitimate production while stopping leakage to illegitimate users. But it is harder than it might seem to find solutions that combine watertight controls with the politically necessary assurance of secure supply to all customers, and with the essentially *commercial* (profit making) nature of the transactions involved (Fedchenko, 2006). In principle,

---

16 Since 1994, Sweden has had an Export Control Society (details at http://www.chamber. se/exportcontrol) designed both to inform business people on developments in Swedish and other official regulations, and to receive their comments and advice.

the most appropriate system might be one based on multinational commercial consortia (such as already exists for European nuclear power production) plus supervision and control by an international authority like the IAEA and/or the UN, rather than by the USA or any self-appointed 'rich men's club'. The combination of such disciplines on active production with analogous internationalized approaches to spent fuel handling, and an intensification of the already well-established national and multilateral efforts to dispose safely of surplus and obsolete WMD-related materials,[17] might at last offer the prospect of something like a secure nuclear cycle. However, even more important in the longer run will be the success of industry, science and the engineering community in identifying ways of producing nuclear energy that are significantly more 'proliferation-resistant' than today. This is because these use fusion rather than fission, focus on materials other than HEU and plutonium, are engineered to physically block certain transformations, and/or have an ownership and management structure militating against individual nuclear 'break-out'.[18]

Governance Solutions: tame the market, or go with the flow?

The above analysis indicates that there can be no single instrument or one-size-fits-all regulatory solution, neither for the practical problems of managing the private sector's role in modern-day security, nor for the normative concerns that ensue. That point would become even more clear if the discussion could be extended to cover important fields unrelated to weaponry and conflict, such as the maintenance of critical infrastructures or the handling of epidemics and natural disasters (where business not infrequently finds itself in the front line). Some solutions for specific 'new threat' issues have already been touched on, but in this final section we return to the question of governance approaches in a more generic mode, starting with a reminder that the underlying issue is about maintaining or modifying the classic duality of the state and the market. While the distinctness of these two things in the (largely) post-Communist world is incontestable, there is a separate judgement to be made on where the *normative* centre of gravity lies in their relationship. If we take the position that 'business works for its own interests and those of a few (although nowadays often not so few) shareholders' while 'government protects the

---

17 The reference is to the activities launched by the USA's Nunn-Lugar programme to assist WMD disposal in the former Soviet Union, now usually called 'cooperative threat reduction' (CTR) or the Global Partnership (GP), after the related action programme of the G8. The Nordic states have contributed substantially to such work in Northern Russia. It demands the cooperation of specialized Western, as well as local, companies and some of the most significant obstacles hitherto have arisen on the commercial and legal front. On this aspect see Anthony (2004), and for a recent detailed policy study of European CTR efforts see Stockholm International Peace Research Institute (2005).

18 In a sense, and without advancing as far as the use of novel technologies, the multinational cooperative solutions that have been mooted for letting Iran and North Korea receive more nuclear-generated power without themselves performing suspect transactions are aiming at the same kind of 'proliferation resistance' in nationally tailored form. The nuclear industry is exploring more general possibilities in the course of research and development work on 'fourth generation' nuclear reactors.

whole population', it is clear that public security and welfare are values to be defined as well as maintained by government, against business if necessary. If we assume that the tendency of business is to exploit people and things while the business of government is to guarantee their well-being and their rights, then the more social kind of security demands that the state should either curtail business activities or do something to cushion and counterbalance their effect on individuals. From such a starting-point, the natural response to the question of how to deal with business impact on any and all dimensions of security would be to (a) impose/reimpose direct state control (and ownership if necessary) over the processes involved, or at least the most vital and sensitive of them; (b) control and limit business impact by means of legislation, regulation, and the normal state panoply of enforcement.

Other options could be opened up by considering the possibility that those determining the course of business affairs share some of the same values as the state and society that they spring from (or operate in), or that they may want to make it look as if they share them. Alternatively, that they arrive at some of the same conclusions for their own more materialistic reasons (e.g. preserving a calm environment for their operations and increasing the number of healthy and wealthy consumers for their products), and, crucially, that the market itself does not automatically penalize and eliminate such behaviour. On this view, solutions could include: (c) using market processes and mechanisms to induce and reinforce right actions: (d) the voluntary or induced development of appropriate standards, codes, mutual help movements and so on by business itself (sometimes called 'soft regulation'). Under both approaches, there is prima facie need for (e) dialogue, consultation, information exchange and ongoing communication and monitoring between the public and private sectors.

The reader may already have guessed, especially from the introductory discussion above, that this author finds the second normative hypothesis more sustainable than the first and would advocate a mixture of all five generic governance solutions. To explain or excuse this position, the remainder of this text will go back over the set of ideas above and look at the merits and elements of each type of solution in more detail.

Method (a), the reappropriation of a security-related function by the state ('re-nationalization' or re-establishment of a state monopoly) has two aspects that may or may not be combined. The state authority may reclaim ownership and resume operation of the given asset/function, and/or it may formally prohibit the private conduct of the same activity. The former method is not unknown today, but the most salient recent cases of this have involved the state seizure of energy sources and facilities, or at least renewed state control of the operating enterprises in a number of developing countries and the Russian Federation. Western governments have been consistently critical of such acts,which is not to say that they will not be continued and even extended. Market ideology aside, the main obstacles to Western countries opting for re-nationalization themselves – even in cases with a more direct security linkage and perhaps more legitimacy – are economic and financial. European nations' budgets in particular are neither sized nor structured to carry the costs involved. On the contrary, an increasing number of governments are seeking part-private financing – 'Public–Private Partnership' – even for cost-heavy (and normatively sensitive) projects falling well within their still-intact areas of responsibility, such as building prisons, bridges, airports and hospitals. What is most likely to be realistic is the retrieval or re-centralization by government of limited, relatively low-cost elements of activity that are important for control and for citizens' protection: notably, security inspectorates and perhaps some other aspects of infrastructure management.

By comparison, legal prohibition of a given private activity costs nothing, and may be a particularly appropriate way of 'drawing the line' in cases where a field of action is likely to have to remain divided for some time between the state and the market. An example would be a law that did not prohibit private security companies but made it unlawful for them to carry out specific activities involving, for example, extreme violence or executing punishment or intelligence collection either at home or abroad. Most countries already have laws forbidding private citizens (except for enterprises directly supplying the state) to own certain more powerful kinds of weaponry. UNSC 1540 (discussed in the previous section) established the same concept worldwide for private ownership of WMD, and one could imagine parallel measures being extended to torture instruments or certain non-lethal techniques reserved for government use in maintaining law and order.[19] However, as these last references should remind us, not every state authority in the world can be trusted to use such instruments wisely either. Any too-absolute or generic recommendation for the resumption of state control – in this or any other field vital for human welfare – would tend to clash with the growing tendency in international thinking to *relativize sovereignty* in precisely such life-and-death connections. The principle of a government's 'responsibility to protect' its people, as solemnized in the UN Summit Outcome document of September 2005 (United Nations General Assembly, 2005), leads to interesting reflections here. It implies condemnation of any government that lets the means of delivering security slip so far out of its hands that its citizens became each other's and anyone's prey. But it also holds out the threat of intervention against state authorities that use their monopoly (or lion's share) of violence to prey on their own people. State control, it would seem, is no longer to be regarded as an absolute good but is increasingly treated as part of an interdependent loop with *good governance*.[20]

Regulation of a security-related activity – method (b) – raises no comparably profound or difficult issues because it happens in the sphere of the market all the time. Laws govern companies' structures and methods of registration, their treatment of employees, standards for the goods they produce, their impact on the environment, the honesty of their advertisements, and increasingly, the small details of their internal governance. One of its general merits is that it is a *transparent* approach and, in the case of major legislation, subject to parliamentary and other democratic control. Another is its variety and flexibility: it can define spheres, conditions and methods of activity, establish answerability and monitoring procedures, define penalties for infraction or make offences justiciable through the courts, set special

---

19 The distinction should be kept clear between such measures and those that are proposed to stop anyone (including state scientists) from carrying out certain activities, like certain kinds of genetic manipulation.

20 This linkage is particularly clear in the context of international efforts for Security Sector Reform in developing, post-Communist, or post-conflict nations.

rules for emergency situations (especially relevant to infrastructure and energy security and to public health as described above), and even reassert government's control of individual transactions where it creates a system of *licensing*. Rules and laws can be made in consultation with business as well as other constituencies, and can be adapted in the light of representations from those who experience their impact as well as of changing circumstances.

This method offers at least partial solutions for issues arising in all the fields discussed above, but it does merit a few caveats of its own. Quality of regulation is important, and getting it right particularly means not having *too much* regulation, making it too complex, or allowing duplication and perhaps contradiction with measures initiated in other (including non-security) contexts. Over-regulation hits smaller firms especially hard, which some people would feel goes against liberal economic and social norms. But it is also counter-productive from a purely practical viewpoint, since finding the right way to guide smaller actors often proves especially important for blocking abuses that are diffused throughout the market. Even more important in today's globalized conditions, a purely national approach to regulating a security-relevant market phenomenon will often be mistaken because the threat in question is transnational, or because the firms controlling the activity are multinationals, or because disparate national rules can interrupt normal international exchange and competition. This explains why, in practice as well as principle, an increasing number of the issues involved are being tackled at the level of regional organizations like the EU, or globally in the WTO, the UN and its specialized agencies. Last but not least of course, *enforcement* has to be adequately provided for, which often means sensitizing government agencies and servants to the security overtones of activities they have been used to controlling from a mainly economic viewpoint. Customs officers may be used to looking for smuggled guns as well as drugs and cigarettes, but until very recently they were unlikely to know what WMD-relevant components would look like. Multilaterally adopted measures clearly pose difficulties of their own here.

Method (c), making use of the market's own tools and dynamics, could work in principle even on the assumption that business is purely a 'target' and cannot be expected to do anything helpful itself. The most obvious example is when the delegation/authorization of a given private activity (like a commission to a private security provider, an order designed to establish a state's drugs stockpile or a request to design a strategic IT system) takes the form of a contract, binding under commercial law. The state has only itself to blame if it does not frame the contract in a way that sets out all relevant qualitative and normative as well as practical requirements, and anticipates every kind of mal-performance or abuse.[21] The very decision to grant an important state contract to one private entity rather than another can and should be based on evidence of good performance and behaviour along all relevant security dimensions. Similarly, at the macro-level, the state still has power – even under systems far gone in privatization – to adjust features like tax rates

---

21 Examples of commercial and human rights abuse arising during the Iraq war from large US government contracts given to favoured private firms with minimal specificity or safeguards are quoted in Holmqvist 2005.

and tax breaks, state credits and subsidies, export credit guarantees, but also safety standards and consumer protection rules, in ways that will foster the desired security-relevant behaviours by making them ultimately more profitable than the reverse.[22] It is also worth noting that the more clearly the criteria of good and bad security conduct are set out and followed in any such field, the more likely it is that those providing secondary services to active companies, such as bankers and insurers, auditors and those involved in evaluating possible mergers and acquisitions, will *mark companies up or down accordingly*, thus providing strong extra incentives without government having to lift a finger. This already happens, at least in the West, with regard to Sarbanes-Oxley compliance and performance in the recognized parameters of Corporate Social Responsibility (CSR),[23] while some share-buying and share-holding communities also choose between companies on the basis of their 'green-ness' and of other ethical standards relevant to human welfare abroad as well as home (more on this below).

Mention of CSR also draws attention to the fact that the business sector itself – admittedly under NGO and consumer pressure – has proved capable of taking initiatives to define, inculcate and monitor standards in a variety of security-relevant fields (method (d) above). Most often, as with the trade in 'conflict diamonds' (triggering the so-called Kimberley process), the protection of the environment, or (in Europe) the avoidance of genetically modified ingredients, such efforts have been made only after sustained consumer pressure made it clear that profits would suffer otherwise. However, there is evidence that business people can nurture a more general desire to show support for community norms,[24] also at an international level, even if only because they feel that is what is expected of them, and cases of genuine humanitarian effort from companies helping, exist, e.g. in the aftermath of Hurricane Katrina.[25] Perhaps the most easily commendable form of such an initiative is when companies get together to spread knowledge of and better implement the standards set in 'hard' official regulation. Thus, the US-based Business Executives for National Security collect and disseminate information on official strategic export controls. However, when the transactions in question take place fully within the private sector and/or where a diversity of behaviours needs to be controlled for the sake of one security aim, it may be logical for business to construct its own 'codes' with or without help from concerned NGOs. This has happened particularly in the case of guidelines for operating in conflict zones where the International Committee of the Red Cross has made a special effort to educate business, and where the initiators of

---

22 States, of course, have mercenary motives of their own and may not want to do this if it conflicts with maximizing public revenue.

23 As a further example, a US investors' group has called for companies to be formally obliged to disclose the amount of 'risk' they carry in relation to climate change. including the risk of penalties for non-compliance with related norms (Maitland 2006b).

24 A McKinsey poll published on 25 January 2006 showed that 70 per cent of managers wanted their firms to respond better to social pressures and needs in areas such as climate change, health, privacy and 'ethically' produced goods: 90 per cent of Indian executives said that business should play a responsible role in society. (Maitland 2006b).

25 For an example of an organization ('Business Humanitarian Forum') set up expressly to coordinate such efforts see http://www.bhforum.ch/.

the UN's (voluntary) 'Global Compact' with Business recently published a special guidance document.[26] Aside from any specific criticism of particular codes sincerity or effectiveness, however, two major concerns arise from any effort to survey this gradually expanding field of initiative.[27] First, security-related initiatives are still very partial and dispersed, and no attempt has yet been made to link them, as would seem logical, with the private sector's single largest code-making exercise on Corporate Social Responsibility. This has now become more than self-sustaining with a whole new segment of the private sector earning money from promoting and monitoring it! This reflects some reluctance by CSR experts to 'dirty their hands' with difficult security issues as well as the security sector's own frequent distaste for surveillance and transparency. An interim solution might be to develop a set of 'Corporate *Security* Responsibility' principles separately, while drawing on methodologies used successfully for CSR. Last but not least, these initiatives are overwhelmingly found among larger enterprises of the developed world, whereas the most burning need today would be to get Russian, Chinese, Middle Eastern and other non-Western business on board as well.

Method (e) – communication and consultation between the public and private sectors – hardly needs more discussion since several examples of its relevance have been offered above. It can also fit many pictures of what the public–private balance of control should be, including exclusive state guidance. The only remarks that may be added are, first, that the form and target of contacts always needs reflection – formal or informal, precautionary or reactive. And who precisely should government talk to? Secondly, that the material requirements for rapid and secure communication need attention, especially in emergency response (or when working with business in conflict management abroad), and that more-than-national dialogue mechanisms are needed when the challenge, the context of regulation or the structure of business itself lies above the national level.

The argument for viewing a combination of all of the five methods mentioned above as the best overall solution can now be quite swiftly made. All of them have strengths, but also weaknesses which the use of the others can compensate, and a multi-instrument approach fits best with the extremely multi-dimensional nature of the problem (including the way that the public–private balance of roles and authority varies from sector to sector). The question may still be posed whether the totality of such means is capable of solving the problem. Part of the answer lies in the observation that the potential of all the methods is very far from having been exploited by governments and inter-governmental groupings up to now, and that comprehensive (multi-sectoral) and strategic approaches have been particularly lacking. Another point – deliberately reserved for this closing section – is that government is not, or should not be, alone in its effort to discipline and harness the business sector's growing security power. In the story of improvements to relevant business behaviour up to now, more has been achieved (and on a wider global scale) by NGOs, popular

---

26 For ICRC guidance see http://www.icrc.org and for the Global Compact guidelines of 2005, http://www.unglobalcompact.org/HowToParticipate/guidance_documents/.

27 One, certainly incomplete list of security-related private sector groups and networks, is in Appendix B to Bailes and Frommelt (2004).

campaigns, shareholder action and consumer action than by governments. Except in the most directly military fields, government will very rarely be more important (and profitable) to business as a consumer than is the great ordinary public – with obvious implications for where the real power lies.[28] This does not imply that NGOs should simply criticize and persecute business in every way possible: special-interest and single-issue movements have sometimes pushed business in directions that are not necessarily the best for broader public interests,[29] and it is a valid question who will control the bona fides and responsible behaviour of the NGOs themselves.[30] However, in the big picture today, the problem is not an excess, but a deficit of NGO agitation on specifically security-related issues compared, say, to those of purely ethical, humanitarian, or social concern. Anti-nuclear activity focuses much more on civil nuclear power than on the need for military disarmament or non-proliferation; anti-weaponry agitation is almost exclusively focussed on small arms and purely humanitarian issues, and more NGOs try to drive big companies out of sensitive conflict zones than try to drive them back to help in reconstruction following a conflict. Debating what more civil society actors all around the world could do to address the whole range of challenges discussed above as part of a *triangular* pattern of influence and control between state, business and society would be an exciting and promising way forward, even if for the moment it may sound a little quixotic.

Consideration of civil society's powers also offers a basis to revisit the question posed in the introductory paragraphs: Should the basic aim of policy today be to retrieve security functions from the private sector, or to cope smoothly with their transfer? Given the shift of threat profile and priorities especially for Western societies and the processes of democratization and empowerment of individuals as well as privatization and marketization, the reality is that power has moved from the state apparatus *both* to the private sector and to society as a whole – as well, of course, as outwards to the transnational sphere. Ordinary people are actors, for good or ill, as well as victims and targets in any given kind of modern catastrophe: they can combine to lobby for security-related ends at multinational and global level almost as simply as they can at home.[31] Re-regulating the balance between state and

---

28 As a recent example, a poll in summer 2006 found that 91 per cent of top world firms who responded had liaised with NGOs on human rights issues while only 54 per cent had discussed the issue with governments (Williamson, 2006: 3).

29 Animal rights extremists come to mind, but contrary views have also been expressed about the impact of anti-fur agitation and about those NGOs that have forced Western oil companies to withdraw from conflict-prone parts of Africa.

30 To tackle this question, three leading NGOs recently signed a new 'accountability charter' of their own ('Greenpeace, Amnesty and Oxfam agree code of conduct', *Financial Times* 3/4 June, 2006: 3).

31 This raises the intriguing question whether 'global public goods' can only be created by governments and institutions using collective resources, as the literature has so far tended to assume, or whether some forms might not be created by the public itself. The importance of non-governmental financial transfers for development and humanitarian aid is, for instance, noted by the Swedish Foreign Ministry (2001). According to Newsweek (2006), the privately-funded Gates Foundation spent only slightly less in 2005 ($844 million) than Finland ($897 million) which in turn was the world's 17th largest state donor of aid that year.

business by re-nationalization measures, or even by a quantum jump in regulation, according to this author, would be very difficult to do without calling widely-valued rights and roles of civil society into question as well, even if governments were able to defy the great bulk of historical precedent by showing themselves able to provide better service than business anyway. Lines can and should be drawn to remedy some transfers of authority that have gone too far too fast, or had unintended consequences, and to reassert greater control over further transfers for the future. For the main part, however, history and economics seem to offer few alternatives to a public policy based on *adaptation* to seemingly irreversible changes and trends, If the analysis above has any merit, this can and should be achieved through the broadest possible multi-sectoral approach to defining challenges and goals, and through the skilful use of multiple governance solutions. The hopes for success will be greatest of all if governments can exploit the full potential of a triangular approach where the people – the ultimate object of all good security policy – can fully play their part.

References

Ahlström, C. (2003), 'Non-proliferation of ballistic missiles: the 2002 Code of Conduct' in *SIPRI Yearbook 2003: Armaments, Disarmament and International Security* (Oxford: Oxford University Press).

—— (2005), 'The Proliferation Security Initiative: international law aspects of the Statement of Interdiction Principles' in *SIPRI Yearbook 2005: Armaments, Disarmament and International Security* (Oxford: Oxford University Press).

Allison, G. (2004), *Nuclear terrorism: the ultimate preventable catastrophe* (New York: Times Books).

Anthony, I. (2004), 'Reducing Threats at the Source: A European Perspective on Cooperative Threat Reduction', *SIPRI Research Report*, 19 (Oxford: Oxford University Press).

—— (2006), 'Reflections on continuity and change in arms control' in *SIPRI Yearbook 2006: Armaments, Disarmament and International Security* (Oxford: Oxford University Press).

Bailes, A. J. K. and Frommelt, I. (eds) (2004), *Business and Security: public-private sector relationships in a new security environment* (Oxford: Oxford University Press).

Bauer, S. and Bromley, M. (2004), 'The European Union Code of Conduct on Arms Export', *SIPRI Policy Paper* no. 8. Full text available at <http://editors.sipri.se/pubs/policypaper8.pdf>.

BHF Newsletter, Business Humanitarian Forum, last edition accessed 4(4) of December 2006, <http://www.bhforum.ch>.

Biersteker, T. (2004), 'Counter-terrorism measures taken under UN Security Council auspices' in Bailes, A. J. K. and Frommelt, I. (eds), *Business and Security: Public-Private Sector Relationships in a New Security Environment* (Oxford: Oxford University Press).

Blix, H. et al., (2006), 'Weapons of Terror – Freeing the World of Nuclear, Biological and Chemical Arms', *Report of the Weapons of Mass Destruction Commission*. Full text at <http://www.wmdcommission.org/files/Weapons_of_Terror.pdf>.

Bunn, M. (2000), 'Nuclear Smuggling' in *The Next Wave: Urgently Needed New Steps to Control Warheads and Fissile Material* (Washington, D.C.: Carnegie Endowment for International Peace and Harvard Project on Managing the Atom).

Fedchenko, V. (2006), 'Multilateral control of the fuel cycle', in *SIPRI Yearbook 2006: Armaments, Disarmament and International Security* (Oxford: Oxford University Press).

Financial Times (2006), 'Greenpeace, Amnesty and Oxfam agree code of conduct', 3 June: 3.

Hagelin, B. (2004), 'Science- and Technology-Based Military Innovation: the United States and Europe' in *SIPRI Yearbook 2004: Armaments, Disarmament and International Security* (Oxford: Oxford University Press).

Hart, J. and Kile, S. N. (2005), 'Libya's renunciation of nuclear, biological and chemical weapons and ballistic missiles' in *SIPRI Yearbook 2005: Armaments, Disarmament and International Security* (Oxford: Oxford University Press).

Holmqvist, C. (2005), 'Private Security Companies: The case for regulation', *SIPRI Policy Paper*. Full text available at <http://www.sipri.org/contents/publications/Policypaper9.html>.

International Committee of the Red Cross, <http://www.icrc.org>.

Lau, L. and Stiglitz, J. (2004), 'China's alternative to revaluation', *Financial Times*, 24 April 2004.

Lee, R. (2000), *Smuggling Armageddon: The Nuclear Black Market in the Former Soviet Union and Europe* (New York: St. Martin's Press, 2000).

Lenain, P. (2004), 'The economic consequences of terrorism' in Bailes, A. J. K. and Frommelt, I. (eds), *Business and Security: Public-Private Sector Relationships in a New Security Environment* (Oxford: Oxford University Press).

Maitland, A. (2006a), 'The frustrated will to act for the public good', *Financial Times*, 25 January 2006: 10.

—— (2006b), 'Companies urged to reveal climate risk information', *Financial Times*, 15 June 2006: 6.

Newsweek (news summary), 8 July 2006.

Powell, B. and McGirk, T. (2005), 'The man who sold the bomb', *Time Magazine*, 14 February 2005.

Proliferation Security Initiative (PSI) official website, <http://www.state.gov/t/np/c10390.htm>.

Roffey, R. (2004), 'Biological weapons and potential indicators of offensive biological weapon activities' in *SIPRI Yearbook 2004: Armaments, Disarmament and International Security* (Oxford: Oxford University Press).

Roffey, R. and Kuhlau, F. (2006), 'Enhancing bio-security: the need for a global strategy' in *SIPRI Yearbook 2006: Armaments, Disarmament and International Security* (Oxford: Oxford University Press).

Statens kärnkraftinspektion [Swedish Nuclear Power Inspectorate] (2000), 'Report on Combating of Illicit Trafficking', *SKI Report*, 00:3.

Stockholm International Peace Research Institute (2005). 'Strengthening European Action on Non Proliferation and Disarmament: How can Community Instruments contribute?' Conference Papers <http://www.sipri.org/contents/expcon/euppconfmaterials.html>.

Sveriges Exportkontrollförening [Swedish Export Control Society] <http://www.chamber.se/exportcontrol>.

The National Security Strategy of the United States of America, version of September 2002, at <http://www.whitehouse.gov/nsc/nss.pdf>.

The New York Times (2004), 'Interview with Mohamad ElBaradei', 23 January 2004.

United Nations General Assembly (2005), *2005 World Summit Outcome*, <http://www.un.org/summit2005/documents.html>.

United Nations Global Compact home page on Conflict Prevention, 'The Role of the Private Sector in Zones of Conflict', <http://www.unglobalcompact.org/issues/conflict_prevention/index.html>.

United Nations Security Council (2001) Resolution no. 1373 of 28 September 2001 on Threats to international peace and security caused by terrorist acts, S/RES/1373(2001), text at <http://www.un.org/Docs/sc/unsc_resolutions01.html>.

United National Security Council (2004) Resolution no. 1540 of 28 April 2004 on Weapons of mass destruction, S/RES/1540(2004), text at <http://www.un.org/Docs/sc/unsc_resolutions04.html>.

Utrikesdepartementet [Swedish Ministry for Foreign Affairs] (2001), *Financing and Producing Global Public Goods*, <http://www.egdi.gov.se/dev_financing/documentID43161.htm>.

Williamson, H. (2006), 'Global companies "keener to avoid rights scandals"', *Financial Times*, 1 September: 3

Chapter 4

European Military Forces: Integration by Default

Ståle Ulriksen

The European armed forces have been downsized, reorganised and restructured for a decade and a half. During that period European forces have been engaged in a large number of operations ranging from classical peacekeeping to full-scale, high-intensity war and have operated within several international institutional frameworks and settings. In this process the European armed forces have had to incorporate several major changes.

The deepening integration of Europe has led to the Common Market, the introduction of the euro and expanded foreign policy cooperation. During the last decade, 15 states and almost one hundred and fifty million people have joined the EU and NATO. This has had a multitude of effects, of course, one of which has been to move the European political focus away from the military issues that dominated the agenda during the cold war. Simultaneously, military and defence issues seem to have lost their status as 'high politics' with ensured budgetary priority above most other issues. Military spending as a percentage of GDP has decreased dramatically in Europe since the end of the cold war.

The changes triggered in the 1990s by the American re-launch of the concept of Revolutions in Military Affairs (RMA) enhanced the consciousness of an ongoing rapid qualitative change in military technology. The possibilities created by the vast and rapid improvements in information technology lay at the basis of the change. In many ways, this initiated a paradigmatic shift in military doctrine.

The changes of foci from the either/or divide between full-scale war and UN peacekeeping during the cold war to the very demanding handling of complex emergencies, caused major changes in European military doctrine. During the 1990s European forces became traumatised in a series of post-cold war peace support operations in the Balkans and in Africa. The resulting new European military doctrines provided guidelines on how to use force that was very different from both full-scale war and traditional passive peacekeeping (Tardy, 1999: 55–78; Thornton, 2000: 41–62; Findlay, 2002). These changes also made the parts of the European technological base that were designed to wreck as much destruction as possible upon Warsaw Pact forces irrelevant, as the new doctrines demanded more precision and less collateral damage.

The change in strategic and geographical focus implied devaluation in terms of relevance for the European forces: changes in strategic thinking on both sides of the Atlantic emphasised power-projection and thus devalued territorial defence.

For most Europeans, the cold war was about preparing to defend their own territory. Their forces were recruited, trained and equipped accordingly. This meant that there was a huge need for rather simple capabilities for strategic transport and logistic support. Still, these capabilities were not easily acquired as defence budgets declined and several key states faced serious economic problems.

These sets of changes made European military transformation more complex and far more difficult than, for instance, the parallel transformation of the US Armed Forces. The US process was mainly focused on the introduction of new technologies and the development of doctrines and structures to maximise the effect of these technologies. The US cared little for 'military operations other than war'; the US armed forces already had a huge power projection capability and the US military did not suffer the large budgetary reductions that hit the European armed forces.

As a result of this range of economic, political and military factors, military integration in Europe deepened and widened to an unprecedented level. This led to a large number of cooperation projects where an increasing number of European states took part in binational and multinational projects in the research and procurement of military equipment, international mergers in the arms industry, binational and multinational training programs, agencies and military units. The process was linked to developments in NATO, the West European Union (WEU) and the EU, but not restricted to any of these institutions. It consisted of a web of cooperative projects, each with its own dynamics and motivation, rather than a planned and controlled process. It was a process of decentralised military integration, or military integration by default (Ulriksen, 1996).

This chapter commences by sketching the present state of the European armed forces. This is necessary because European military capabilities are often portrayed in a rather bad light, mainly because the methods of evaluation are based on comparisons with US armed forces, and because the American way is often seen as the state of the art. It is also necessary because EU estimates of progress do not register all military capabilities of the EU member states. The Capabilities Improvement Chart I/2006, for instance, shows no progress in carrier-based air power, helicopter carriers or strategic sealift since 2002 (Council of the EU, 2006). The fact is that since 2002, Italy has built a new aircraft carrier/amphibious ship, France has built two helicopter carriers/command ships and Britain has built two large assault ships and introduced a class of four large amphibious vessels. These ships also represent a large increase in strategic sealift capabilities. The second part of the article discusses multinational forces and how such units create dynamics that rebound to shape the future military geography in Europe. The third part discusses the range of institutional options available for European states in military operations.

The State of the European Armed Forces

A large number of European states are still implementing major changes in their military structures, often including professionalisation in the sense that conscription is being supplemented with other forms of recruitment, or phased out. Most of these states aim to increase their capability for operations abroad within multilateral frameworks. Some states have been through repeated restructuring processes resulting in more or less continuous downscaling since 1990. Finally, some states seem to have found workable, balanced and more or less sustainable structures. Still, Europe's armed forces vary greatly in form, function and their current situation.

Five key functions may be identified: sovereignty enforcement and defence against terror; territorial defence; peace support operations (PSO) or stability operations; global rapid reaction, and global power projection. *Sovereignty enforcement and defence* against terror is about border control, protection of vital resources and functions, surveillance and intelligence. It may include both military and paramilitary organisations and assets as well as police. But it does not require large scale military forces intended to fight battles: *Territorial defence* does. This is about the defence of the territory and the nation against major military threats. Its credibility rests upon the ability to mobilise most of societies' resources for war. Traditional territorial defence depends upon conscription and the maintenance of large reserves that may be mobilised when the need arises. The standing military organisation is heavily tasked with education and training of conscripts to sustain the reserves.

PSO and stability operations require the ability to sustain force levels in the long term, mostly low intensity operations abroad. Sustainability rests upon the ability to train new forces continuously, or to rotate standing forces in a cycle of phases that includes operations, recovery and training. Most European states recognise that to keep one unit in the field continuously, a total of three to six such units are required. A cycle with six phases, including one in operations, could be considered ideal for normal military units. Heavier operational workloads create stress which causes experienced personnel to quit, and to decreased recruitment. If the forces are required to switch between operational roles, modes and tasks, much training is required. If the time between deployments is cut, so is time for training for other tasks.

Global rapid reaction capabilities depend upon high readiness as the units will have to be able to move fast into operations. It will also depend on flexibility in tasks as the units will have to cover a range of potential situations, and easy access to means of transport as the area of operations may be almost anywhere. The tasks themselves are normally limited in time and space. Readiness is very expensive. Flexibility requires much training and several sets of equipment for different tasks. Ready access to fast transport normally means that a fleet of expensive transport aircraft has to be maintained. Units trained and equipped for rapid reaction are normally much more expensive to maintain than ordinary standing forces, and far more expensive than similar units in reserve.

The high end of *global power projection* is about the ability to deploy substantial military resources and to sustain high intensity military operations over long distances. Depending on the scale and intensity, it rests on a spectrum of capabilities in intelligence, reconnaissance, communication, logistics and supply, tanker aircraft, air and sea transport as well as on a range of actual forces. The latter includes long range or carrier-borne aviation, amphibious capabilities, precision strike capabilities, and so forth.

European armed forces vary considerably in their ability to carry out these five tasks. Many of the smaller states concentrate almost exclusively on sovereignty enforcement. Most southern European states have large paramilitary organisations like the *Gendarmerie*, the *Carabinieri* and the *Guardia Civil* dedicated to such tasks. Most Mediterranean navies have dedicated more ships to patrol their territories at sea now than during the cold war. In the north, the Scandinavians have largely retained their Home Guard for such roles, and the Danish and Norwegian Coast Guard services and ocean patrol capabilities have been strengthened.

Some states have retained a system for large-scale mobilisation in defence of the territory. Greece and Finland stand out here, but Bulgaria, Italy, Poland and Romania also maintain large forces intended for territorial defence. These mobilisation forces are numerous. Finland, for example, can mobilise 22 brigades. Most of them receive little training and are equipped with very old equipment. Most West European states have disbanded their mobilisation forces, and on paper the cuts appear drastic. Norway, for example, used to have 13 brigades: today there is only one. However, most of those 13 brigades were equipped with obsolete material and would have had no value whatsoever for present Norwegian security policy. The Norwegian defence budget is is at a similar level to that prior to the cuts in absolute terms, a fact that indicates the expense of readiness and flexibility.

Most European states contribute regularly to long-term PSO operations, but some states, like Ireland, have specialised almost exclusively in such roles. Half the German army is reserved for low-intensity PSO operations. The EU Headline Goal of 1999 called for the EU to be able to deploy a corps of some 60,000 troops in a stabilisation operation for one year (Lindström, 2007). That goal has not been stressed later in the process, but the EU is undertaking such an operation in Bosnia and may take over Kosovo as well. NATO has designed its force structure in order to be able to take on three corps-size operations simultaneously. NATO needs nine deployable corps HQs, and a large number of deployable forces to do that. In 2007 at least nine such HQs will be available. Eight of these will be led by member states of the EU and these assets may be available to the EU as well.

Most European states have committed rapid reaction units to the NATO Response Force (NRF), and the European Union Battle Groups (EUBG). Forces rotate in and out of periods of readiness of six months, normally once every three years. From January 2007, there will always be one NRF and two EUBG on readiness, and a similar number of units in preparation for the next rotation. Thus, one NRF will have some 25,000 soldiers, sailors and airmen, and a full three year period of rotations will include 150,000 personnel. While Canada, Turkey and the US contribute troops, most of the personnel are likely to be from member states and states associated with the European Union. The EUBG are smaller units and hitherto the rotation only includes ground forces, headquarters and airlift, a total of some 2,000 troops. But from 2008 the EU hopes to have an aircraft carrier with its air wing and an escort group in readiness as well. Such a force may well include 4,000 sailors and airmen. If so, two EUBG and a carrier group on readiness continuously in three year cycles may include up to 48,000 personnel in that period. Each unit is committed for a full year that includes six months of training. Although the NRF and the EUBG may train and operate together, the earmarked units cannot stand in readiness for both the NRF and the EUBG or any other force at the same time. All in all, the NRF and EUBG systems will employ up to 200,000 personnel for one year every three year period. Those forces may be available for other operational tasks as well, but not if the 1:6 rotation cycle mentioned above is to be maintained.

Most European states will be able to contribute some forces to global power projection, and some may provide a substantial contribution. Even so, only France and Britain are doing this more or less across the board of military capabilities. France and Britain are maintaining their nuclear capabilities and investing heavily in power projection capabilities for their navies, with new large aircraft carriers, command vessels and amphibious ships. They are procuring very advanced fighter aircraft equipped with a range of precision munitions. Regarding the European capability to fight conventional wars far away from home, it should be noted that the British contribution to the war in Iraq in the spring of 2003 was larger than that of 1990–91 in absolute, but particularly in relative terms. Britain deployed a full division along with a large number of fighter aircraft and naval vessels. The number of personnel peaked at 46,000 in March and April 2003. That force was slightly larger than the force deployed in the Gulf War of 1991. And while the British armed forces had 306,000 under arms in 1990, they had only 210,000 in 2002. Britain deployed 15 per cent of its forces in 1991, and 22 per cent in 2003. Even so, the British forces were deployed with greater ease in 2002–2003 than in 1990–91. Moreover, the British contribution in 2003 made up a much larger part of the total coalition forces than in 1991. In 1991, the US deployed almost ten division equivalents, and Britain accounted for one of the six non-American divisions. At the start of hostilities in 2003, the US fielded three division equivalents and Britain one division.

Even if all the forces of each European state had reached a very high standard in a national setting, any European army would face huge operational difficulties in high intensity, high tempo warfare. Modern high-tempo operations require that the whole organisation, including fairly low-level officers, understand the operational concepts, the doctrine and the tactics. Lack of an integrated system of command, control, communication, and intelligence, reconnaissance, surveillance (C4IRS) is the major weakness of the combined European armed forces. This is not simply a question of technology: the huge variance in military doctrine, leadership philosophy, language and language skills, and the existence of strong inter-state as well as inter-service rivalry, dwarf the mere technological problems. The whole organisation must share a common understanding. This has been difficult to achieve even in the USA, where work to increase 'jointness' has given priority since the mid-1980s. In the US armed forces there are five main services: the Army, the Air Force, the Navy, the Marine Corps and the Coast Guard. In a European system with 30 participating states, there are more than one hundred such services if the para-military organisations under the various ministries of defence are included. Each and every one of these services will have its own collective identity, own schools and colleges, own routines and doctrines, and frequently their own research institutes as well. All in all 30 states, 30 ministries of defence and some one hundred services have to be co-ordinated if an all-European military force capable of *efficient high intensity warfare* is to be created. This simply does not seem possible.

In the short term the only solution to this problem would seem to build operational capabilities on 'Lead Nations' or 'Framework Nations'. Basically this means that one state provides the basic infrastructure and critical assets of a multinational unit, and that other states provides different sub-units and capabilities to complement it. This makes military sense, but it may prove more difficult politically as being a Lead Nation may come to mean just that. Obviously, the Lead Nations will attain powerful positions. But they may also be qualitatively different from other states in that since they own critical assets for command and control they will retain a much higher level of military independence than those states providing only tactical units. The states capable of being a Lead Nation will be in a league of their own, the integrated European equivalent of the Great Powers. This is one of the real key issues of intra-European military politics in 2007.

Even among the Lead Nations there will be a pecking order. In many ways, the relative weight of the large European states in security policy has changed dramatically as their military relevance has changed. During the cold war, the West German army used to be the backbone of NATO's central front. It had 12 manoeuvre divisions with 48 armoured, mechanised and infantry brigades in 1990, and was the strongest army in Western Europe. In the plans of 2006 the army had only four such divisions with eight brigades, an army of the same size as those of Britain, France, Italy, Poland and Spain. Four of the eight German brigades, so-called *Stabiliserungskräfte* or stabilisation forces, were only meant for operations of low and medium intensity. Consequently, the German Army will only be able to contribute four brigades plus supporting forces in high intensity operations. The German Navy has been denied the amphibious ships that were envisioned as an important enabler for participation in international operations, and has no assets for naval command (Kujat, 2002). If Europe is to play a larger military role in the world it will depend on British and French leadership.

The Military Structures

In spite of improvements made during the last few years, there is still a gap between military ambitions and the budget to maintain, recruit, equip, train and actually deploy military units in most European states. Most European armed forces are constantly struggling to adapt to reduced budgets or increased operational activity. Indeed, European reluctance to contribute more to international operations is often a result of budgetary limitations rather than lack of available forces. Few states have been able to balance budgets and ambitions, and there is a constant search for savings and more cost-effective solutions.

During the last decade-and-a-half most such solutions have been a mixture of market-oriented economic ideas imported from business, privatisation and internationalisation. All require the state to ease its direct control over the security and defence sectors and to accept greater international interdependence and the increased influence of the market and private companies. This trend has grown even stronger after the turn of the millennium, but the states are still mainly in control, and most of them are not prepared for radical solutions like functional division of military tasks between states where each state concentrates its efforts in national military niches. States are reluctant to commit themselves to large-scale, long-term visions of an integrated European defence. The Headline Goal 2010 that was endorsed by the European Council in 2004 repeatedly underlined the prerogatives of member states in defence matters (Council of the EU, 2004). Still, when it comes to concrete decisions on practical matters like the procurement of new weapons or military equipment, on the joint preparation for operations or for the design of a multinational unit, such lofty questions are not addressed at all. Nevertheless, when hundreds of such decisions go more or less in the same direction, towards more bilateral and multilateral cooperation on almost all military levels, a more coherent European military system is slowly and incrementally taking place.

Joint assets

The EU and NATO all depend on the same forces provided by their respective member states, but the two organisations have different command structures. These headquarters and chains of command have become more harmonised during the last few years although there is still some friction. NATO has one operational Strategic Command (SHAPE), which includes an EU cell; three operational level commands, and six commands at the component/tactical level. Additionally, NATO has four Combined Air Operations Centres. In a military operation, the EU military chain of command will include headquarters at three levels. The *Operation Command* will handle the strategic level from Europe; the *Force Command* will handle the joint operational level in the theatre and co-ordinate the *Component Air, Sea and Land Commands*. If the operation uses NATO assets, a NATO HQ will take on the Operation Command while a Combined Joint Task Force, or similar HQ, will function as Force Command. NATO's command structures have many more resources, and are far more capable than those of the EU. Nevertheless, the EU has access to national joint operations commands in Britain, France and Germany. These will be in charge of all EUBGs.

In practice, EU operations of a certain scale, independent of NATO, will rely on the leadership and substantial involvement of Britain, France or Germany at the strategic and operational levels. However, such operations also depend on a range of specific capabilities. The lack of independent European sensors and navigation systems is a very serious drawback in any high-intensity scenario independent of NATO. The most efficient way to use a precision guided missile (PGM) is to link it to a Global Positioning System (GPS). Currently, only the US operates such a system globally.[1] Indeed, the possession of a very comprehensive C4IRS infrastructure in space is probably the most valuable of all the military assets of the USA. In March 2002, the European ministers of transport gave the go-ahead for Galileo, a European GPS system that may be used for both civilian and military purposes when it is operational, hopefully by 2008 (Europemedia 2002a and b). Until then, Europe will have to depend on the USA to allow the use of its GPS.

Since 2003, the number of European satellites for surveillance and reconnaissance has increased dramatically. The French Helios optical surveillance satellites have been followed by German, Italian and Spanish systems. Helios 1 was financed by France, Italy and Spain, while Helios 2 is a French venture with a small Belgian

---

1 The Russian military also operates a GPS, the Glonass.

participation. Germany is building a constellation of all-weather radar satellites, and Italy a network of Cosmo radar and optical satellites. Spain also plans an optical satellite system. France has concluded agreements for cooperation with Germany and Italy. The two French satellites may be used globally, while the Italian will cover the Mediterranean and the German central and eastern Europe. Satellite information must be processed to be useful. The EU (formerly WEU) Satellite Centre in Torrejon provides the EU and WEU with information vital to crisis handling.

Britain and France already operate a total of 11 airborne warning and command systems (AWACS) for surveillance of air space and command of air forces. NATO operates a jointly owned fleet of 18 such aircraft. The French Navy operates a few American E-2C aircraft. Sweden and Greece have bought a total of 10 Erieye aircraft for airborne early warning and control. Britain is presently building Airborne Stand-Off Radar (ASTOR) to survey movement on the ground which will give Britain and Europe a capability similar to the US J-STAR. Additionally, France has equipped some Cougar helicopters with similar radars for tactical use. Several European states have Unmanned Aerial Vehicles (UAVs) in service, and more such systems are being developed. Regarding collection of intelligence, Europe is doing a lot in terms of investment in hardware. The coordination of these assets does not seem to be working well at all at a European level.

France, Britain and Italy operate military communication satellites, while Germany and Spain are developing their own systems. Other European states such as Sweden, plan to utilise civilian satellites for military purposes. There are no European international programs on communication satellites. It should be noted that all the states having Lead Nation ambitions at the operational level are building their own systems which may then be offered to the EU as part of the command and control package. The conservation of national sovereignty and independence in this area, as opposed to Europe-wide co-operation, is striking.

In terms of capabilities for PSO, the implementation of present plans will be more than enough in the near future. European capabilities at the strategic and operational levels, both in terms of headquarters and hardware, are improving very rapidly. However, these improvements are mainly the result of the efforts of individual states, and not of collective efforts in the EU as such. The main exception is Galileo, the future European Global Positioning System, but then Galileo was mainly a civilian initiative.

The navies

European naval forces are far more integrated in terms of common routines, language and communication equipment than their respective armies. Most European navies have sent their ships to the standing NATO-forces in the Atlantic or the English channel (STANAVFORLANT and STANAVFORCHAN) for decades. Although French forces have not been part of NATO's integrated military structures since 1966, French naval ships regularly participate in combined exercises. During the last few years, French ships have been included in British flotillas and vice versa. The navies of the new NATO and EU members took part in Partnership for Peace exercises for several years prior to joining. The Polish, Romanian and the small Baltic navies have acquired Western ships and equipment.

As from 2007, four European deployable naval headquarters will act as maritime component commands of the NATO Response Force. These are deployed on British, French, Italian and Spanish ships command ships and carriers. These HQs will, of course, also be able to command future naval components working with the EUBG.

Presently, European states have six aircraft carriers, three British (one in reserve) and one each from France, Italy and Spain. Only the French *Charles de Gaulle* is equipped with catapults and capable of operating heavy aircraft. The others all operate versions of the Harrier. In practice, the ship-borne Harriers have to limit their load of fuel and weapons, and thus represent less offensive capability per aircraft than the Super Etendards and Rafaeles of the *Charles de Gaulle*. Nevertheless, these ships represent a very valuable capability for most PSO scenarios.

This capability is set to grow strongly during the next decade. The second Italian carrier will enter service as the *Andrea Doria* in 2007, and a second Spanish carrier was ordered in 2006. Both ships will be able to combine the carrier role with an amphibious capability. They will be joined by three much larger classic aircraft carriers in 2012–2015. Britain will replace its three *Invincible*-class carriers with ships almost three times as large, and France will build a similar, but probably even larger ship. The total number of European aircraft carriers will increase from six to eight in less than a decade. But the capability will increase far more than that: the total displacement of the carrier fleet will increase from some 135,000 tons to more than 320,000 tons.

European amphibious capability increased during the 1990s, and will increase even more in the present decade. Britain has the helicopter carrier HMS *Ocean* as well as the *Bulwark* and *Albion,* two brand new Landing Platform Docks with command facilities. Britain is also building four amphibious transport ships based on the design of the Dutch-Spanish *Rotterdam*-class. At some 16,000 tons they will be almost three times as large as the ships they replace. France has two modern Foudre-class Landing Platform Docks (LPD), each capable of carrying a mechanised battalion and seven helicopters as well as two new helicopter carriers, the *Mistral* and the *Tonnere*. All four vessels will have advanced command and control facilities. The Dutch and the Spanish have already built or ordered two Rotterdam-class amphibious transport ships; Portugal and Belgium and Luxembourg plan to build two similar ships jointly. Denmark has built two smaller multi-purpose support ships that may also carry troops. These ships will be supplemented with six British and at least one Norwegian civilian roll on-roll off (ro-ro) ships from different civil–military arrangements. Several of the Rotterdam-class and the four British and French ships will have advanced command and control facilities.

The increase in capabilities for naval aviation, amphibious transport and landing, and for command and control at sea, add up to strongly increased capabilities for offensive operations from the sea. A corresponding increase in the number of ships designed for area air defence makes such operations more credible. Without efficient ship-borne air defence to protect the fleet in power projection missions in high-threat environments, the carriers will have to use most of their capabilities for self-protection and have little left for strikes against land targets. By early 2007, at least

25 modern air defence destroyers or frigates of between 5,500 and 7,200 tons will have entered service, are being built or are on order. The British have ordered six air defence ships (with an option for a further six), France, Italy, The Netherlands had Spain will each have at least four, and Germany will have three. Additionally five Norwegian frigates will have long-range air defence radars which may be fitted with missiles later. These 30 ships will use three different radars and two different long and medium range air defence weapon systems, but will nevertheless represent a huge improvement of the European ability to protect its ships against aircraft and missiles. This will make it possible to utilise carrier air power more efficiently for offensive purposes. Additionally, the increase in helicopter carriers and LPDs combined with the introduction of advanced attack helicopters in several European states will make it possible both to give troops ashore close air support and to provide them with efficient heliborne reconnaissance. Many of the above-mentioned ships and a large number of planned smaller frigates and different classes of submarines will be equipped with missiles for strikes against land targets. To some extent, the increase in these maritime capabilities will ease the strain on the weak deployable support services for the air forces.

This increase in power projection capabilities has come at a price. There have been large cuts in smaller escort ships, frigates and corvettes, in submarines, as well as in the number of mine countermeasure vessels and fast attack craft (FAC) for operations in the littorals. On the other hand, there has been an increase in ocean and costal surveillance vessels for sovereignty enforcement. Many of the smaller escorts and FACs have been transformed to patrol vessels for border control, environmental surveillance and ship inspections.

The european air forces

Although both France and Britain have developed deployable capabilities to command and control air operations, the Europeans depend more heavily on NATO for such assets for the air component than for the ground and naval components. Standardisation and interoperability in NATO air forces has reached a very high level, and it would not seem very wise to build parallel European structures as long as NATO assets are available in operations. European cooperation and integration in the shape of pooling of resources, common development and production projects and combined operations, have come further in the air forces than in ground forces and the navies.

In 2004, the 25 EU members had more than 4,000 combat aircraft in operational and training units or in store. Those aircraft belonged to an amazing 27 different main types and an even larger number of sub-types. There was no need for such a huge number of airframes, and the vast variance in types was of course very expensive and highly inefficient in an European perspective. Both the total number of aircraft and the number of types have decreased dramatically since 2002 and the process continues. More than one thousand new JAS-39 Gripen, Rafales and Eurofighter Typhoons are being delivered. When these replace older types, most of the remaining aircraft will be also be relatively modern, often updated, F-16s, F-18s, Mirage 2000s, Tornadoes and Harriers. Many European states are also partners in the development of the American Joint Strike Fighter (JSF), and during the next decade several hundred JSFs may enter service in European air forces.

Aircraft are not weapons. By the turn of the millennium most European air forces were still mainly equipped for air defence, for combat against other aircraft, or for attacks on the logistic infrastructure of the huge armoured armies of the Warsaw Pact. Fuel and ammunition depots, airfields and railway stations, traffic choke points and so on, are large targets. They can be destroyed by 'dumb' bombs filled with high explosives, penetration bombs, or cluster bombs scattering hundreds of sub-munitions in all directions. Those weapons are very ill-suited for destroying a command post in an urban neighbourhood if one wants to avoid killing civilians. The Europeans had very few systems for precision attacks from the air. After Kosovo and the initial campaigns in Afghanistan, this situation has changed rapidly. By 2007, most European air forces have acquired precision-guided bombs, and several are introducing cruise missiles like the French-British Scalp/Storm Shadow and the German-Swedish Taurus. These missiles, weighing some 1,200 kg, have a range of 250 to 350 km (Hewson, 2002).

European forces lack large transport aircraft to lift heavy equipment over long distances. For years, most European states have depended on renting Russian and Ukrainian civilian Antonov 124s for such tasks. Such services may not always be available. Hitherto the only strategic transport aircraft in Europe are the four C-17s of the Royal Air Force. The RAF plans to buy another C-17, and a consortium of 16 European states plan to build a joint fleet with an initial three C-17s. However, within the decade between 200 and 300 Airbus A-400 transports will be procured. The A-400 is a smaller aircraft than the C-17 and will only be able to take on loads up to 35 tons. While strategic transport services might be bought in emergencies, this is not the case for airborne tanking. Europe has approximately 70 tanker aircraft, which might prove too few in a theatre with large-scale air operations, few bases and long distances. Regarding medium-sized transport aircraft the situation is far better. The European states have some 300 C-130 Hercules and C-160 Transall, and about 150 even lighter aircraft such as the G-222, C-212 and C-235.

The combat capabilities of the European air forces are improving rapidly with the modernisation of existing aircraft and introduction of new aircraft and weapons. The ability to support operations with strategic transport is not that bright. The lack of strategic air transport is not a critical shortcoming as regards Europe's ability to run PSOs in Europe or in the vicinity of Europe. It will not be critical in areas where very heavy equipment will not be needed in large quantities. However, the further away from the sea and existing bases the theatre of operations are situated, the heavier will be the strain on air transport. In Central Africa, for instance, all or most fuel as well as all the water needed might have to be brought in by aircraft.

The armies

By 2010, it may be expected that the British, French, German, Italian, Polish and Spanish armies together will have around 50 deployable brigades. Nineteen smaller European states should be able to field the equivalent of at least another 30 to 40 brigades. A large number of independent battalions and forces for combat support and for combat support services come in addition. It is important, however, not to put too much weight on such numbers as brigades are not standardised units in size, training level, preparedness, equipment and availability. Neither are brigades necessarily the most relevant unit of measure. Rather, the point here is rather to provide a rough estimate of potential: if the Europeans have a total of 90 deployable brigades, and maintain a cycle of operations of 1:6, then they should be able to sustain 15 brigades in the field continuously. If each brigade comprises 3,000 troops, and if one assumes a 1:1 ratio between the manoeuvre forces and the support forces, then Europe should be able to keep around 90,000 ground troops in the field continuously on a sustainable basis. Note that almost all of these units have accumulated much experience in operations in the Balkans, Iraq, Afghanistan and Africa. Note also that most British, French, German, Italian, Spanish and a large number of the Polish brigade and division headquarters have accumulated experience as regional HQs in the operations mentioned.

The European armies vary considerably in terms of their priorities. There have been major reductions in heavy armoured formations, and with few exceptions the remaining heavy units are rarely deployed abroad. For many years it was assumed that the main battle tank was obsolete and that European armies were 'tank heavy'. However, most of the tanks in European arsenals after the cold war were old or not very well protected. Recent experiences from Iraq and Lebanon may prove that the tank is still needed. If so, the few thousand really modern tanks left in European armies may be valuable but scarce assets. The German and Dutch cuts in armour have placed many second hand Leopard 2 tanks on the market. They have replaced older tanks in the arsenals of a large number of states. The advantage of this is an increased standardisation of European armies.

There has been a relative increase in light and lightly mechanised infantry units. These are well suited for most PSO. Very few marine, airborne or helicopter-based air assault units have been dissolved in Europe since the cold war. The Netherlands and Italy have even converted mechanised brigades into air assault units equipped with both attack and transport helicopters. Amphibious forces, or marines, have been equally prioritised. France and Britain will also place attack helicopters procured for the army aboard ships in order to increase the punch of the marines. It appears that present European armies are first and foremost designed for PSO and for rapid reaction. It is highly questionable though, if European armies have retained their cold war skill in large scale armoured warfare.

Multinational Forces

From the early 1990s, a large number of multinational forces were created in Europe. Such units were created in all services and at many levels, although changes have been strongest in the ground forces. I have therefore chosen to focus on multinational ground units here. Quite briefly, ground forces have traditionally been organised into companies, battalions, brigades, divisions and corps. A unit is composed of from two to five lower level units with support units added at each level. Battalions (400–800 troops) are normally composed exclusively of one arm, such as infantry, armour and artillery. Traditionally, the brigade (2,000–5,000 troops) is the smallest unit where different arms are combined in order to support one another. From the brigade level and up, a step from one level to the next represents a leap in the fighting qualities of the units. Thus the strength of a division (15,000–25,000 troops) is regarded to be greater than the sum of the strength of its brigades. The corps 50,000–100,000 troops) represents yet another step towards increased efficiency.

A high degree of standardisation and integration had taken place in NATO during the cold war. In then navies and air forces, standardisation of communication systems and operating procedures had eased cooperation to such a degree that a pilot from one country could easily serve in a fighter squadron of another. On the other hand, the ground forces mainly operated in large national units. On the central front those units were the nine allied army corps that were lined up in Germany. In other words, the building blocks of the multinational forces on NATO's Central Front were very large units. As the corps were separated geographically, the troops and even division commanders did not need to have much contact with allied forces. They could operate in their own language and follow their own doctrines.

In 1990–91 NATO embraced a force structure with six multinational corps on NATO's central front. This was primarily a measure to strengthen solidarity and display commitment within the alliance at a time when re-nationalisation was one of the ghosts haunting European security (Pallin, 1995). Multinational units may be perceived as rather potent symbols of cooperation and as instruments to engage allies and influence their way of military thinking. The Franco-German brigade created in 1987 was to a very large extent a political statement protesting against what was perceived as President Reagan's unilateral *détente* with the Soviet Union. For years, the brigade was mocked as a paper tiger and an extremely expensive language school. Still, in the late 1990s the brigade participated in operations in Bosnia and Kosovo and in the latter half of 2006 it forms the core of the land element of the NATO Response Force. The unit has evolved from being a symbol of European cooperation to a credible and deployable military force. The same story could be told for the Eurocorps that caused such fierce controversy when it was created in 1991.

The multinational units were also created as measures of economic rationalisation. Most states found it difficult to maintain the corps level in their shrinking armies as defence budgets were reduced. The result was that national units at the level of the corps were disbanded or fused into multinational units. This was not the case, however, for the two German–American corps established in 1993. One German division joined the US V Corps, while one US division joined the II German corps. But all corps-level support units were national and the command of each corps would be permanently in the hands of the lead nation. These were loose arrangements compared to the more complex multinationality found in the Eurocorps and Dutch–German Corps. Thus, the Americans kept a distance to multinationality in NATO's force structure. Consequently, integration of forces in NATO became an almost completely European process.

The creation of the multinational forces was also a struggle for political influence: five of the corps were planned as main defence forces, designed for territorial defence. The sixth corps, however, was to give NATO a capability for rapid reinforcement of crisis areas. The corps was to become known as the Allied Command Europe

Rapid Reaction Corps (ARRC). Here, actual military capabilities mattered more than political symbolism. The leadership of such an important unit would obviously give the lead (or framework) nation both influence and prestige. The fact that the ARRC spearheaded NATO forces in Bosnia in 1995, in Kosovo in 1999 and in Southern Afghanistan in 2006, underlines the point. Much to the disappointment of the Germans the command of the ARRC was given to the British army which had just proved itself capable both of being deployed overseas and of fighting intense battles during the Gulf War (McInnes, 1993). The British also suggested the creation of a European Reaction Force and tried 'to endow the ARRC with a WEU command in case of out-of-area operations' (Smith, 1992). This would have given Britain a central military position in both NATO and the WEU. France strongly opposed the idea. Both the French and the Germans felt snubbed and reacted very strongly to what was perceived in Bonn and Paris as a British coup in the spring of 1991 (Menon et al., 1992: 98–118; Moens, 1993; Stein, 1993). The *Eurocorps* was created in 1991, at least partly in response to the ARRC.

The Eurocorps and the ARRC represented different models of integration. The headquarters of the ARRC and the Eurocorps are able to command four divisions in the field. Although the number of 60,000 troops has often been cited to describe the potential size of the corps, it is more likely that such a force would approach 100,000 troops. The ARRC could draw on a force of well ten allied divisions. Several of these divisions had brigades assigned from yet other states. The Eurocorps had four dedicated divisions, one from each of the framework nations (Belgium, France, Germany, Spain). In terms of these assigned forces the ARRC, with its combination of heavy and light forces, had greater flexibility than the Eurocorps. But throughout the 1990s the links between HQs and subordinated forces became less permanent and the composition of units decreased in importance. Still, as the NATO-deployable corps may become more important in force generation processes, the importance of permanently assigned forces to the corps may yet increase again.

There was a more important difference. The ARRC was built around British structures, the key enabling units are British and so is sixty per cent of the HQ staff. The commander is always a British general. The design allows the lead nation 'to unhook from multinationality and use its corps headquarters for any possible non-Alliance or unilateral action' (Seitz, 1992). In theory at least, the lead nation design preserves sovereignty for the lead nation,while the other contributors will always play second fiddle. The Eurocorps support structures were multinational and command-rotated among the framework nations. They would all gain some experience, influence and prestige from command of the corps. In Eurocorps, a small state like Belgium could be an equal partner with France and Germany. It is probably no coincidence that after the latest restructuring in 2005–2006 the German army only contributes divisions to corps based on rotating commands. This may leave Germany without a national champion in the same way that the ARRC is for Britain. It may reflect the strong German commitment to integration, and it may give Germany major influence in a large part of the force structure. It may also reflect a reluctance to take on highly profiled national roles in military interventions.

The ARRC and the Eurocorps were defined as reaction forces, and intended to have a high level of readiness and an ability to move to crisis areas. Two other multinational corps developed as main defence forces. The 1ˢᵗ German–Netherlands Corps was established to replace one German and one Dutch corps in North-eastern Germany between 1991 and 1995, and included one division from each state. The composition of support units and the permanence of the chain of command made it the most integrated multinational corps in NATO. The unit that ended up as the Multinational Corps Northeast (MNC-NE) was based on the allied forces in LANDJUT, a corps level unit created in 1962 to command NATO in the defence of Schleswig-Holstein and Jutland. As Poland joined NATO and MNC-NE in 1999, the corps headquarters moved to Szczecin in Poland. The corps was the first to include forces from a new member state. Each state would contribute one division, and command of the corps would rotate between the three states.

In the force structure of 1991, only a fraction of the forces were meant to be deployable over long distances and to maintain a high state of readiness. The NATO force structure, adopted in July 2001, called for the transformation of the whole structure into deployable units, albeit with differentiated levels of readiness. One lesson learnt from the operations in the Balkans was the value of rapid reaction forces like the ARRC. This organisation had spearheaded the NATO operations in Bosnia in 1995–96, and in Kosovo in 1999. Additionally, the Eurocorps had provided the core of NATO's headquarters in Bosnia for 18 months during 1998–99 and taken command of the NATO forces in Kosovo in 2000. A permanent headquarters was far more efficient than one created ad hoc and on location.

The new structure called for nine headquarters at the corps level (Deni 2005). Three were to serve as High Readiness Force (Land) HQs (HRF-L), and six more as headquarters at a medium level of readiness. The former were meant to be ready to deploy within two weeks after the start of a crisis and be in command of a full corps of up to four divisions in two to three months. The latter were to be capable of providing relief for the HRF-L HQs after six to twelve months of preparation. Each of these corps would also be capable of leading the type of force envisaged in the EU Helsinki headline goals of 1999. Each corps was suited for commanding an operation of the SFOR or the KFOR type.

Twelve candidates presented themselves. No less than nine of these, including the US V Corps in Germany and the 3ʳᵈ Turkish Corps in Istanbul, wanted the most demanding roles as HRF-L. By March 2002, only six candidates for the HRF-L HQ remained. Notably, the US V Corps was no longer among the candidates. Ostensibly, the reason was that the US would give the Europeans the opportunity to modernise their forces. One effect, however, was to reinforce the impression that multinationality in NATO was a European process in which the US armed forces did not participate.

In 2002–2003 the ARRC, the Eurocorps, the Dutch–German Corps, the Spanish, Italian and 3ʳᵈ Turkish corps were all certified as HRF, while the Greek C Corps and the MNC-NE were certified as forces with lower readiness. Additionally, France announced that it would provide a seventh HRF-L HQ from 2007 and Poland proposed the II Polish corps as a third lower readiness HQ. The candidature of the II Polish corps is still uncertain; the costs may simply be too large for Poland (Golawski 2005b). The French, Greek, Italian, Spanish, Turkish and corps were all purely national units and had to invite allies to contribute. The lead nations had to invest substantially in upgraded command and control capabilities of the headquarters, and had to commit large support units to them.

The process described above has left hardly any national corps-level units in Europe. Those corps that still exist have been, albeit to varying degrees, transformed into multinational units. Most of the rest have been disbanded. The multinational corps were also given important operational tasks. From 2003 they have rotated in command of the International Security Assistance Force (ISAF) in Afghanistan. The six High-readiness corps also rotate as Ground Force Component Commands for the NATO Response Force. As with the Eurocorps and the ARRC in the late 1990s, such operational tasks have caused all the deployable corps to evolve into much more credible military units.

Moreover, since these are the only corps-level units left they tend to form the cores of regional clusters of cooperation between armies. The MNC-NE, for instance, has attracted participation from the Baltic States as well as the Czech Republic and Slovakia. The existence of the MNC-NE and Poland's role in Iraq seems to have established Poland as a lead nation for large parts of Eastern Europe. In the summer of 2003, the 12th Polish Mechanised Division from Szczecin took control of the occupation of parts of central Iraq. The 12th was the Polish contribution to the MNC-NE and was used to operate as part of a multinational force. Poland provided one of the brigades of this division. Poland's close partner, Ukraine, provided another brigade, and most Eastern European states contributed forces. Polish troops had some experience in leading smaller multinational formations like the Nordic–Polish brigade in Bosnia, but this was a far more challenging task. From 2003 onwards, several Polish divisions and brigades gained experience in Iraq. Simultaneously, the MNC-CE was developed as a multinational headquarters until it was certified as a NATO deployable corps at lower readiness by NATO in late 2005. Further, the Czech Republic, Slovakia, Latvia and Lithuania had joined the MNC-NE. All were either cooperating closely with Poland in Iraq, or in multinational forces at the brigade and battalion level. Building on this accumulated experience, Poland was able to accept command of the International Security Assistance Force (ISAF) in Afghanistan in 2007 with the MNC-NE as its headquarters (Golawski, 2005a).

Most multinational brigades in the NATO Response Force and several of the European Union battle groups have been generated from existing cooperation in multinational corps: the Eurocorps, with contributions from France, Germany, Belgium, Luxembourg and potentially Spain; the I German-Netherlands Corps with German, Dutch and Finnish contributions; the Multinational Corps North-East with troops from Poland, Germany, Slovakia, Latvia and Lithuania. Four more are generated from existing cooperation at division or brigade-level: one with the participation of Italy, Hungary and Slovenia (the so-called Multinational Land Force); a second with contributions from Italy, Spain, Greece and Portugal, is built on the Spanish–Italian Amphibious force; a third is drawn from the UK–Netherlands amphibious force, and a fourth was built on Nordic cooperation, with Sweden, Finland, Estonia and Norway as contributors (Anderson, 2005; Kerttunen and Jepson, 2005). The last four battle groups are provided by regional groupings of states: one from France and Belgium, one from Germany, Austria and Czech Republic, a third from the Czech Republic and Slovakia, and the last from Greece, Cyprus and the candidate countries

Bulgaria and Romania. Ireland and Denmark are not taking part in the battlegroup system, though for different reasons.

Several battle groups are generated from larger units which also provide forces for the NATO Response Force. This is a clear advantage as experience gained in one institutional setting would more or less automatically be transferred to the other. Of course, dual-hatting means that rotation cycles need to be coordinated. Such coordination will in itself increase the institutionalisation of both forces as planning and commitments need to be agreed on well in advance of readiness periods.

Integration in Operations

Contemporary European nation states have multiple institutional options for military operations. They may act on their own; they may act in ad hoc coalitions with other European states, with the USA or with other partners; or they may direct their efforts through the UN, NATO or the EU.

The existence of many options has probably had both negative and positive effects on European military integration. With other options available it has not been necessary for the Europeans to push the development forwards. On the other hand, it may also be that the existence of many options has made it possible to go slow with military integration until the time is ripe. The development within each of these categories may tell us something about the strengths of the different options, and perhaps if the time is ripe…

National operations

Several European states are capable of undertaking small evacuation operations or Special Forces operations abroad on their own. Some may be capable of carrying out larger operations closer to home. Still, in essence only two European states are both capable and willing to undertake complex military operations in a national setting far beyond their own borders. Those states are France and the United Kingdom. Their power projection capabilities are dwarfed by those of the USA, but still larger than those of anyone else. The British intervention in Sierra Leone in 2000, and the French actions in Côte d'Ivoire from 2002, both involved thousands of troops, sailors and airmen. If not heavily involved elsewhere, both Britain and France are able to deploy much larger forces if the need arises. Indeed, the British forces would be better suited to carry out a Falklands operation today than it was in 1982. The Royal Navy has two aircraft carriers in service and another mothballed. It has a helicopter carrier, two brand new amphibious command ships as well as six new large amphibious transport ships under construction. The only reservation to such a claim is the withdrawal in 2006 of the air-to-air capable Sea Harrier and its replacement with the Harrier Gr.9 which is more of a ground attack aircraft. But even that weakness will be rectified with the introduction of two new carriers in the next decade. These ships will displace some 65,000 tons, around three times that of the ships they will replace. France plans to build one similar ship to complement the still relatively new *Charles de Gaulle*.

As seen above, European military capabilities for power projection depend heavily on those of Britain and France. These states alone possess the range of strategic instruments necessary both to command and to implement national military power projection operations.

It should be noted however, that both France and Britain have moved towards multilateral solutions even in those regions where they traditionally have acted very independently. The British operation in Sierra Leone and French operations in the Central African Republic and Cote d'Ivoire were carried out, after the initial phase, in close cooperation with the UN and regional organisations. One should also note that the European Battle Groups were designed and dimensioned exactly for this kind of task: assistance to UN operations in crisis (Ulriksen et al., 2004).

Ad hoc european coalition operations

In situations where there has been neither the will nor the time to engage NATO or the WEU or EU in operations, groups of European states have acted together outside these institutions. The European Rapid Reaction Force which entered Bosnia in the summer of 1995, led by French and British forces, is one example. The Italian-led Operation Alba where troops from most South European states, plus Denmark, entered Albania in 1997 is another. Most such operations, however, have been carried out to evacuate Europeans and other foreigners from war-stricken African countries. At least seven ad hoc coalitions were used in such evacuation operations in Rwanda, Zaire/DR Congo and Guinea-Bissau. Besides France and the UK, Portugal and Belgium – both states with a large number of citizens living in former colonies in Africa – have been the most active participants in these operations. In December 1997, Portugal and Belgium signed a declaration of intent to create a joint deployable Air Task Force tailored for evacuation operations in Africa. (*Atlantic News*, 1997). Note here that these few states, when carrying out such operations, also evacuated other Europeans. In this sense they provided a common European good. In 2007, however, such evacuations are likely to be handled by one of the European battle groups in service.

Other ad hoc coalitions

Several European states have strong ties to their former colonies and dependencies. Britain and France still have defence agreements with many of these states. British forces regularly exercise in Malaysia, Kenya and Oman, for instance. France has a number of defence agreements with African states. From the mid-1990s, France and Britain cooperated in supporting the build-up of African forces which could take on regional peace support operations, each mainly providing assistance to their own partners. Simultaneously, Portugal was trying to build up the Lusophonie so that the Portugeese-speaking community could take on Peace Support operations.

By 2006 much of the focus had shifted towards European support for the African Union (AU) and its regional standby brigades. While the European Union was hardly visible in African security affairs in the mid-1990s, the EU is now a major partner of the AU.

United Nations operations

Until the mid-1990s, a number of European states provided the bulk of forces for UN peacekeeping operations. After the disasters in Somalia, Rwanda and Srebrenica, few European states have contributed substantial forces over time to UN operations. There are two reasons for this. First, most European states have been hard pressed to provide forces for NATO operations in Bosnia, Kosovo and Afghanistan. The main exceptions were non-NATO members such as Ireland. Second, after the three disasters mentioned above, the Europeans stopped trusting the UN's ability to command and control military operations. A group of small European states, led by Denmark, tried to rectify that by creating a Standing High Readiness Brigade (SHIRBRIG) for the UN. SHIRBRIG HQ has become an important asset to the UN, but it cannot compensate for the lack of forces. Most European states still remain sceptical. When Italy and France agreed upon taking the lion's share of the burden in the expanded UNIFIL in Lebanon in 2006 they insisted on creating a new headquarters in New York to command that single operation. The new HQ was comparable in size to the whole existing UN military command apparatus responsible for all other ongoing operations. This scepticism is also reflected in the European Battle Group concept. The battlegroups are built to *support* UN operations, *not to become part of them*.

This far, the development of national operations, ad hoc European coalition operations, operational cooperation with former colonies and UN operations all seem to point in one direction – namely the strengthening of the European dimension. Most tasks formerly carried out in such settings are now channelled through European arrangements.

Operations in coalition with the USA

From late 2001 and until 2006 the US-led Operation Enduring Freedom (OEF) in Afghanistan was carried out in tandem with the international security assistance force in Kabul. This division ran counter to the principles of unity of objective and unity of command, two of the central principles in military theory. NATO's role grew from giving assistance to the Dutch–German corps in 2003 until most US forces were placed under British NATO command in 2006. At the time of writing (spring 2007) the situation seems highly perilous. Most European NATO forces contributed to OEF. Several European armed forces experienced the heaviest fighting since the Second World War. Denmark and Norway, for instance, provided Special Forces and F-16 fighter aircraft that were directly involved in heavy combat. It is likely that these experiences have contributed strongly to the development of more professional forces in Europe (Ulriksen, 2006).

The Gulf War in 1990–91 and the first phase of the ongoing War in Iraq, in the spring of 2003, are the largest conventional military operations (large-scale, full-spectrum, high intensity campaign) conducted by Western forces since the end of the cold war. Both operations included large European contingents, but in 2003 only Britain and Poland contributed to the conventional war campaign. The initial Polish contingent consisted of some 200 troops from the GROM, Poland's famous Special Forces unit. Later, the Poles took on command of a full multinational division.

Belgium, France, Germany, Greece, Luxembourg and Slovenia did not contribute forces. Italy, Spain, The Netherlands and Denmark contributed relatively large forces to the occupation, while most other NATO states provided smaller contingents in the initial occupation phase. By the end of 2006, the following European NATO members still had forces in Iraq (ranked after the size of forces in Iraq): Britain, Poland, Denmark, Romania, the Czech Republic, Latvia, Slovakia, Lithuania and Estonia. Most of these had warned that they were planning reductions or withdrawal. Note that only two of the old NATO allies remained, Britain and Denmark. The following had withdrawn (ranked after the size of the contributions at their peak) Italy, The Netherlands, Spain Bulgaria, Hungary, Norway, Portugal and Iceland.

Like the failures of the UN in Somalia, Rwanda and Bosnia, the failure to stabilise Afghanistan from 2002 to 2006 and the failed stabilisation of Iraq from May 2003 are likely to become major learning experiences to be incorporated into European military thinking. In early 2007, it seems very unlikely that the primary conclusion from these lessons will be that ad hoc coalitions with the USA will be the best institutional choice for interventions in the future.

NATO operations

After the NATO intervention in Bosnia in 1995 and Kosovo in 1999, Europe seemed as dependent on NATO as ever. The Europeans would eventually carry the lion's share of the burden in the occupation of Kosovo as they had in Bosnia. Nevertheless, as US air power was seen as the key to success in both conflicts, these operations reinforced a pattern in which the Americans would fight the war and the Europeans would come in afterwards to carry out long-term peace support operations. That was also the predominant attitude in the Pentagon after 9/11. Still, the EU has already taken over NATO operations in Macedonia and Bosnia and is likely to take over in Kosovo as well.

There is little doubt that the events following 9/11 when the US by-passed NATO in Afghanistan and the crisis over the war in Iraq has weakened European trust in the USA, and thus their faith in NATO. For NATO, and perhaps also for the European Security and Defence Policy (ESDP), much depends on how Afghanistan is handled. There can be little doubt that the quarrel over caveats and contributions are extremely harmful in times where several allies take severe losses. Overt displays of lack of solidarity within the alliance undermine the whole idea of NATO. If NATO fails in Afghanistan the alliance will be weakened, especially as a military organisation. If NATO is perceived to fail in Afghanistan because of lack of internal solidarity between Europeans, the ESDP is likely to be damaged as well. But the EU is more likely to survive such a blow than NATO as a military organisation.

As seen above the major projects in NATO after Kosovo, the multinational corps and the NATO Response Force, have been carried out almost exclusively by European forces. If some kind of balance between the US and the Europeans is not found, what presently comprises NATO's integrated military structure may easily become Europe's contribution to a redefined Atlantic alliance. In such a perspective, the future of NATO is as much a question of American preferences as of those of Europe.

EU operations

In the late 1980s and early 1990s, the Europeans operated under the auspices of the Western European Union (WEU) in the Persian Gulf, the Adriatic and the Danube. The perceived failure of Europe in Bosnia effectively stopped the development of the WEU as a militarily operative organisation. No new WEU military operations were launched after 1992. This clearly illustrates the fact that during the 1990s the Europeans failed to develop and institutionalise the conceptual and physical infrastructure necessary for European autonomous military actions to be perceived as credible. Still, a series of European multinational operations in Bosnia, Albania and Africa was carried out as ad hoc arrangements. Most were quite successful and would have enhanced Europe's image as a credible military actor if they had been conducted within an EU or WEU framework.

From 2003 to 2006 the EU has launched 18 operations, most of them civilian. Still, the takeover of the NATO operations in Macedonia and Bosnia proved that the EU was capable of running long-term PSOs (although Bosnia may yet provide surprises). The two operations in the Congo in 2003 and 2006 showed that the EU was capable of conducting independent operations a long way from home. Gradually, these successes have strengthened the EU as a military actor.

Compared to any traditional great power the EU still has a long way to go as a military actor. But the brief discussion above clearly suggests that since 2003 the EU is increasingly the preferred institutional option when European states are taking part in peace support operations.

Conclusion

The ongoing military integration in Europe is best understood as a decentralised process in the sense that it is not guided by a single political or military plan, or organised within a single institutional framework. Rather, European military integration is a complex web of cooperation and commitment between states on many levels and in many fields. The practical results of the integration process are joint technological projects, trans-national defence industry mergers, bi-national or multinational military units, and multinational operations. Military organisation and doctrine are becoming steadily increasing technology-intensive. Money is far more important than manpower, and the financial cost of maintaining a first-class defence increases very quickly. This means that for all small and most medium-sized states the possibility of keeping a national balanced military force that is recognised as credible is diminishing very quickly. This technologically-propelled inflation is one of the key inputs in the ongoing restructuring of West European armed forces. With stable budgets, the only way to keep a first class defence is to cooperate with other states. As mentioned above, the end of the cold war and the political developments in its immediate aftermath served to promote fast growth in the number of multinational forces in Western Europe. There is presently a clear tendency that such forces replace national structures for both economical and operational reasons. The combined logic of military and economic efficiency and international commitments will force integration further unless some really dramatic event forces a change of course. The fact is that unless someone puts a foot down and actively stops it and presents a credible alternative, the integration process will follow its own logic.

The present situation is characterised by a complex, rather decentralised network of multinational cooperative projects – the number of participants in each project varying from two to more than ten. Almost every state cooperates, in one way or another, with almost everybody else. Nevertheless, the climate of the cooperation network is not one of consensus or harmony. Rather, it should be described as cooperative rivalry. Not surprisingly, states are competing for influence and positions. In contrast to what is the norm in the international system at large, threats to use armed force, or the actual use of it, is irrelevant to interstate relations in the European subsystem. That does not mean that military might is unimportant, the influence and rank of each state in military policy of the whole depends very much of the size of the contribution that each state brings to the negotiation table.

While most of the above has focused on internal drivers for military integration in Europe, the brief discussion on different institutional options for operations also shows how such internal drivers interact with external processes. For the time being it would seem that both internal and external forces are pushing in the same direction.

References

Andersson, J. J. (2006), *Armed and Ready? The EU Battlegroup Concept and the Nordic Battlegroup* (Stockholm: Swedish Institute for European Policy Studies).

Atlantic News (1997), 'Belgium and Portugal: Creation of a joint air force', *Atlantic News*, no. 2972, 10.12.

Council of the European Union (2004), *Headline Goal 2010*, endorsed by the European Council of 17 and 18 June 2004, <http://www.consilium.europa.eu/uedocs/cmsUpload/2010%20Headline%20Goal.pdf>.

—— (2006), *Capabilities improvement chart I/2006* <http://www.consilium.europa.eu/ueDocs/cms_Data/docs/pressData/en/esdp/89603.pdf >.

Deni, J. R. (2005), The sources of military doctrine: The NATO Rapid Deployment Corps (Washington DC: UMI).

Europemedia.net (2002a), 'Transport ministers approve Galileo', 26 March 2002, downloaded November 2002 <http://www.europmedia.net>.

—— (2002b) 'European parliament supports Galileo project', 11 February 2002, downloaded November 2002 <http://www.europmedia.net>.

Findlay T. (2002), *The use of force in UN operations* (Oxford; SIPRI/Oxford University Press).

Golawski, A. (2005a), 'On Course for Afghanistan', MNC-NE homepages, 12 October 2005 <http://www.mncne.pl/?menupage=p_article.browse&root=6375d6 8b7ca97b0ed809d6106721a128&category_id=9392841ae6669847bfaae82447927 18a&product_id=205>.

—— (2005) 'Entry pass to the first league', MNC-NE homepages 8 December 2005, translated from Polska Zbronja 21 November 2005, accessed on 20 May 2006 at

<http://www.mncne.pl/?menupage=p_article.browse&root=6375d68b7ca97b0ed8 09d6106721a128&category_id=9392841ae6669847bfaae8244792718a&product_ id=221>.

Hewson, R. (ed.) (2002), *Jane's Air-Launched Weapons*, Issue 39 (London: Jane's Information Group Ltd).

Kerttunen, M. et al. (2005), *EU Battlegroups: Theory and Development in the Light of Finnish-Swedish Co-operation* (Helsinki: Department of Strategic and Defence Studies).

Kujat, H. (2002), 'Vortrag des Generalinspekteurs der Bundeswehr, General Harald Kujat, Zum Stand der Reform der Bundeswehr', [On the state of the reform of the Bundeswehr] in the Übersee-Club in Hamburg 22 Januar 2002 <http://www. bundeswehr.de/index_.html>.

Lindstrom, G. (2007), *The Headline Goal* (Paris: The European Institute for Security Studies), updated January 2007, < http://www.iss-eu.org/esdp/05-gl.pdf>.

McInnes, C. (1993), 'The Future of the British Army', *Defence Analysis*, **2**(9).

Menon, A. et al. (1992), 'A common European defence?' *Survival*, **34**(3) 98–118.

Moens, A. (1993), 'The European Security and Defence Identity and the Non-Concert of Europe', *European Security*, **2**(4) Winter.

Palin, R. H. (1995), *Multinational Military Forces: Problems and Prospects* (London: IISS) Adelphi Paper 294.

Seitz, R. (1992), *NATO's new Troops: Overcoming Obstacles to Multinational Ground Forces* (Carlisle PA: Strategic Studies Institute, US Army War College).

Smith, D. (1992), 'Arms and equipment for a European rapid reaction force', *Military Technology*, no. 3.

Stein, G. J. (1993), 'The Euro-Corps and Future European Security Architecture', *European Security*, **2**(2) Summer.

Tardy, T. (1999), 'French policy towards peace support operations', *International Peacekeeping*, **6**(1).

Thornton, R. (2000), 'The role of peace support operations: doctrine in the British Army', *International Peacekeeping*, **7**(2).

Ulriksen, S. (1996), *Desentralisert militær integrasjon? Forsvarspolitikk i Vest-Europa etter den kalde krigen* [Decentralised military integration? Defence policy in Western Europe after the Cold War] (Oslo: NUPI-rapport nr 208, Oslo, June).

—— (2004) Requirements for Future European Military Strategy and Force Structures, *International Peacekeeping* , **11**(3) 457–473.

—— (2006) 'European Military changes since 9/11', in Giovanna Bono, *The impact of 9/11 on European Foreign and Security Policy* (Brussels: VUB-Press).

Ulriksen, S. et al. (2004), 'Operation Artemis: The shape of things to come' in *International Peacekeeping*, **11**(3) Autumn.

Chapter 5

Dangerous Dysfunction?
Governing Integrated Military Force
in Europe

Janna Haaland Matlary

In this chapter we analyse the political governance of multinational forces, asking whether this has remained a national domain subject to national control, or whether there is some degree of supra-national or international governance structure at work. We look at both *ad bellum* and *in bello* decision-making with a focus on the three international organisations (IOs) where Nordic military force is deployed, viz. NATO, the EU, and the UN. However, it is first necessary to analyse why it is so important to participate internationally in optional wars. Why not simply opt to retain maximum national control by remaining at home, preparing for attacks on one's own territory?

The Political Importance of International Deployment

Small states in particular seem to seek power within international organisations as they do not have the 'great power' option. The typology of power suggested by Barnett and Duvall (2005) is useful in this regard. Power can be *direct*: A makes B do something B would not otherwise do. But it can also be indirect, in the form of institutional rule-making. When A cannot compel B to do something, he can create conditions for B's freedom of action that sets the agenda or precludes certain types of decisions.

This perspective on power permits an analysis of strategic action on the part of states *inside* international organisations. When *ad bellum* is to be decided, it is usually via a United Nations Security Council (UNSC) mandate or Art. 51 of the UN Charter by one or several states. When *in bello* is governed, it is almost always inside an IOs, the UN, the EU, or NATO, and states have power as a function of their military contribution. However, the 'actorness' of the state is no less inside the IO than outside it, in the case of a direct power relationship to another actor. Only if a state provides relevant military resources to NATO or to the EU can it expect to be included in the decisive inner group of states regarding decision-making. Small Nordic states must therefore maintain relevant national military resources in order to contribute to the international operations of the organisation in question, and in the case of NATO, to maintain a threshold level of defence at home. There is no choice between national and international contributions – states that are not willing to contribute internationally, do not count in either organisation.

Thus, being passive, keeping one's military tool statically deployed behind one's own borders is unimportant and counterproductive in both the NATO and the EU settings. The importance of being active within IOs in order to increase one's standing in them is what counts. For the post-modern European state, 'national control' is therefore only interesting as an analytical category when we speak about relative national importance *within* an international setting, be it in the IO or in the field.

In such an international setting, a plethora of questions arises: How can national control be retained when military contributions are deeply integrated, for example in an EU battle group? How can it be retained when troops are under another state's command? And how can non-state actors and private military and security companies be controlled, if at all?

Drivers of Internationalisation

Before we can assess the degree of political governance over military assets in international operation, we must discuss the driving forces of internationalisation and what this means in terms of the military tool. States opt for participation and the interdependencies that this entails as argued in the preceding section, and because this is in their interest, as argued below. However, they are also compelled to respond to the increasing military integration that takes places because of shrinking military budgets. Military modernisation is so costly that no small or medium-size state in Europe, in an age of non-existential enemies, has the political will to pay for a so-called balanced defence structure on their own. The 'peace dividend' after the cold war resulted in 30 per cent decrease in national budgets on average, and the downward trend continues while the increase in procurement and other costs rose by more than the average rate of inflation (Norwegian Defence Study FS07). Thus, military integration and/or privatisation is clearly necessary.

In addition to the cost factor (which necessitates cost-sharing) comes the political need for risk-sharing through participation in multilateral organisations and even the need to have an IO as a scapegoat. As Conor Cruise O'Brian remarked about the UN: It serves as 'a scapegoat for the follies and vanities of statesmen…it is a large part of its utility to state leaders' (cited in Berdal, 2006: 37). In this section the cost drivers are initially discussed, followed by the political drivers of internationalisation.

Cost

The twin drivers of military internationalisation are threats and budgets, but one possibility is that 'Europe only recognises as much threat as it can afford' (Lindley-French, 2006). Even if the official version is that strategic considerations dictate budgets, European states on average are below their own goal adopted by NATO of 2 per cent of GDP for defence. Cost is therefore a major driver of international integration of the military tool, be it in R&D, procurement, maintenance or deployment.

The situation after the cold war is often termed 'diffuse' (*Forsvarsdepartementet*, 2004), and the lack of a clearly identifiable existential enemy leaves security policy in limbo. The traditional threat of invasion is obsolete in Europe, but territorial defence has nonetheless remained, and Article 5 has not been redefined. The 'optional' non-article 5 has usually been designated 'out of area', whereas the real threat, so to speak, is at home, 'in area'. Franzten (2005: 182) has shown how NATO has been reluctant to adapt to another, more realistic threat picture for political reasons:

> By 1999 'defence' still had very much a territorial meaning in NATO. NATO could have adjusted defence conceptually by including it in the wider security agenda. This has not been done formally ... too many allies were not willing to accept the consequences flowing from an expanded concept of defence.

Thus, while the NATO strategic concept continues to distinguish between 'in area' and 'out-of area', the reasons for this are not strategic: they are political.

If the territorial threat to European states, and between them, is a historical bygone, it would make eminent sense to integrate European militaries and have a supra-national command and political governance system. This would save money and allow for optimal use of resources in deploying in international operations. However, we are still very far from this reality, and may never experience it – given how the states' monopoly on the use of military power remains a central constituent of the states themselves. Most countries reluctance to abandon 'balanced' defence structures must be seen in this light. Yet the trend in military budgets is such that small and medium sized states cannot maintain a traditional military structure for very much longer. The military integration that currently takes place is primarily driven by budgetary considerations, but the process is nevertheless a very real one. In his annual briefing on the status of the Norwegian armed forces, chief of defence General Diesen (2006) made it clear that unless the budget line follows the real cost of procurement, up to 25 per cent of Norwegian capacity will have to be discontinued in the near future, and the whole structure will disappear in the next 25–30 years. Yet the history of Norwegian defence budgets does not suggest that increases are likely, and this is not atypical of other nations in Europe.

Ulriksen details how military integration now takes place also below the corps level after an initial period of creation of multinational corps like Eurocorps, the 1st German–Netherlands Corps and the Multinational Corps Northeast (Ulriksen, 2007). These corps have been deployed in several operations, especially in the International Stabilisation and Assistance Force (ISAF) and on rotation in NATO's Response Force (NFR). Ulriksen remarks that these two tasks have put concrete and heavy demands on the multinational corps of Europe, and this in turn means that they train together in a much more committed and well-defined way than hitherto. Multinational forces have moved away from the drawing board and into the field. This makes for real integration in action, especially when we move to the lower level of battle groups.

The EU decision to form 13 battle groups and to rotate them two by two biannually was spearheaded by the UK and France who also have lead nation roles. In addition comes Spain and Italy: 'One should note that the four states that provided national battle groups (in the EU) are also lead nations in NATO deployable corps,' Ulriksen points out. This implies that these states are able to dominate a military deployment and in a sense, to gain maximum influence within it. A lead nation role in command and control is not realistic unless one contributes significantly on the ground, as we saw in the case of command of UNIFIL II in the Lebanon where France initially offered only a couple of hundred troops yet wanting command of the mission. This was heavily criticised, and France had to 'increase the offer' tenfold in order to be lead nation.

The four states in question have clearly understood this principle, and as stated, are contributors in such a manner as to make lead nation status warranted. This means that the four enjoy a political lead nation role as well. Big states are therefore dominant in military integration schemes because they can offer HQs as well as entire units such as battle groups.

But being on rotation also implies responsibility to act, and thus binds states within the EU and NATO. Ulriksen mentions the reluctance of Germany to lead the EU mission to DR Congo for the election observation in June 2006: 'Since a German battle group was on guard in the readiness rotation cycle, Germany was expected by its European allies to lead the operation' (ibid., p. 10) But domestic resistance in the end required that both France and the UK assumed major responsibilities in the mission. Ulriksen's assessment is that 'influence depends upon contribution, competence, and credibility' (ibid.).

In conclusion, we see that even 'bottom-up' military integration initiated by states themselves has important implications in the form of 'self-binding'. In addition come the attempts at 'top-down' military integration in both the EU and NATO. In the EU, the creation of the European Defence Agency (EDA) is intended to result in a rational process of common planning for both the R&D and the procurement as well as military modernisation phase, whereas the NATO process of setting up the NRF (Nato Response Force) and the defence modernisation process led by Allied Command Transformation (ACT) have the same purpose. By being on rotation, be it NRF or the battle group, state contributions must be interoperable and co-trained. This works to create real military integration as well as real political obligation to deploy, regardless of individual states' national interests. Further, the driving force towards multinational cooperation and even integration in military procurement, training, and operations discussed above, contributes to sovereignty pooling. The EDA in the EU and the NATO 'transformation' process are *loci* for directed change, and the usefulness of some kind of direction to multinational integration is obvious. European states are now on the verge of realising this. The bottom-up process is dysfunctional, and EU states, especially small and medium-sized states, stand to lose if the bottom-up process continues.

In the EU, the EDA has been set up to direct the process of rationalising military planning for research, procurement, and cooperation. There is a clear incentive to match the dominance of US actors in this field – the US exported weaponry to the value of 18.5 billion USD in 2005, while export sales in the three European states discussed in this article totalled 7.2 billion USD (*Berlingske Tidende*, 2006). The EDA has proposed a common research fund 'to give up the last remnant of national sovereignty in this field' (ibid..) in order to counter the market dominance of the US.

Although there are many obstacles to such a development, it is clear that both the weapons industry as well as military integration among two or more states is the way ahead for European states (Agrell, 2005; Khol, 2005; Matlary, 2005; Sköns, 2005).

Few, if any European states, can afford such monumental changes alone. They therefore seek multi-national cooperation and integration both in terms of use of equipment, maintenance, forces, and sometimes personnel. This process is a bottom-up, *ad hoc* process, spear-headed by some states *in cooperation* with each other,[1] but encouraged by both the NATO transformation process and by the EU development of battle groups, the EDA, and capability building.

The battle groups of the EU illustrate the discrepancy between the military integration commitment and the intergovernmental nature of political decision-making. Although the EU council will decide on deployment by consensus, only those states that are military contributors are likely to matter in real terms. We know that the coalition of leaders regarding the use of force in the EU consists of France and the UK, with the support of Germany, but that no request for an EU deployment arises without prior consultation with troop-contributing states. In the case of Operation Artemis, the UN knew that France would bear the brunt of such deployment, and asked for troops once this was agreed (Ulriksen et al., 2006). We can assume that the EU will remain vague on the question of 'grand strategy', and will be willing to deploy only on an *ad hoc* basis as in the case mentioned. Thus, the consensual character of the decision-making process will remain in formal terms, but the real decision-making will evolve around those states that are on rotation with a battle group, always involving the major states France and the UK. In the case of multinational battle groups, all contributing states are bound to deploy together even if the formal option of defecting exists. As Andersson points out in his study of the Nordic–Baltic Battle Group, even non-EU member Norway is formally 'consulted' on the decision to deploy (Andersson, 2006: 39). In theory, states can withdraw their contribution. In reality, this will be a total blow to credibility for the battlegroup member state that does this.

In sum, whether it is 'bottom-up' or 'top-down' military integration, *European states incur political obligations to deploy as they co-train and rotate in fixed military units like battle groups.* Such obligations are greater for small states than for major states for two reasons. First, small states integrate in the battle group itself, thus not having full battlegroups. They therefore depend both on partner states within the battle group as well as on the IO for which they rotate. Second, major states usually also field HQ capacities, thus commanding their own forces, i.e. their own battle group. Even if this is not the case, major states are much more likely than small states to be in lead positions.

Further, the rapidity of deployment in both battle groups and the NATO Response Force (NRF) implies that there is no time for the usual, slow political process. Crises that demand responses are not plugged into political cycles of intergovernmental decision-making. The use of force may therefore come about with much more rapidity than anticipated when these organisations were designed.

---

1   Conversations with Norwegian, Dutch officers and staff at NATO Defence College, Spring 2005.

Finally, since both the NRF and the battle group have a deployment time of only a few days, these units have to be on high readiness, meaning co-trained to a very high standard. This factor means real military integration, which in turn demands that politics follow military facts. Also, the fact of rotation means that specific states are under obligation to contribute at specific times. One cannot 'free ride' or opt out as before.

As states integrate in common R&D, procurement and maintenance schemes, they consolidate military integration for the longer run and commit to common deployments through such common capabilities and their interoperable systems. Military integration in Europe, driven by cost factors, will likely continue and deepen with regard to both these aspects. The political level continues to work on formal intergovernmental terms while the military tool is rapidly and increasingly integrated. Moreover, political sensitivies about sovereignty preclude any principled discussion about political integration in this field. These developments mean a loss of national control of own forces in the sense of olden days, but it is also the precondition for gaining influence, as argued above, albeit in a mode of interlocking interdependence.

Politics

Another driving force of internationalisation is political: the sharing of risk and the ability to have an IO as a place to direct blame if need be. Having a multilateral 'cover' becomes increasingly important and makes for a precarious balance between commitment in ongoing operations and domestic public opinion. Western elites increasingly lack the experience of war and a 'war ethic', and the same must be said for Western publics. When media report from the battle field, criticism mounts, and NGOs and media request detailed information on targets, weaponry, calibration, etc. (Frantzen, 2005). They demand the right to change views on deployment as fighting progresses, and are often easily swayed by day-to-day events in the field. Only in operations without much media coverage can one still maintain elite control – political and military. But almost all military operations today are highly 'medialised'. Media are often 'embedded' in operations themselves, and in general, operations must count on much media interest once military force is employed. Post-national security policy, as most policies, is still firmly vested in a national structure of democratic accountability and national power-plays. Nothing can 'back-fire' as quickly as deployment of one's own forces. What was heroic and acclaimed one day, is often the object of devastating criticism the next. From the Iraq and Afghan wars there are reports of US[2] and Canadian politicians[3] who try to minimalise media

---

2   The restrictions on reports of American losses in Iraq in 2004 and 2005 are well known.

3   Prime Minister Harper of Canada is accused to refusing to fly the flag at half-mast for the fallen in Afghanistan, 'Canada leader accused of trying to de-emphasize danger to troops', *International Herald Tribune*, 26 April 2006.

coverage of their own losses, and fierce debates about dangerous deployments.[4] One's own losses are increasingly hard to accept for politicians seeking re-election. Both President Bush and PM Blair experience tremendous domestic problems over Iraq, to the extent that they staged a *mea culpa* press conference in Washington, DC in mid-May 2006 where errors were openly admitted. Kosovo was almost unbearably difficult for NATO governments because their publics demanded changes and recalls, detailed information on military choices and strategies, etc. (Clark, 2003).

Further, both NATO, the EU, and the UN ask for more troops, and there is a constant problem of procuring what is necessary for all three international organisations. As we have seen, governments want to participate more in order to keep NATO going, build the EU, and strengthen the UN – and they want to gain international power and prestige. The military tool is one which gives much status and influence, especially as the risks involved are such that many states shy away from commitment. Cimbala and Forster's (2004) study of NATO burden-sharing shows that all member states are keen to participate and willing to take risks despite the danger of national losses and domestic unpopularity: 'cheque-book' diplomacy is not accepted as a substitute, they point out.

What can a government do about this dilemma? It has to 'deliver' in two arenas – at home and internationally, where the demands are conflicting, even oppositional to each other. The reality of this dilemma is increasingly evident in European politics. Many states have withdrawn forces from Iraq after domestic opposition – Norway, Spain, Hungary, Italy – to mention some, and the debate about ongoing deployments in Iraq is very strong in Denmark. Former PM Berlusconi's statement that 'I am against the war' to the Italian newspaper *la Repubblica* on 31 October 2005 underlined the absurdity of the 'two-level' game elites may play in this regard. In order to become re-elected in 2006 and to appease a critical public opinion, Berlusconi suddenly turned against the war, but to please Washington, Italian forces were still present in Iraq with more than 2,500 troops as of April 2006. Most state leaders cannot get away with this type of inconsistency. They have to make painful choices. The BBC reported from Kabul that both the UK and the Dutch force increases for the extended ISAF would be smaller than promised at NATO ministerial meetings.

In the model of 'two-level' games developed by Putnam (1988), governments want maximum autonomy not only abroad, but also vis-à-vis their publics. Participation and even integration in international organisations tends to increase governments' power over domestic actors, and they may find the trade-off between domestic and international power in favour of strengthening their national hand through 'self-binding' or collusive delegation. It follows from this that a government which is weak domestically in an issue area will seek international 'self-binding'. Such 'tying of hands' may make the government able to change domestic agendas and marginalise various actors in pointing out that international obligations narrow or even determine national freedom of choice. The need to transform domestically as

---

4   Recently, these have taken place in The Netherlands and the UK regarding deployments to Afghanistan, and in Germany regarding deployments to DR Congo. All three cases are discussed below. See also: 'Canada: Accentuating the positive', *The Economist*, **3**, March 2007: 52.

a result of binding agreements within NATO and/or the EU is one example of such an international argument used in the Norwegian domestic debate where politicians use the NATO-argument extensively (Heier, 2005).

Returning to the initial issue of national control of the military tool, we see that the 'Swiss option' is only meaningful for states that have no security policy in terms of international commitments or needs for embeddedness in international structures. Given the interest in participating internationally, states invariably face constraints on their national control over the military, but they also stand to gain from collective political efforts.

The following section looks at how small Nordic states fare with regard to *ad bellum* and *in bello* decisions in the relevant organisations. I proceed with an analysis of these two decision-making situations for the three major IOs: the United Nations, the European Union, and NATO. I concentrate on general decision-making – on the role of state actors versus other actors – not on Nordic states in particular.

The UN

The UN is unique in bestowing legitimacy for the use of force – *ad bellum* – but faces severe problems in carrying out operations – *in bello* (Findlay, 2002; Matlary, 2006; Berdal, 2006). The brunt of military contributions comes from developing countries which have a net income from these, and the lack of Western troops means a lack of modern capabilities that are expensive, such as air lift, helicopters, support functions, intelligence, etc. Thus, whereas the world's states look to the UNSC for the *ad bellum* decision, they look away when the call for contributions is made. In the following we look at the question of political governance of both decisions: Do Nordic states retain any influence in these?

Ad bellum

Decision-making on the use of force is predominantly made by the UNSC, which has a unique mandate in this regard. However, it should be noted that also regional organisations, such as the EU, NATO, and the African Union, can decide to use force without a UN mandate. There is no explicit text in any of these organisations' relevant documents that reserves the use of force to situations with an explicit UNSC mandate. The case of Kosovo comes to mind where NATO acted without a mandate. Further, the emergence of the so-called 'responsibility to protect norm' (R2P) at the same time as terrorism challenges the conventional interpretation of Article 51, combine to make reliance on a UNSC mandate less realistic (Matlary, 2006).

However this may develop, it is clear that most decisions on the use of force take the form of a UNSC mandate. The number of such mandates under Chapter VII of the UN Pact and interventions has risen tremendously in the post-war period, making for a change away from traditional peacekeeping to militarily robust peace enforcement. The actual decision to use force is a political one which has almost nothing to do with legal canon or precedent. In fact, the interpretation of the pivotal phrase 'threat to international peace and security' of Chapter VII has by now become so stretched that almost any case can be argued to be covered by it (Matlary, 2002). This in turn means that legal precedent in this regard is of scant importance. As Findlay (2002: 7) puts it: 'The drafting of such mandates is an intensely political process, driven by various considerations that are not relevant to the use of force issue.' In addition, the use of force is treated with great conservatism: it is much easier and cheaper to remain aloof than to implicate the UN in a war with unpredictable outcome and to have to supply troops in addition. One must also add that the veto ensures that only cases where there is no forbidding great-power interest will come onto the agenda of the UNSC.

In sum, the UNSC makes supra-national decisions for the entire UN membership on the use of force (as all states are politically bound by its decisions). Each of the UN Security Council P5 wields a double veto – one to prevent agenda-setting on a conflict where one has national interest;[5] one to stop a mandate once the agenda is set; non-permanent members only play a role when neither veto has been exercised, and great power politics play the key role in making decisions on mandates. The Middle-East conflict is not on the UNSC agenda because of the US veto, and intervention for humanitarian purposes is always endangered by Russia and China, both wary of any weakening to the intervention norm.

Thus, *the key decision-maker in the world regarding the use of force is not democratic or even intergovernmental*, but is most accurately characterised as great power politics. As in most periods of history, the decision to use force is made by the great powers according to their interests. Non-membership, the normal status of the Nordic states, has no influence on the *ad bellum* decision. The UNSC is a supra-national decision-maker, and national sovereignty has been transferred from states to the UN Pact.

In bello

Once a mandate, what happens next? In the cases where a coalition of states, or so-called regional organisations such as NATO, the EU, the African Union (AU) etc., are assigned to the task, they command the military operation. But in the many cases of UN-led operations it is in fact the Secretary-General who acts as commander-in-chief. This was a practice developed by Dag Hammarskiøld in Katanga, in the absence of the initially planned military structure of the UN itself. This practice, deficient as it may seem to an officer, has been wide-spread:

> The organisation's operations in Somalia and Bosnia found the Secretary-General conducting himself as a commanding general and making final decisions having to do with the application of air power, the disposition of ground forces, and the dismissal of commanding officers (Findlay, 2002: 10).

---

5   Bachrach and Baratz's classical study of the power of non-agenda setting and non-decision. It is well-known that in this manner Russia prevented a mandate on Kosovo, and that China 'exchanges' its veto power with African states and possibly Iran. Having the veto is thus a source of power that is gaining in value the more the UNSC is seen as the world's 'legitimator'.

Activist Secretary-Generals have meddled in military affairs in this manner, whereas those with less inclination in this direction have appointed a deputy secretary-general to act as superior to an in-theatre force commander from one of the contributing states. The lack of command and control at UN HQ has not impeded this practice, and the story of unprofessionalism, failure, scandal, and bitterly 'learned lessons' is a long one. After a thorough analysis of all UN operations up to 2002, Findlay (2002: 351) concludes:

> On the whole, the way in which the UN has dealt with the use-of-force issue has been unimpressive. Neither the UNSC, successive Secretary-Generals, nor indeed peacekeepers themselves can be given high marks ... in general the use of force by UN peacekeepers has been marked by political controversy, doctrinal vacuousness, conceptual confusion and failure in the field.

In sum, Norway and the other Nordic states are thus without influence in the *ad bellum* decision unless they happen to be non-permanent members of the UNSC in a situation where no veto has been used. As regards the *in bello*, they have influence to the extent that they offer relevant military contributions. Generally, the lead nation of a UN operation will be a major power which is willing and able to offer the largest contribution. However multinational the force, the main rule is that a small Nordic state's contribution will be under the command of an American, British, French, or German general[6] if the operation is run by a regional organisation, i.e. NATO or the EU. In the cases where these capacities are integrated to begin with, such as the Norwegian Telemark Battalion in the 2. Dutch–German corps, the commander will be either German or Dutch. In the case of the Nordic Battle Group in the EU, the commander will be Swedish since Sweden is lead nation for this particular battle group. In an operation run by the UN itself, the chances of assuming leading roles in command and control functions depends on Nordic contributions, as is the main rule for all operations.

Nordic states may be given key posts in HQs and even influence at a strategic level when they make relevant and desired military contributions. In his doctoral study, Heier (2006) found that the special forces that Norway contributed to Operation Enduring Freedom in 2003 provided it with direct access and even influence at the strategic level in the Pentagon, and that this influence vanished the moment these troops were withdrawn.

In a situation where 'sovereignty is status', even a small state may increase its power through contributions in the field. The willingness to assume risk while offering relevant contributions is particularly valued in NATO according to Forster and Cimbala's study (2004), and it gives one-to-one influence. The less risk-willing states are, the more power that accrues to those states that do contribute.

---

6   An exception is the Norwegian General Skiaker who commanded KFOR V in 2004.

The European Union

The EU has developed its security policy role over the last ten years, and at a brisk pace. The capacities for planning and commanding operations are miniscule compared to NATO, but the EU has nonetheless a rudimentary planning capacity at the polico-strategic level in the military staff of about 200 officers. It also has a growing experience in running operations, and commands a host of civilian tools that NATO lacks. These tools are of increasing relevance in modern wars that concern stabilisation and democratisation as the main security strategy.

Decision-making for using force – *ad bellum* – is also potentially an EU matter, although the EU has never made such a decision on its own: it has always acted on UN mandates. However, in the European Security Strategy (ESS), which is the EU strategic plan, there is no explicit condition for such a mandate. In a given situation the EU can decide to use force autonomously, as did NATO in the case of Kosovo.

Ad bellum

The EU has launched four peacekeeping and peace enforcement operations, two using the command and control assets of NATO ('Berlin plus') – two using national HQs. All of these have had UN mandates.

In bello

Formally, the EU has an intergovernmental decision-making structure in security and defence policy, which is limited to robust peace enforcement. However, in practice the system is one of differentiated integration whereby some lead states decide on deployment after a formal request from the UN (or some other IO). Such a request is only forthcoming when there is a genuine will to respond favourably, as was the case with Operation Artemis in Bunia province in the DR Congo. Thus, the real decision-making on *in bello* is made by the contributing states.

The formal decision-making procedure proposed in the text of the constitutional treaty is named 'permanent structured cooperation' (Article III, 213) which allows for 'avant-garde' groups in this area. This text is not adopted, pending the future of the treaty itself, but it should be noted that the EU battle groups were adopted under this rule, initially by France and the UK, and by including Germany as the third state when the modalities were already decided by these two states. This is important to note because the possibility of avant-gardism does not rely on a treaty rule, but can be the result of an agreement between two or more states to go forward. It is then up to the others to associate themselves with these proposals, and although the possibility of the veto exists under the formal intergovernmental scheme, it is rarely used, if ever. This is in line with the general foreign policy logic of the EU whereby some states suggest policy, and those that resist usually abstain:

> Collective decision-making remains subject to the national veto, but there is at the same time a preference for constructive abstention in which governments do nothing to undermine a collective policy if it is agreed by a majority of EU states (Forster 2006, p. 141).

However, there is no strategic consensus among EU states on which missions to undertake or how to develop in the security and defence area. Whereas France and the UK are able to conduct coercive diplomacy with global power projection, smaller and medium-sized states prefer non-military EU foreign policy, among these particularly the formerly neutral states. This concern revolves around the risk of being involved in war-fighting at the high end of the spectrum and when the battle groups were agreed in 2004, the possibility of an opt-out for states was important in reaching an agreement. The question is whether the possibility of avant-gardism will be impeded by these states or not. The French model of an independent EU security policy is pitted against the UK model of NATO–EU complementarity. However, the willingness on the part of other EU states to develop coercive diplomacy is dubious. This means that in the areas where there may be UK-French agreement to launch a mission, the support of the remaining member states is not automatic.

With the deployment of the new EU battle groups, decision-making will be more critical as these groups are in a formal system of rotation and involve military contributions from many EU states. For the EU member states, it will no longer be a question of accepting a British or French operation with high risk (the concept of the battle group is rapid intervention in an on-going crisis), but of deploying one's own forces. We can safely assume that the EU member states contributing to the battle groups in rotation will take a close interest in their deployment. Research on the relationship between political vulnerability and own casualties shows that vulnerability increases inversely with the political interest in the mission: *the less existential the threat, the more vulnerable a government becomes* (Arreguin-Toft, 2005). This is not unexpected, but provides a good prediction about EU missions, which are all of a non-existential character: they will tend to be deployed for less dangerous operations. This also fits with the traditional main thrust of EU foreign policy, which is 'civilian' (Duchene, 1972). The intention on the part of the EU to engage in coercive diplomacy when moving beyond its borders (Cooper, 2004) is factually correct, but not likely to play the role it ought to.

Among the Nordic states in the EU, Sweden has been an eager participant in EU missions. Denmark has a national caveat which prohibits such participation due to the national compromise over the Treaty of Political Union dating from 1993, and Finland has few forces for international deployment. The case of Sweden illustrates the strategic possibility for a medium-sized state in gaining international power and standing in this issue-area. It volunteered to play an active role in EU security policy from the very beginning of its membership in the organisation in the logic that participation equals influence (Matlary, 2004; *Utrikesdepartementet*, 1996). Moreover, one wanted to show that Sweden not only took an interest in Northern Europe where it is likely to have national interests, but also in areas that are important to the EU as a whole. To be a 'constructive EU citizen' is extremely important within an organisation that calls itself 'a union' and which relies on a high degree of commonality. To pursue one's own national interests too often and too openly is scorned upon in this political culture. Instead, the key to legitimacy and trust is to be in the 'inner core' of the EU, and the way to such status is through general commitment to EU goals. Using this logic, Sweden and Finland have both consistently pursued policies to land them in this 'inner core', with Finland picking some few areas where they excel in common expertise and problem-solving ability, such as Russian affairs. For its part, Sweden is active in the Euromed-strategy and peace enforcement in Africa, such as in the Democratic Republic of the Congo in 2003 and 2006. This is both geographically and functionally far beyond the traditional area of Swedish national interests.

Both Finnish and Swedish elites have worked hard to ensure that something akin to an 'Article 5' does not develop in the EU. This would have made them into 'second class'- members in the organisation. On the definition of the security policy of the EU, these two states therefore made a major, common effort (Bailes et al., 2006: 12). Also in the area of effecting domestic change that these governments otherwise could not have, they both sought to redefine 'neutrality' through making it compatible with all EU security policy. The impact of the EU on domestic Swedish and Finnish security policy is very well documented in recent scholarship (Miles, 2006; Rieker, 2006). As for Norway, this nation remains wholly on the outside of *ad bellum* decisions in the EU, but has ensured that Sweden will keep it informed of all details on this with a gloss of decision-making power. In return, Sweden will 'consult' with Norway on all aspects of battle group decision-making in the EU and ensure that Norway also agrees to decisions about deployment (Andreassen, 2006). However, the Norwegian say in the matter is bound to be illusory, as one 'defection' from an actual deployment means that Norway will not be trusted in the future. Credibility is a major asset in defence policy. But when we look at the impact of EU policy on defence modernisation, there is little evidence of any influence from EU institutions themselves, apart from the recent policy proposals from the EDA on R&D, procurement and common projects. The potential of the EDA to direct military integration is a major one, but it is too early to tell whether states will opt for pooling in this field. So far, the EDA meets considerable British scepticism about common projects, and there seems to be a fear that it is designed on a French model of supra-national EU security policy (interviews, Brussels, 11 December 2006).

NATO

The CPG (*Comprehensive Political Guidance*) adopted at the Riga summit in November 2006 makes interesting reading for those who still think that Article 5 operations are restricted to NATO territory. The main threats listed as facing NATO in the next 10–15 years are de-territorialised threats: 'Terrorism, increasingly global in scope and lethal in results, and the spread of weapons of mass destruction are likely to be the principal threat to the alliance'(CPG, p. 1). These threats 'hibernate' in failed states and are to be met where they originate. This implies that Article 5 changes in terms of substance since the alliance is tasked to defend citizens, territory and values. The CPG explicitly states that Article 5 today has a new de-territorialised meaning: 'The character of Article 5 is continuing to evolve. Large-scale conventional aggression against the alliance will continue to be highly unlikely, however, as shown by the terrorist attacks on the US in 2001 following which NATO invoked Article 5 for the first time. Future attacks may originate from outside the Euro-Atlantic area and may involve unconventional forms of armed assault' (CPG,

p. 2). This text clearly states that defence of the allies now means global 'out-of-area' defence against terrorism. Whereas non-Article 5 operations remain those of crisis management and by now uncontroversial, the core task of NATO, Article 5, has been redefined in terms of threats, response, and geographical scope. The declaration of Article 5 in the case of 9/11 is a Copernican point in this regard. This major change has not been debated much politically and may even go unrecognised. As is always the case when 'stuff happens', to quote former Secretary of Defence Donald Rumsfeld, major change may simply result without much further ado.

The 'new' and global Article 5 implies further military integration in NATO, both in terms of rapidity, capacity, and versatility. One must be able to 'respond quickly to unforeseen circumstances' and to meet challenges 'from wherever they may come' (CPG, p. 3). To this end, forces must continue transformation 'including conceptual and organisational agility, and the development of robust capacities that are deployable, sustainable, interoperable, and usable' (CPG, p. 3). In sum, this means increased cost, increased common training, continuous stress on readiness, agility, global deployability, etc. Small and medium-sized states have no choice but to go further along the path of military integration. Today, NATO struggles with the gap between ambition and troop contributions, especially in Afghanistan, which is the major deployment. In total, about 50,000 NATO soldiers are deployed in five missions, and these are all 'out of area' in terms of NATO's territory.

The NAC (North Atlantic Council) makes *ad bellum* decisions, which always entails *in bello decisions* as well. It does not make sense to distinguish between these in a military alliance. The formal procedure is consensual, but it is a well-known fact that there are three groups of states in NATO: the power projection states comprising the US, the UK, and France; the peacekeeping states led by Germany; and the protected states of the former Soviet bloc which want to retain 'old NATO' and try to develop American good-will for this through international deployments (Lindley-French, 2006). The Nordic member states are active in the 'Atlanticist' camp where Denmark is closer to US policy than Norway with regard to both Iraq and to deployments in the south of Afghanistan.

Ad bellum

The *ad bellum* decision in NATO is consensual and taken by the North Atlantic Council (NAC), which consists of the member states. To date, only two such decisions have been made – apart from undertaking regional operational roles under UN mandates – viz. the attack on Kosovo and the decision to define the terrorist attacks of September 11, 2001, to be an attack under Article 5 of the Washington Treaty. The US did not want to avail itself of NATO in this case, however. In the Kosovo case, the US was the main actor driving the process, whereas in the 9/11 case, European states headed by NATO's secretary-general sought to define a role for NATO (Lindley-French, 2007).

NATO policy in terms of deterrence – the main activity in the cold war – has always been dominated by the US, which undoubtedly is more than *primus inter pares*. There are legion transatlantic crises in NATO's history for this very reason, so much so that crisis must be termed the normal condition for the alliance. But only after the cold war has NATO faced *in bello*-decisions

In bello

The case of Kosovo is very important in this respect and illustrates how European allies were ignored in target selection and military choices, but also how these allies are unable to operate with the US. Henriksen (2006) gives evidence of how the NAC was 'tricked' into phase three of the military operation because it was clear that domestic opposition to the bombing campaign was mounting in several European states:

> General Naumann explains that both he and Secretary-General Solana understood that NATO would never formally endorse stage 3 of the campaign ... Naumann admits to being the architect behind the 'Phase two Plus trick' (Henriksen, 2006: 15).[7]

This was a way to ensure 'mission creep' into the third phase of bombing which included controversial dual-use targets without making this transition entirely clear to the NAC. The method was simple enough: to let Solana sum up a very long meeting, adding to his summary that he would himself examine and authorise such targets. This worked, and as the British evaluation of the campaign concluded: '... the formal decision to move to strategic bombing of Serbia (Phase Three) was never put directly, in quite those terms, to the NAC' (ibid.).

This rare glimpse into the real decision-making in NATO illustrates two factors: first, that the US is the dominant actor, and secondly, *in bello* decision cannot be too intergovernmental and protracted. Decision-making on targets would seem to belong to the military professional, but as publics and press are very engaged via modern communication, this is no longer the case. The political desire during this campaign was to end it much sooner than it actually did, and pressure in this direction was formidable. Moreover, even the UK was extremely annoyed at American dominance of the decision-making, and as Wesley Clark (2003) shows, the irritation went both ways: The American swore never again with regard to 'war by committee', whereas the Europeans decided that they had to do more in the military field in order to avoid such American dominance again.

The *in bello* decision-making was a reflection of the influence-contribution function. With such military superiority, the US reckoned that political clout was implied. This one-to-one relationship between power and contribution is also illustrated by the European reaction that one must be able to contribute more and better.

The style of decision-making in NATO is the so-called 'silent procedure'. It means that a decision is taken unless one or more states object within a set time-frame, usually 24 hours. In rare cases is there open disagreement, although the history of NATO is replete with crises, as Lindley-French (2006) points out. In the

---

7   My translation of Henriksens article in Norwegian. The article is based on Henriksen's PhD thesis *Operation Allied Force: A Product of Military Theory or Political Pragmatism?* Luftkrigsskolen, Trondheim.

case of Turkey's request for Article 4 preparations on the eve of the attack on Iraq in 2003, this was opposed by France, Germany, Belgium, and Luxembourg. According to one diplomat, this was a 'near-death' experience for the alliance, and the crisis was also recognised by then secretary-general, George Robertson. France dares to oppose within the alliance because it has an European strategy for strengthening the EU in security policy and therefore seeks to limit the role of NATO to its traditional military alliance role. France opposes the development of NATO in the direction of military–civilian standardisation as debated at the Riga summit, and also that it should become too much attuned to American security interests on a global scale. Since France rejoined the alliance structures from 1996, there has been a tension between this European model of the EU/NATO relationship and the Atlanticists where France has been willing to field strong opposition – to the point of obstruction – in meetings, even up to the eve of the Riga summit (interviews, Brussels, December, 2006). However, the new CPG (Comprehensive Political Guidance) emphasises that NATO must develop towards global partners and in global roles, and moves far in the direction of embracing terrorism as the main threat to be countered.

In the actual operations, states that do not have lead nation status, are subsumed under the command of another state, but as seen in the case of ISAF, national caveats abound when the risk is a major one. In Afghanistan, the various states have their own 'turf' in the country where they are responsible, with their own logistics and support. Multinationality exists in terms of cooperative agreements about sharing capacities such as air power, and in emergencies, the commander may actually command all forces without prior acceptance in national capitals. However, the realism of this remains to be seen. ISAF strikes one as a good case of underlining how limited military and political integration actually is. The co-training in battle groups in the EU and in the Rapid Response Force (RRF) is much more integrative than the national deployments of ISAF.

In sum, in NATO decision-making all states have the veto in NAC, but this has a clear cost, as in the EU. France is the most exceptional state in NATO, opting many times to disagree with the Atlanticists. NATO has taken *ad bellum* decisions twice – in the case of Kosovo as well as in the case of 10/11, the day after the attack on the Twin Towers, where it declared the latter to be an Article 5 operation. In terms of operations, the contributors decide according to contribution, and relevant military capacities that are in demand wield proportionately more influence than standard contributions. Heier (2005) found that the Norwegian special forces which were used in Operation Enduring Freedom in 2003 gave much influence for Norway in Washington, a finding consistent with the general literature on this topic (Cimbala and Forster, 2005).

In NATO, as in the EU and the UN, small states have limited influence, but can increase this through relevant and sought-after military contributions. Only in the EU and NATO do these states influence *ad bellum* decisions, but which, however, are rare.

Conclusions

In conclusion, small states remain rather powerless in all multinational settings, despite the formal influence on the *ad bellum* decision in both NATO and the EU for members. But the political cost of vetoing such a decision in either organisation is forbidding, especially for a small state. The 'shadow of the future' implies that one may be severely punished for this in later negotiations. Further, the importance of achieving 'standing' and status through active participation is much greater now than in the cold war security policy picture, as argued above: passivity is not a good strategy.

As regards *in bello* governance, states influence according to their contribution, although it remains true that small states very seldom come into commanding positions. The prevalence of national caveats is indicative of a strong urge to control national contributions, and one may assume that this imperative increases with risk of own losses. The political logic of multinational operations is dysfunctional: it works against multi-nationality when the going gets tough. This is amply evidenced in ISAF, and is not surprising. Here we see a tension between the state's desire to play two-level games – i.e. share cost and risk at the level of the IO, and the desire to avoid risk. The fact that small states play a role at all in the *in bello* phase is, however, historically recent. In international law prior to the UN Pact, great powers could use force as a normal tool of foreign policy. Even the League of Nations did not outlaw force, its covenant proposed arbitration as an alternative as well as a mandatory 'cooling-off' period of three months. Small states used to have only one legal 'opt-out', viz. neutrality, which had to be granted and guaranteed by the great powers.

In the light of this, it is an improvement in terms of small states' power that they can now exert influence in the operational phase, largely in proportion to their contribution, and that they can periodically wield some influence as a member of the UNSC. But as we have argued, the option of neutrality or 'passive membership' in security policy is much less attractive than it used to be. Today, a state uses military force as a *general foreign* policy tool in order to enhance its status and standing. Whereas the success of a mission remains vital, 'showing the flag' remains at least as important to any one state, and this is where dysfunction enters between military and political interests. The state desires to satisfy domestic political needs and to achieve international power simultaneously: ideally no risk, no losses, and no integration of the military tool. Military requirements demand interoperability, real multinational command, and even integration of small states' contributions. The drivers towards military integration are at work, but there is much less political incentive to follow suit. The result is ubiquitous 'muddling-through' – intergovernmentalism remains the decision rule formally, but the exigencies of the situation demand few and assertive actors once an operation is ongoing. In reality, few regretted General Naumann's 'trick' at the NAC in 1999.

However, the lack of coercive political ability in both NATO, the EU, and the UNSC makes sophisticated security policy impossible to achieve in a multinational setting. As long as 'least-common-denominator logic' dictates *ad bellum* decisions, only unitary, strong states will be able to undertake coercive strategic diplomacy, which is the essence of security policy. The multinational setting for current security policy serves to provide risk, cost and blame-sharing to national governments, but also makes strategic action near to impossible. In addition, only when 'stuff happens' to an extreme degree – when crises are so bad that they must be dealt with – will multilateral action be forthcoming. As Ulriksen's chapter shows, military integration happens by default. In theatre, when wars turn hot, national caveats can always be imposed. The conclusion is that the state retains all its national control over its own contributions if it insists, but that these 'brakes' impede effective outcomes and thereby, ultimately, the success of IOs like NATO and the EU. This is nothing less than the classical free-riding dilemma where free-riding is a rational choice only up to a point.

There is a political tension between the need to satisfy the domestic, democratic need for accountability, and the military need for functional integration in the field. There is also a tension between the intergovernmental character of the decision-making procedures in the IOs here discussed, and the need for rapid deployment and rapid shift of tactics and even strategy.

References

Adler, E. and Barnett, M. (1998), *Security Communities* (Cambridge: Cambridge University Press).

Aggestam, L. (2005), 'A European Foreign Policy?' Paper presented at the Centre for European Studies (ARENA), University of Oslo, 22 February.

Agrell, W. (2005), ' Fra forsvarspolitikk til teknologipolitikk – svensk forsvarsindustri hinsides det nasjonale eksistensforsvaret' [From defence policy to technology policy – the Swedish Defence Industry beyond National Defence], in Matlary, J. H. and Østerud, Ø. (eds).

Andersson, Jan Joel (2006) *Armed and Ready? The EU Battlegroup Concept and the Nordic Battlegroup*, (SIEPS, Stockholm).

Arreguin-Toft, I. (2005), *How the Weak Win Wars* (Cambridge: Cambridge University Press).

Avant, D. (2005), *The Market for Force* (Cambridge: Cambridge University Press).

Bachrach, P. and Baratz, M. (1962), 'Decisions and Non-Decisions: An Analytical Framework', *American Political Science Review*, **57**, 632–42.

Barnett, M. and Duvall, R. (eds) (2005), *Power in Global Governance* (Cambridge: Cambridge University Press).

Berge, A. (1914), *Listerlandets kystværn og kaperfart 1807–1814* [Pirateering in the Lister-area, Norway, 1807–1814] (Tønsberg: Tønsberg aktietrykkeri).

Berlingske Tidende (2006), 'EU vil indhendte USAs store forsprang i våpenteknologien' [Will the EU catch up with the USA's lead in arms technology] 21 April: 10.

Buzan, B. and Wæver, O. (2003), *Regions and Power: The Structure of International Security* (Cambridge: Cambridge University Press).

Chayes, A. and Chayes, A. (1995), *The New Sovereignty* (Cambridge: Harvard University Press).

Cimbala, S. and Forster, P. (2004), *US, NATO and Military Burden-Sharing* (London: Frank Cass).

Clark, I. (2005), *Legitimacy in International Society* (Oxford: Oxford University Press).

Cooper, R. (2004), *The Breaking of Nations: Order and Chaos in the 21st Century* (London: Adelphi Papers).

Comprehensive Political Guidance, NATO, Adopted at Riga Summit 2006, Annex 1. SG (2005) 0918.

Diesen, S. (2006), The Chief of Defence's Annual Address to The Oslo Military Society.

Findlay, T. (2002), *The Use of Force in UN Operations* (Oxford: Oxford University Press and SIPRI).

Forsvarsdepartementet [Royal Norwegian Ministry of Defence] (2004), *Relevant Force – Strategic Concept for the Norwegian Armed Forces* (Oslo, Ministry of Defence).

Frantzen, H. (2005), *NATO and Peace Support Operations, 1991-1999* (London: Frank Cass).

Heier, T. (2006), *Influence and Marginalisation. Norway's Adaption to US Transformation Efforts in NATO, 1998-2004*, Phd Thesis (University of Oslo, Department of Political Science).

Henriksen, D. (2006), 'Demokratisk underskudd i NATO under Kosovokrigen' [Democratic Deficit in NATO during the Kosvo War], in *Norsk militært tidsskrift*, **12**(6).

International Herald Tribune (2006), 'Canada Leader accused of trying to de-emphasize danger to troops', 26 April.

Kennedy, P. (2006), *Of War and Law* (Princeton: Princeton Univerity Press).

Koenig-Archibugi, M. (2004), 'Explaining Government Preferences for Institutional Change in EU Foreign and Security Policy', *International Organization*, **54**(1) 137–174.

Khol. (2005), 'Ongoing Cooperation Between Europe's Armed Forces', in Sven Biscop (ed.), 'E Pluribus Unum? Military Integration in the European Union', *Egmont Papers* no. 7. (Brussels: Royal Institute for International Relations).

Lindley-French, J. (2006), 'The Utility of Force: The NATO Challenge'. *Hva kjennetegner dagens og morgendagens anvendelse av militærmakt?* [What characterises the current use of military power?] Report from Forsvarets Stabsskole, Oslo, Avd. For Militærmakt, [Norwegian Defence Staff College].

Matlary, J. H. (2002), *Intervention for Human Rights in Europe* (London: Palgrave Macmillan).

—— (2006), *Values and Weapons: From Humanitarian Intervention to Regime Change?* (London: Palgrave Macmillan).

Matlary, J. H. and Østerud, Ø. (eds) (2005), *Mot et avnasjonalisert forsvar?* [Towards a denationalised defence?] (Oslo: Abstrakt forlag).

Merk, R. (2006), 'Census Counts 100,000 Contractors in Iraq', in *The Washington Post*, 5 December.

Naumann, K. and Ralston J. (2005), 'European Defense Integration: Bridging the Gap between Strategy and Capabilities', *CSIS Report* (Washington D.C.: Center for Strategic and International Studies).

Putnam, R. (1988), 'The Logic of Two-Level Games', *International Organization* **42**, 427–460.

Singer, P. W. (2003), *Corporate Warriors. The Rise of the Privatized Military Industry* (Ithaca: Cornell University Press).

Sköns, E. (2005), 'Omstruktureringen av vesteuropeisk forsvarsindustri – markedskreftenes logikk' [Restructuring Western European Defence Industry – the Logic of the Market Forces], in Matlary, J. H. and Østerud, Ø. (eds).

Smith, I. R. (2005), *The Utility of Force* (London: Penguin).

—— (2006), 'Requirements for Effective Military Interventions', in R. G. Patman (ed.) *Globalization and Conflict: National Security in a 'New' Strategic Era* (London: Routledge).

Ulriksen, S. (1996), *Desentralisert militær integrasjon? Forsvarspolitikk i Vest-Europa etter den kalde krigen* [Decentralised military integration? Defence Policy in Western Europe after the cold war]. NUPI-rapport 208, Oslo.

—— (2007), 'European Military Forces: Integration by Default'. In this volume.

—— et al. (2006), 'European Military Forces: Integration by Default', Unpublished working paper.

Van Creveld, M. (1999), *The Decline of The State* (Cambridge: Cambridge University Press).

Wagner, W. (2005), 'The Democratic Legitimacy of ESDP', *Occasional Paper* no. 57. (Paris: EU Institute of Security Studies).

Wulf, H. (2005), *Internationalizing and Privatizing War and Peace* (Basingstoke and New York: Palgrave Macmillan).

PART 2
National Defence Beyond the State

Chapter 6

Public–Private Partnership in the New Norwegian Defence

Ragnvald H. Solstrand

Cooperation between the Norwegian armed forces and civil society is a well-established *leitmotif*, yet simultaneously a new theme. It is highly topical and controversial, both politically and within the defence organisation. At the same time it is a normal part of the defence activities. Public–private Partnership (PPP), which is the current official designation, encompasses a broad spectrum of contrasting principles and practical arrangements. A number of these have long been incorporated by the armed forces, constituting a pragmatic operational relationship. Others, however, are new and partly unknown, and require evaluation and decision-making both from a political and an operational standpoint.

If we look back to the 1970s, we find that the Norwegian armed forces in many ways constituted a society within society. The organisation possessed most of what was required to ensure its functions. The various military establishments were more or less autonomous units, with everything from their own recruitment and training activities to own mechanical workshops, kitchens, and transport and caretaker services. The one major and strategic link to civil society was the right of the armed forces to draw upon the civil infrastructure and civil resources in the event of war – the concept of so-called 'total defence'.

Comparing this with the current situation, the picture is fundamentally different. The primary role of the armed forces is now to contribute to international peace operations together with the forces of other nations. It has been realised, sometimes painfully, that the armed forces are totally dependent upon the contribution of the private sector in deploying and supporting the forces which engage in these missions. At home, we purchase a broad range of services from civil enterprises, everything from canteen operations and transport to maintenance of important and complex technical equipment. Experience so far has generally been positive.

The Norwegian defence sector is undergoing dramatic internal as well as external changes, and the challenges raised by increased PPP should be examined in this new context. The Norwegian MoD and armed forces have already gone a long way towards developing the formal and structural basis for using PPP. This provides a framework for examining the objectives and consequences, in depth and from different standpoints.

The remainder of this chapter will be structured as follows. First we provide an account of what is 'new' in the 'new Norwegian Defence', and how PPP can be adapted as a strategic tool-box in the ongoing process of reorganisation.

We continue with a brief review of the conceptual and methodological basis for PPP in defence as it currently exists in the development stage. The aim is to offer a critical survey of some of the more diffuse and challenging aspects of developing PPP as a useful tool. Thereafter, we look more closely at the motivation behind the adoption of these means – that is, the contribution to increased efficiency, rationalisation and cost-cutting. We ask under which conditions the various categories of PPP measures can be applied, and which factors are critical to its success.

In the final part of the chapter we briefly discuss the difficult and sensitive question of the boundary between those activities which may be privatised, and core activities which must remain within the defence organisation and under its full control. Political aspects will only be touched upon briefly. We examine in greater depth the question of what, from a purely functional standpoint, must be regarded as core activities – that is, functions which in the long term must be developed and managed on the basis of national interest, readiness and not least, national control.

New Defence, Old Problems

Throughout the last fifteen years the permafrost of the cold war and its philosophy gradually released its grip on the Western nations' defence. Fundamental questions about the military organisations' primary objectives and functional organisation were placed on the political agenda. In political circles many quickly reached the conclusion that the future could be expected to be more 'peaceful', and the need for military forces significantly lower. The so-called 'peace dividend' was spent on other important functions of the state with the result that defence budgets in many European countries were considerably reduced.

There were no clear answers regarding future challenges, but a new conceptual approach gradually emerged, based on permanent uncertainty and a continual need for adaptation and flexible structures. The strongly US-inspired watchword for this in NATO was *transformation*, a state of continual alert, changing strategic goals and organisational realignment.

Some time passed before this change had any impact in Norway. The reasons for this are complex and well worth including in a separate study. Here, we must be content to note that the defence budget did not decline dramatically after 1990, but stabilised at around 3.5 billion euros. The result of this was that no pressing need for dramatic restructuring was felt. First in Parliamentary Report 45 (2000–2001), the long term plan for the period 2000–2005 (*Forsvarsdepartementet*, 2001) was the need for a substantial re-thinking addressed. The pressure for reorganisation and modernisation continued in Parliamentary Report 42 (2003–2004) relating to the period 2005–2008 (*Forsvarsdepartementet*, 2004). Compared to previous plans, Norway was now developing a completely different defence structure, both quantitatively and qualitatively. It is therefore appropriate to refer to 'the New Defence'. The Army has been reduced to a single brigade, yet the requirements of international operations are increasing. The Navy's fighting strength has not been drastically reduced as yet, but the resources available for necessary training and upgrading of equipment are very limited. The Air Force is in a similar situation, with the paramount question being the purchase of new fighter aircraft. Not feasible within a realistic ordinary defence budget, it will inevitably have to be considered in the context of waste and extraordinary appropriations.

The existential problems of the 'new defence' are to be found in the domain of planning, administration and finance. For several decades the armed forces focused on long-term structural developments for which there was no real budgetary basis. This has long been recognised, but a number of systemic weaknesses have prevented national policies and organisational practice within the armed forces from being harmonised. During the 1970s and 1980s Norway attempted to maintain an army comprising 13 brigades. The result was that by the early 1990s, only three of these brigades had the necessary minimum of materiel to be operational.

The Defence Commission of 1990 focused on the structural imbalance between goals and resources, and outlined a plan for a considerable reduction in both the territorial defence and peacekeeping roles of the armed forces. In subsequent studies, and in the long-term programmes submitted to the *Storting,* reorganisation, reduction in manpower, and trimming of the entire organisation were predominant. The major provisions and objectives were essentially financial. The intention was to halt the increase in operating costs through rationalisation and a slimming-down of non-operational activities, assuming that an immediate annual increase in budgets of 0.5 per cent in real terms would be granted. Only in very general terms did the documents deal with the operational functions and strength of the armed forces. Participation in international operations was to be limited, but even here, finance was a predominant – yet unspecified – theme. It was proposed that extra expenses incurred by involvement in international operations should be financed in addition to the ordinary defence budget.

Subsequent parliamentary bills (St. prp. no. 45, 2000–2001, and St. prp. no. 42, 2003–2003) focused more on challenges to security and the tasks facing the armed forces in a new era. But also these documents and the accompanying political processes were focused on questions of finance, not on structural and operational implications. The restructuring during the 1990s had not achieved the desired results: operational costs continued to increase though there were no budget increases. Concurrently, defence equipment was increasing in cost at an annual rate 3 to 4 per cent above the nominal rate of inflation for which compensation was made. During the last ten years, the real increase in wages and salaries in the military organisation amounted to 44 per cent compared to the mean of 26 per cent for Norway as a whole. Briefly, this meant that the real purchasing power of so-called 'flat budgets' was declining by about 2 per cent per annum. Taking these factors into account, it becomes apparent that efficiency, reorganisation and slimming of the organisation became the predominant strategic management focus.

PPP for a more cost-effective defence

Tools within the sphere of Public-Private Partnership were seen as important, if not crucial, to come to grips with these problems. In a parliamentary bill (St. prp. no 42 (2003–2004), the main goal of PPP was stated as 'channelling a larger portion of resources into the modernisation and transformation of the operational forces'. In this bill it is also stated: 'In order to meet urgent requirements of force availability and cost effectiveness, increased importance will be attached to strategies other than traditional acquisitions, including PPP.' Further, it is emphasised that 'it is important that, where feasible, the armed forces use the private sector, nationally and internationally, to supply products and services'.

The new centre–left government that took office in 2005 has clearly signalled a lower profile for PPP efforts, however, without changing the main thrust of previous policies. In another parliamentary bill (St. prp. no. 1, 2006–2007) it is pointed out that the military sector depends on collaboration with civilian partners to acquire and maintain important military capabilities. Such collaboration is also seen as a means to support national industries and create jobs. International collaboration is encouraged, however, in rather general terms. PPP is no longer portrayed as a potential key contribution to solving the economic problems of the defence sector. Rationalisation and the improvement of internal processes are now seen as being more important vehicles to counter cost escalation and cope with shrinking defence budgets. PPP will be focused on those areas where internal means fall short.

Public–Private Partnerships: The Norwegian Approach

The Norwegian MoD is currently in the process of carrying out essential work in defining the taxonomy and developing concepts and methods for utilising PPP. In consultation with the Ministry of Finance, the Ministry of Defence selected the term 'Private–Public Partnership' to encompass three types of enterprise: outsourcing, partnering and Public–Private Cooperation (PPC).

Outsourcing implies the delegation of a specified part of the activity to one or more external contractors. An agreement is entered into, normally of 3 to 5 years' duration, which (under certain conditions) commits the supplier to deliver prescribed goods or services to the defence organisation. It is this type of agreement with which the armed forces have most experience. A typical example is canteens, although the list is long. Outsourcing is that category of operations which immediately stands out as an object for competitive tendering, partly for the purposes of comparison with continued internal enterprise, but also with the aim of finding the best external supplier. Even though this is the simplest form of PPP, administrative challenges remain. Evaluation, decision-making, and follow-up will, in total, require significant administrative and analytical skills whereby the final accounts will be able to illustrate the net advantages of outsourcing.

Partnering comprises a variety of arrangements based on mutually binding, long-term agreements between a public sector and one or more private parties, with the aim of providing specific goods or services. For the armed forces, partnering is seen to be most relevant for large procurement programmes. The MoD will normally provide the funding required, while the private partners make available the core expertise and take responsibility for the delivery and follow-up of the equipment throughout its entire life-time. Used properly, partnering is mutually beneficial for all parties involved. The private partners can allocate their resources optimally in a long-term perspective, securing cost-effective processes and supporting creativity and innovation. The armed forces can focus on their unique areas of competence, such as operational requirements and performance specifications. It is clear that successful partnering requires a high degree of integrated work processes, underpinning common thinking and harmonisation of strategies. Therefore, competition is not a dominant feature in partnering arrangements.

Public–Private Cooperation (PPC) has similar characteristics to partnering. The agreement between partners is normally concerned with material supplies or development, and is based upon a long-term strategic plan. The fundamental difference between partnering and PPC is that the latter implies that the private partners are responsible for the major part of financing and own the physical product; the public partner leases the product for a predetermined period such that the defined functions may be carried out as required.

The current guidelines state that PPC shall only be entered into when this proves to be the cheapest method for the armed forces to acquire a specified output, seen in a life-cycle perspective. The arrangement also incorporates several incentives and mechanisms to increase cost efficiency. Fixed costs can be distributed among several users. The distribution of risks and gains is another central issue. Risk is an important element in cost calculations involving a major long-term project. In principle, risk management shall be assigned to that party which has the greatest possibility to control such risk. A party which has the overall responsibility both for acquiring the physical product and operating and servicing it over a long period has the strongest inducement to find cost-effective solutions in order to increase the profit margin.

Can PPP be practised in the defence?

No doubt, PPP measures may also be practised in the defence sector, with varying degrees of success. However, this raises some significant challenges. Experience has already been gained in the USA, the UK and several other countries, but it appears that much of this experience is either not accessible or directly relevant to Norway. Other public sectors in Norway have ten to fifteen years' comprehensive experience with privatisation, but the lessons drawn here are not directly applicable to the armed forces. Far-reaching privatisation in defence, similar to that of the Norwegian Telecommunication Administration in the 1990s, does not feature on the political agenda and the armed forces as such will continue to be a state monopoly in the provision of national security against external threats.

Experience from exposure to competition within sectors such as transport and health may be of value for the armed forces, but does not appear to have been documented in any systematic manner. There is a considerable distance between the general theories and a solidly based practical approach required for the armed forces to benefit from PPP measures. Access to good empirical and applied research within this field is extremely limited.

Outsourcing: Shedding Light on the Problem

Outsourcing distinguishes itself from Partnering and PPC regarding both content and implementation. It is concerned with identifying clearly demarcated areas of activity which hitherto have been operated by the armed forces, but which are suited to outsourcing in its entirety to an external supplier operating in a commercial market. In spite of some contacts with other public bodies and the business sector, the armed forces have remained a quite 'closed' and self-sufficient organisation. A number of candidate projects for successful outsourcing should therefore be expected.

It was possibly this recognition that led the MoD to regard outsourcing as one of the central elements in the restructuring of the Defence. It is worth noting that this occurred as recently as 2002, well ten years after the fundamental problems of internal imbalance lay on the politicians' table. Outsourcing was first and foremost regarded as a means of saving money and reducing the number of employees, to establish a balance in the over-strained Defence budget.

In April 2002, a document entitled *Concepts and methods for outsourcing activities* was approved by the Ministry of Defence (*Forsvarsdepartementet*, 2002). The Ministry was quite specific in its formulation of the requirements: the process was to be given high priority, and rapid progress was demanded. The now defunct Defence General Headquarters followed up these orders with an implementation directive, and considerable resources were invested to ensure a rapid realisation. Initially, this was to proceed for a trial period of two years. Until mid-2005, some 30 items for outsourcing had been defined, of which only a few had not yet been followed up due to limited manpower. Of the others, five had resulted in outsourcing contracts, ten were at a stage where contracts were expected to be signed in the near future, and ten had been terminated without any decision being made on outsourcing. Of the ten latter projects, most have been continued as part of other initiatives. Progress from mid-2005 to mid-2006 has been limited, and seen in relation to ambitions and possibilities, the results hitherto must be considered as modest.

The Norwegian guidelines strongly emphasise that outsourcing shall be *totally* profitable financially. However, total economic analyses are complicated by a number of circumstances. First, the internal 'tender' must realistically take into consideration the potential for improvement inherent within the existing structure of the armed forces. Experience from other sectors confirms that internal tenders can be equally competitive. Secondly, the total financial estimates must take into consideration liquidation costs of the ongoing internal activity in the event of an external supplier being selected. Winding down within a relatively rigid and tightly regulated organisation like the armed forces can have long term and unpredictable consequences which affect the entire organisation's finances and mode of operation. As public employees in the regulated Norwegian job market, the terms of contract for many of the defence staff provide them with sound job protection. Salaries and other personnel-related costs do not necessarily quickly dissipate when activities are outsourced. The armed forces, going through a period of dramatic staff reductions, have already paid out several billions of *kroner* to encourage early retirement by extensive redundancy packages. In principle these types of costs should be included in total financial calculations for outsourcing. In practice, however, it is problematic to distinguish and ascertain costs of such personnel flows in a large organisation undergoing major staff reductions. A corresponding problem exists with property, buildings and plants where the whole defence sector is in the middle of a comprehensive disposal process. Restructuring expenses and income from sales have been shown to be highly uncertain elements.

The time perspective for total cost calculations is also a problematic factor. As the defence leadership is primarily interested in utilising outsourcing as an economic means in the ongoing demanding restructuring process, it is natural to search for measures which can result in considerable savings within a 3 to 5 year horizon. Restricting cost evaluations to such a short period simplify them considerably, but imply a risk of short-sighted decisions. Outsourcing possibilities which might yield extensive advantages in the long term, might be overlooked.

As mentioned, savings provided the main motive for the defence leadership's strong reliance on outsourcing. But the approved guidelines are exemplary in relation to the overall presentation of all important factors and circumstances which have to be considered. The consequences for defence personnel must be accounted for and negotiations must be entered into with the staff organisation. Legal and commercial aspects must also be considered. This implies that the MoD and armed forces must have a solid expertise in these areas which can be supplemented by external consultants as and when necessary. It is especially important to have clear, objective and flexible contracts.

Evaluating the results of outsourcing initiatives, the initial factor for ensuring satisfactory supplies is that the armed forces (as a customer) and the supplier have a clear and mutual understanding of what is to be supplied and under which circumstances. As the client, the armed forces must clearly define and specify the required services. Outsourcing of canteen services has confirmed that the supplied services do not always come up to expectation on quality. The problem is considerably larger when more complex services are to be described in terms of utility and how the armed forces can benefit from the suppliers' technological and organisational development throughout the contract period. The Norwegian defence has adopted the so-called 'balanced scorecard' method to support development and implementation of outsourcing strategy at all levels in the organisation. Balanced management-by-objective has become the designation of this approach, and which may also be considered appropriate for the formulation and follow-up of outsourcing strategies (Bakke, 2004b). The primary objective of outsourcing is broken down into subsidiary goals with associated attributes and indicators, capable of being measured or evaluated so as to provide the basis for an overall evaluation.

In the short term, where economic factors are of primary importance, there is little to suggest that outsourcing of activities will make any notable imprint on the hard-pressed defence economy. In the longer term, savings may well make a significant contribution to stabilising operating costs. One assumption is that the Defence establishes solid routines for outsourcing which place relatively few demands on the leadership, leaving them free to concentrate on essential internal problems.

It is not difficult to find reasons why the efforts in outsourcing can fail (Bakke, 2004a). Two risk factors which can have major consequences and should be emphasised are insufficient basis for impact assessment, and a lack or preparedness for dealing with discontinuation of outsourced services. The problems associated with long-term cost analyses are already mentioned. Long and complex chains of economic cause-and-effect relationships must be understood and incorporated into the model. No less difficult is the need to acquire data on future costs. In order to undertake cost analyses which will support the decision-making process, an overall measure of uncertainty is needed.

There will always be a risk that a supplier will not be able to fulfil the agreed contract, and that it will not be possible to find an alternative source. It is therefore necessary to be prepared to quickly re-establish activity within the defence structure, dependent upon how critical the service is. In practice, it will be very difficult to maintain a level of preparedness over time in an organisation which is under severe economic pressure. Outsourcing is seldom reversible, and in most cases it will take a considerable time to re-establish an activity internally. Consequently, the armed forces can only secure themselves against unacceptable risks by ensuring a strong control over the selection of services to be outsourced, both with respect to the probability and the consequences of any discontinuation of the service. Where the service is truly critical for the ability of defence to function, it will be mandatory to ensure a minimal likelihood of interruption of supplies.

Considering the risk of dramatic changes occurring over a period of ten to fifteen years, this realisation should lead us to conclude that such important functional services should rarely, if ever, be outsourced. This can result in a difficult balance as the major potential for economic saving probably lies with services which are more or less imperative for effective functioning of the armed forces.

Strategic Partnering and Cooperation – Solutions for the Future?

The two other aspects of public–private partnership within the defence sector, i.e. Partnering and Public–Private Cooperation (PPC), are distinguished first and foremost through financing. In partnering, the MoD or armed forces are responsible for the entire or a major part of the financing, while PPC implies private financing and a leasing arrangement. In many instances this is an important distinction. For example, in the case of external financing, there will be a greater possibility to plan the flow of payments over time, and adapt to the annual budget framework. Here, however, these alternative solutions will be examined together.

The primary areas in which partnering and PPC may be applied are those involving procurement of large materiel capacities such as platforms, weapon systems, other categories of operational materiel, buildings and technical infrastructure. The broader concept of procurement has come to replace the traditional concept of acquisition which, first and foremost, is associated with purchase of new materiel under contract with an external supplier. In principle, an evaluation of procurement shall include all methods by which the Defence can achieve a certain materiel capacity, including hire, second-hand purchase, and development of new materiel. Partnering and PPC shall consequently provide the defence organisation with a broader spectrum of options for selecting the best procurement method, all circumstances taken into account.

During the last few decades, the USA and a number of European countries have gained considerable experience with these forms of strategic partnership. Development is largely headed by the major nations where the need and possibilities for strategic partnership are greatest, but smaller nations such as Denmark and The Netherlands have experience which may prove advantageous to Norway. Naturally, these experiences cannot be applied directly, but there is reason to believe that the main trends in this development among our closest allies will also be applicable in Norway. A clear trend is that the political and managerial focus is changing from outsourcing based on tenders to various forms of integrated cooperation and strategic partnership. It is uncertain whether the driving power behind this development is to be found in the military organisations or in the business sector.

The public actors have gradually relegated the financial and short-term economic arguments to the background, to the advantage of the more long-term positive effects of quality and cost efficiency in their broadest understanding within public service production. Strategic partnership and close cooperation in selected areas is to provide impulses and challenges which countervail the too-familiar trends whereby public enterprise becomes inhibited and stagnates in respect of organisation, new methods, new technology, and attitudes towards leadership and employees. In a strategic leadership perspective PPC also becomes a means for opening up the sector to external influence and stimulus.

It is very difficult to acquire an overview of the long-term effects of the increased focus on strategic partnership, let alone quantify and measure these. The effects range over the whole spectrum, from the individual to organisational behaviour and strategy. As many of the mechanisms are long-term, it is necessary to study a cooperation strategy over a period of 10 to 20 years in order to observe the full range of consequences. The MoD requirement that such arrangements must be financially profitable for the defence sector in a broad, long-term context, will certainly be a central issue. For partnership arrangements, total cost calculations will be even more demanding than for outsourcing. Non-economic consequences will probably be of even greater significance to the armed forces. Many of these consequences will be difficult to quantify. In total, this means that it will be difficult to trace the development and to provide clear evidence of the improvements at macro level. Nevertheless, valuable information may be gathered from more limited comparisons at the project level. Some documentation is to be found, particularly from the UK. This shows that projects based on strategic partnership emerge better than other comparable projects concerning avoidance of delays and compliance with budgetary limits. The fact that extensive delays and cost over-runs have been two predominant problems for military procurement in Norway for a considerable time should be an encouragement to increase the focus on partnering and PPC.

In addition to the quantifiable consequences, this form of strategic partnership may be expected to have several other positive effects at the project level. The armed forces and MoD will be able to benefit considerably from private partners' expertise within certain central areas such as technology, operations, the market and finance. Project risk may be spread and controlled more efficiently. The private sector has far greater flexibility with ongoing adaptation to changes in the project's specifications. Economies of scale in the private sector may be advantageous to the customer. When acquiring capacities which can provide services to a larger private market, the armed forces will be able to take advantage of flexible use of resource in cooperation with 'third parties'. This is particularly relevant where the armed forces' operational requirements are so restricted and unpredictable that profitable operation for one user alone is extremely difficult to achieve.

NORTRASHIP – a strategic partnership from the 1940s to the 21st century

One interesting example of successful strategic partnership is to be found in the NORTRASHIP arrangement (The Norwegian Shipping and Trade Mission) which is the principle means of the Norwegian state for shipping preparedness and strategic sealift. The arrangement was introduced during the Second World War with NORTRASHIP as a state-owned shipping company responsible for directing the use of the Norwegian commercial fleet as strategic transport for the allies. The scheme has been modified to meet changing circumstances, both during the cold war and up to the present time when it has become a flexible instrument for gaining rapid access to transport capacity in connection within international military operations. Political responsibility for the arrangement lies with the Ministry of Trade and Industry. Operational preparedness issues are handled by a separate body with representatives from the armed forces, the shipping industry, marine insurance and the seamen's organisations.

By using a PPC agreement with the shipping industry, transport resources may be utilised continually in an optimal manner for private purposes. This is ensured by commercial and operational expertise within the industry, enabling the armed forces to focus on their own key activities. From a cost point of view it would have been completely unacceptable for the military alone to maintain such transport reserves. An alternative solution might have been that a number of nations jointly owned and used such a transport resource, thereby distributing costs. However, such an approach would not solve the problem of simultaneous requirements, as the various nations would often be involved in the same international operation. Consequently, total capacity and costs would be equally as high. The NORTRASHIP arrangement serves to illustrate many of the inherent advantages of a well-planned and executed public–private partnership. One should also easily be able to identify other potential areas of such partnership. More or less randomly selected examples include facilities and equipment for learning and training, buildings and amenities for management units, refuelling capacity at sea, and maintenance capacity for technically advanced equipment. In Norway, a few projects of this category are in operation or under preparation, for example within the coastguard service, and operation and maintenance of marine helicopters. But compared to the potential possibilities, there is little evidence of any real progress in developing these forms of cooperation to their full extent.

Determining the success of PPC

Though PPC is a complex matter, each individual partnership case is not so complicated as to be incomprehensible. But the options, concerning both needs and solutions, are many, and comprise the entire spectrum of aspects from detailed contract law, personnel management and organisational development, to long-term planning and strategic leadership.

In spite of concerns about excessive focus on complexity and totality, it is clear that the armed forces have a central role to play in ensuring progress in the development of strategic partnerships. Strategic leadership is required in determining goals and selecting means; the guidelines must be clear and the means for necessary professional and administrative support must be established. Last but not least, it is necessary to ensure that in practice the requirements of follow-up and control are complied with, legally and financially. These are demanding tasks for the leadership, and represent a significant challenge for the Norwegian MoD, which remains in a exacting phase following the major restructuring which occurred some years ago.

However, it is possible that the most severe restrictions will not be with the Ministry of Defence. Strategic partnership is concerned with the procurement of materiel, facilities and an infrastructure essential to the military part of the organisation. The ministry's main functions will be associated with management, priorities and decision-making through the new programme area structure which is a melting pot for material acquisition. However, it is the military practitioners who will be responsible for the most demanding tasks in specifying needs, identifying good candidates for partnerships or PPC, and to define the concepts and specific solutions. Implementing these projects is the responsibility of the Norwegian defence logistics organisation (*Forsvarets logistikkorganisasjon* (FLO)). Negotiating contracts and ongoing follow-up and control throughout the entire lifetime of the project are also tasks which require expertise and significant resources. The logistics organisation has been undergoing major reorganisation and staff reductions, and it will be of no surprise if the threshold for adopting new solution models will be high. An organisation which is under severe pressure should primarily select well-tried solutions where acceptable. This, however, will perhaps not satisfy the demands of the military and political leadership, both of which have pushed very hard for rationalisation and reorganisation to transfer resources to its 'sharp end'.

In order to achieve the results, the MoD and the armed forces will surely have to look for external assistance, both administrative and leadership in character. A risk exists that the leadership focus and expertise within the organisation is weakened rather than strengthened, and that the ability to maintain strategic control over the development gradually disappears. This finally becomes a question of weighing up the gains against the risks within an appropriate time frame. The risk is that the military may end up in the pocket of the business sector on such scale as to result in undesirable consequences for the economy and the state of preparedness.

Considering the potential that the various forms of strategic partnership and long-term cooperation with the commercial sector hold for the MoD and the military organisation – and bearing in mind the current situation – a certain level of risk should perhaps be accepted.

Will the state of readiness be affected?

One of the doubts which frequently arises when public–private partnership is under discussion, is the danger that the state of preparedness in the defence organisation will be undermined. To a certain extent the armed forces are dependent upon private partners delivering as agreed. The consequences when this does not occur will clearly be negative for the state of preparedness. The problem is indeed both relevant and complicated.

Incomplete, or even a total lack of supplies is a familiar phenomenon for the Norwegian armed forces. The list of examples is long, and includes among other things a large number of brigades 'supplied' with fighter aircraft which, for twenty years, were without their primary weapon, and camps and stores without proper alarm and security systems. These weaknesses, which had major negative consequences for preparedness and combat ability, had little or nothing to do with arrangements which today we would refer to as public–private partnership. A first partial conclusion must therefore be that poor leadership and bad solutions will always have negative consequences for preparedness, whether this occurs within the defence organisation or in a partnership with the private sector.

The next problem concerns the definition of 'preparedness'. The term is frequently used as an overall concept covering a variety of circumstances relating to the ability of the armed forces to perform their primary functions. Basically, preparedness is the state of readiness to carry out those functions which an organisation is required to fulfil. However, this definition is not immediately applicable. If preparedness is essentially synonymous with performance, then the concept has little to contribute to the debate. We are required to make a more precise definition, something which we may do via two alternative approaches: the first related to the point of time of the defence output; the other related to uncertainty.

The time-related approach to preparedness refers to operational capability at some time in the future. The challenges facing the armed forces may, in principle, materialise at any given time in the future, but warning indicators and some time to prepare is expected. Under normal circumstances, one retains a low level of preparedness with contingency plans for raising this in the event of an emergency. Time-related preparedness may be planned, administered and quantified, but relevance is often a problem. This is the traditional understanding of preparedness and which was predominant throughout the cold war, where the Norwegian armed forces never 'operated' but only 'produced preparedness'.

While time-related preparedness focuses on assumed known future threats with a given warning time, the other approach attaches importance to the uncertain or even the unknown. Preparedness is the inherent ability of an organisation to react to and manage a broad spectrum of contrasting situations under diverse circumstances. Uncertainty-related preparedness is basically qualitative by nature and is manifest in attitudes and mode of thought. The main problem is to specify preparedness measures beyond the general expressions of transformation and flexibility, and find out which state of readiness the organisation in fact possesses.

Today, some fifteen years after exiting the cold war paradigm, the role and tasks of the military in the broader Norwegian security context remain unclarified. This means that an essential part of the framework and priorities which should govern our preparedness philosophy is lacking. Today, Norway must plan for a double challenge and parallel tasks: participation in international operations abroad, and the preservation of national security interests at home. Simply stated, preparedness in the first domain is the ability to marshal the military forces that national authorities may decide to offer for international operations in the future. In practice, this results in two specific needs related to preparedness: the ability to rapidly reallocate forces which are already deployed, and – at a later point in time – to marshal forces which Norway does not have today. The first may be referred to as reallocation preparedness; the other as structural preparedness – both being linked to contributions to international operations.

The situation is even more diffuse regarding national preparedness and territorial security. The threat of a major military invasion must now be regarded as no longer a concern for ongoing preparedness. In the meantime, planning takes place on the basis of scenarios which imply a limited transgression of Norwegian territory, by terrorists or conventional military forces. These scenarios may be assumed to entail short warning times and high uncertainty of where and when such incidents can occur, consequently representing a challenge to preparedness. If the new threats to territorial integrity are to be taken seriously, a response will have to encompass the entire spectrum of preparedness measures: the ability to rapidly call home and deploy forces currently engaged abroad; the ability to strengthen and transfer relevant components of the military already based at home; the ability to utilise national and international resources outside the armed forces to relieve, receive, and function together with forces from other nations. Attention to these questions seems limited in the Norwegian defence today.

All PPP arrangements which manifestly do not function according to intention will to some extent negatively effect important areas of preparedness. Where such problems involve over-expenditure, low product quality and restricted delays, this will be a problem for that part of the armed forces which is to receive the supplies, although is not primarily a preparedness problem. Clear exceptions are naturally those occasions where planning, leadership and the execution of a particular preparedness measure is carried out as PPP – where the consequences will have a direct effect on the state of preparedness. The conclusion is not that this particular measure is not suited to PPP: on the contrary, this is where we find some of the best alternatives for PPP regarding costs of covering a specific preparedness function. The previously mentioned NORTRASHIP arrangement is a good example of this. Within one of the most topical areas of preparedness today, the reallocation contingency for international forces, PPP solutions could provide considerably more preparedness for the money than internal solutions. Given the importance of the most central preparedness measures, stringent conditions should be placed on the selection of partners, contracts, and partnership relations. This is probably where the challenges are greatest, and – as previously mentioned – the MoD and the military organisation should seek external assistance in the evaluation, implementation and follow-up of the most important and promising measures.

Regarding the structural preparedness related to international operations, the situation is quite different. Here, the required response time for changing the capacity profile for the available forces may be a few years. We know too little today about what changes may be necessary such that we can plan and ensure sufficient resources in advance. As such, we must handle this as a typical uncertainty-related preparedness. As long as the armed forces manage to maintain a force structure whereby most of the relevant elements exist in one or another form, we will have a sufficient core of expertise to build upon. But building force components will still take time and require significant resources. Because the cost of such structural changes will normally have to be covered within the normal defence budgets, the main problem will probably be that the necessary flexibility to reduce other capacities in order to make resources available will be lacking.

This line of thought points in the direction of partnership with the private sector yielding good solutions. PPC arrangements can provide the opportunity to terminate some leasing agreements and enter into new ones within the time frame required. Resources can be released and the military can draw upon the private partners' expertise to develop prioritised capabilities. Naturally, not all the relevant types of capacity will be available through partnership with the private sector. But as long as international operations continue with the same intensity as today, there will be a significant international market. It is primarily within this international market Norway must seek cooperation.

There are, as seen above, several clearly positive preparedness possibilities with a sensible use of PPP. The negative factors are first and foremost associated with the use of civilians in high-risk operations. Given sufficient intelligence and familiarity with the situation in advance, much of the uncertainty will be eliminated through good supply contracts. Problems can arise if an operation develops unexpectedly into a war-like situation. Hired civilian personnel may then be withdrawn. If, however, their contribution is of vital importance to the further effort, as for example in the maintenance and repairs of essential material, and no replacement exists, this will result in a weakened state of preparedness. With regard to our participation in international operations, these considerations will occasionally simplify themselves – partly satisfactorily, partly otherwise. As an extremely small contributor Norway will rarely have the opportunity to select stand-alone solutions. Normally, we will depend upon arrangements established by the major actors and have to accept the resulting consequences for preparedness. If this is not possible, alternative contributions to the operation or complete withdrawal must be considered.

Further, regarding the PPP arrangements which are meant to function at home, i.e. within Norway, and which may have consequences for our national preparedness, a number of strong connections and interdependencies complicate choices based on purely national considerations. Many of the military capacities will have a dual role, and will be required to cover domestic requirements while having an ongoing primary function internationally. This essentially applies to the Army and the Air Force, to a lesser extent to the Navy, but not at all to the Home Guard. Within the support functions, where PPP solutions are most significant, we clearly do not want one set of support functions for international and another for domestic purposes. Since international operations are continually in focus and ongoing, we must expect that decisions will primarily be made on the basis of international considerations.

These solutions will then have to be adjusted to make them applicable at home when required.

Concerning preparations for war contingencies at home, we can draw upon well-organised public–private cooperation arrangements in transport. Solutions which can be applied in order to secure high preparedness for reallocation between various international conflict areas, will naturally be applicable if our troops are to be rapidly recalled. In addition, purely national arrangements for supplying and transferring forces in the national arena also have a sound potential for strengthening the level of preparedness in a cost-effective manner.

Considerations of preparedness are not a decisive obstacle to a more comprehensive use of PPP solutions. Regarding the most critical preparedness functions, PPP solutions should be avoided until we have sufficiently ascertained that the risks are acceptably low. Preparedness in the defence sector is a composite and complex area where it is difficult to establish which policies and which guidelines are applicable. Continuous and well-informed involvement of the strategic leadership is therefore mandatory.

Defining Defence Core Activities

Are there parts of the armed forces' activities which are of such character that they should be excluded from public–private partnership completely? By which criteria could such activities be identified? In the following, an attempt is made to define the core activities of the armed forces.

There are many references to such core activities in official documents on PPP. An important strategic reason for entering into PPP is to provide the various levels of defence leadership with the opportunity to concentrate on what is most critical for achieving the main defence objectives. As a rule, core activities and PPP should be complementary; but this does not help particularly in identifying core activities, which must be the preliminary step to determining where PPP is applicable.

In accordance with international law, the civil population shall not be engaged in direct combat operations. This places a number of external limits on the legal domain of PPP activity. But what exactly are combat operations? There is a broad grey-zone where multidimensional discretion must be applied. Is the driver of a tank involved in a military operation even though it is another who actually fires the gun? Most would say 'yes'. But does the same apply to the driver of an armoured vehicle transporting infantry to the battle zone? What about the pilot of a transport aircraft carrying autonomous weapons to a drop zone, far from the area of hostilities, weapons that are programmed to detect, identify and hit their targets? If we consider that the pilot is involved in military operations, then will this not also apply to those who programmed the missiles and determined the target coordinates? We could continue this argument, but we have already illustrated that determining the limits is difficult and has to be subjective.

International law is so formulated that it may be interpreted very broadly. A main principle which states that only members of the conventional armed forces, with the exception of medical orderlies and army chaplains, are legal combatants solves nothing. It only confuses the problem and maintains that operational functions are those carried out by forces in operational units, but the term 'operational unit' remains undefined. One can lean on appraisals made by other nations, but the norms behind these appraisals do not necessarily correspond with our own. Based on our own norms and appraisals, we must draw boundaries for PPP which are situated at a reassuring distance from the incontrovertible combatant functions. A 360-degree demarcation could hardly be applied in practice. This indicates that we must be vigilant concerning this problem in each and every PPP case for years ahead, and exercise thorough and critical judgement.

The core functions of the Defence must be something more than the combatant functions, even though these may be defined quite comprehensively. We can attempt to define clear and comprehensive criteria for the core functions based on two different conceptions, both linked to the specific end-product of the activity – combat efficiency at the right place and the right time. This approach, however, is difficult in practice as we are concerned with a complex chain of separate functions, each with its own contribution to the final product. The combatant functions can clearly be defined as core functions, both on account of their proximity and significance to the end-product. But we do not have to go very far along the production chain before these evaluations become more difficult. A complicating circumstance is that importance and proximity can often be linked to the end-product in different ways. One part-function may be of vital significance to the combat ability itself even though its impact may go through many stages. Research, which provides an insight and understanding of central technological development trends and possibilities, is an example of this.

Another approach is to relate the core functions to the strategically important tasks which the defence leadership must master in order to be able to carry out its responsibility for developing the defence sector in the best possible manner with regard to the goals and framework determined by the national authorities. But this criterion is not easily operationalised. The challenge lies in that both long-term and current, more short-term, leadership requirements must be taken into account in a balanced manner, avoiding the pitfall of defining everything that requires the attention of the leadership as a strategically important task.

This may be clarified by posing the question as to how outside actors will react to our choices. How will alliance partners, the national political leadership, and Norwegians in general, regard a situation where the defence leadership itself does not have sufficient expertise to explain the actual circumstances, and to account for those evaluations than have been made? If there is good reason to believe that this will undermine the reputation and credibility of Norwegian defence, then we have probably identified a strategic leadership function.

This brief discussion illustrates the complexity of the problem and indicates those dangers that are inherent in going too far in the direction of standard, general solutions. It must be acknowledged that the concept of core functions only has a practical meaning when linked to a specific application. Here the search is for those elements which are so central that public–private partnerships must be applied with particular caution. As a point of commencement for a brief, concluding discussion, a list of possible core activities can be compiled:

1. Strategic planning
2. Procurement of military capacity
3. Financial management
4. Research and development
5. Media and information service
6. Personnel management
7. Planning and implementation of military operations
8. Operational-related logistics and support.

All these eight points represent essentially broad areas of activity which comprise a number of part-functions. Activities 1 to 6 are core activities in the light of their strategic importance; activities 7 and 8 on account of their close association to the unique primary objectives and the associated end-product of the activity. However, this does not imply that the defence organisation must carry out all part-functions in each of these areas internally. This will vary from one area to the next, and require a far more comprehensive analysis than is possible here.

The activity areas 7 and 8 have been discussed rather extensively earlier in this chapter. Both of them should have a 'PPP-free' zone. Area 7 has a rather extensive zone of this character, while area 8 is less sensitive to PPP, therefore requiring a much smaller 'PPP-free' zone. Even for activities 1 to 6, we must accept that the 'PPP-free' core will vary in extent. Common to all areas is that the MoD and armed forces must have the ability to understand the nature of the problem in an overall perspective, and to formulate and evaluate alternative procedures and solutions; also to communicate the challenges, solutions and consequences to the outside world. Some of the part-functions linked to the administration – preparatory procedures and consequence evaluation – may be good candidates for different forms of PPP. A closer analysis might possibly reveal that this part of the activity is greatest within media and information services, somewhat less in financial control and personnel management, even less in the procurement of military capacity, and virtually none in strategic planning.

Activity 4, Research and Development, is in a special situation. Naturally, the Norwegian defence does not have the resources to carry out research and development on a broad front. The core activity within research must be selected based strictly on the most important defence needs. In a long-term perspective this means that it will be necessary to maintain expertise enabling the organisation to evaluate the scientific and military-technical development which will affect the assumptions behind defence planning. In a short-term perspective research will provide the basis for sound decisions on the development and choice of materials, and on cost-effective organisation and operations. In addition to the internal core activities, the defence sector will have a need to purchase research and development services as an integrated part of larger material procurement projects.

Our conclusion here must be that the search for the core activities in defence will have to proceed with undiminished strength as public–private partnership is increasingly evaluated and implemented. No doubt, some activities are of such character that a PPP solution should not be selected. It is equally clear that the demarcation between such core activities and the other activities cannot be defined in advance, once and for all. We have outlined a picture where the core activities in total do not appear to be so comprehensive that they should prevent us from making a strong bid for further public–private partnership.

Concluding Remarks

The contemporary armed forces face a reality characterised by a high level of activity and demanding tasks, both operational and concerning internal leadership and administration. In order to succeed, the 'New Defence' must develop so as to become a dynamic and open organisation in close touch with the outside world, both nationally and internationally. Transparency towards civil society and the business sector is an important factor in achieving the necessary impulses and challenges to further the development of the organisation. In many respects this implies a form of cultural revolution within the Norwegian defence organisation. The process has started, but there is still a long way to go.

In this situation, attempts to develop public–private partnership should be regarded as a central means in the development of an open and extrovert culture. In the forthcoming years this will most likely be the main objective of PPP. At the same time the Defence must, of course, endeavour to ensure that PPP solutions will yield cost reductions, improved capabilities and a stronger focus on core activities. But these must nevertheless be recognised as long-term goals. Initially, one should prepare for a situation where increased reliance on PPP will result in significantly higher costs – considerably exceeding the direct and short-term gains. But the aim of a more 'transparent Defence' will assist in justifying this introductory investment. So far, the Norwegian MoD and armed forces have struggled in their efforts to develop public–private partnerships, in spite of clearly expressed intentions and strong commitments. It is possible that the difficulties and the efforts required have been under-estimated, and perhaps the time has now come to draw upon external forces such that progress can be made.

Some have expressed concern that the use of PPP in the defence sector will only be to the financial advantage of private contractors and that it will be accompanied by a loss of national control of the development. If we continue to act vigilantly and rationally, these concerns will have no basis in reality. It will be an important task for the military leadership in the on-going process to focus PPP on activities which are not core functions, in the sense that they require the full attention of that leadership. But today there is a rich source of suitable candidates for PPP solutions which clearly do not come under the category of core activities. It is here that we must focus our future efforts. PPP is an important means for the development of the New Defence. It is critical that results are achieved and the motivation reinforced, so that this important development does not stagnate.

References

Bakke, S. E. (2004a), Risks associated with outsourcing (*Norsk Militært Tidsskrift* no. 02, 2004: 32–34)
—— (2004b), Outsourcing; Measuring the quality of output (*Norsk Militært Tidsskrift* no. 03, 2004: 26–32)
Forsvarsdepartementet [Norwegian Ministry of Defence] (2001), *Stortingsproposisjon* 45 (2000–2001) [Parlimantary Bill].
—— [Norwegian Ministry of Defence] (2004), *Stortingsproposisjon* 42 (2003–2004) [Parlimantary Bill].

Chapter 7

Denationalisation of Danish Armed Forces and Militarising of Danish Foreign Policy

Bertel Heurlin

At the beginning of the 21st century, like the armed forces of many other countries, the Danish armed forces are sailing in a sea of change. In Denmark, the changes are radical; the process of denationalisation of the military is profound, almost revolutionary. Further, as part of this process, one may speak of a militarisation of Danish foreign policy in the sense that contrary to the situation during the cold war, the military – now mainly consisting of deployable forces for international missions – is functioning as an important foreign policy tool. (Clemmesen, 2005; Heurlin, 2004a; Heurlin, 2007a).

This chapter describes, analyses and explains these developments, their international and domestic background. Following a brief outline of the changes, a broad survey of the global and international setting after the end of the cold war is presented together with an outline of the new international situation after the US declaration of the global war on terror following the 9/11 attacks. Thereafter follows a description of the militarisation process of Danish Foreign policy after the cold war. The central part of the chapter deals with main issues of defence transformation – the decision making process, conscription, denationalisation and privatisation. The concluding section discusses some perspectives of the future.

Transformation and Vulnerability

Since the end of the cold war Denmark has increasingly denationalised its armed forces. The new Danish Defence agreement 2005–2009 implies not only the end of territorial defence based on mobilised forces; in practice it means the virtual cancellation of military defence of Danish territory. The political mantra is that there is no conventional military threat to Denmark in the foreseeable future. Since 2005, two pillars represent the defence of Denmark: the first being deployable forces for international operations; the second is framed 'total defence', the Danish equivalent to 'Homeland Security'. The new Danish armed forces will contribute only moderately to the 'total defence'. Due to its domestic character, civil public institutions, including the police and the emergency management agency, will generally be in charge of the total defence pillar.[1] However, a reduced home guard will represent some kind of territorial protection but not against traditional attack from outside. This way of organising the Danish defence can be regarded as the ultimate denationalisation. Denmark defends itself by participating in international interventions and other international military missions far from Danish shores (Rasmussen, 2005). The new defence agreement for 2005–2009 is the ultimate organisational answer to the policy of increasing Danish international military activism since 1989. This activism policy has a remarkable record in terms of war-like missions after the cold war. It includes the Gulf War of 1990–91, the tank-battle in the UN-mission in former Yugoslavia in 1994, the NATO–Serbia–Kosovo intervention in 1999, the Afghanistan mission from 2001, and finally Denmark's participation alongside the US and UK intervention in Iraq of 2003 following the position of being part of the coalition's occupation forces (Heurlin, 2004b). Further, Denmark is an active participant in the global war on terror and is increasingly becoming an international military actor. Defence is denationalised, and Denmark – the former military reluctant ally and somewhat pacifistic oriented small country – is practising a kind of a 'militarising' of its foreign policy, meaning using its military forces internationally as a foreign policy tool (Heurlin 1997).

As a consequence of choosing the role as an international military actor, Denmark has to take the challenges posed by what specifically is referred to as the revolution in military affairs, also generally termed the defence transformation, seriously. Currently, Denmark is indeed undergoing a significant transformation in defence matters. At least the political priority is clear and indisputable: more forces on the ground, more soldiering, more focus on operational forces and support, leaner but meaner armed forces. This constitutes a development which already is materialising, indicating a switch in the direction of all voluntary armed forces. But most importantly, the decisive demarcation of denationalisation in the new Danish Defence system is that the military defence of Denmark is based on Danish deployable forces only. How is this situation to be assessed in security terms regarding the fact that Denmark is small and vulnerable?

It seems obvious that in traditional safety terms and as a small state, Denmark is extremely vulnerable economically as well as in terms of national security. Due to its very limited natural resources, Denmark is extremely dependant on foreign trade and international financial markets. In military terms – owing to its flat and small territory – Denmark is unable to defend itself. Consequently, in view of defence and economics, it is necessary for Denmark to rely on security alliances and supranational economic arrangements such as NATO and the EU. In political terms, however, Denmark is less vulnerable since its political landscape is marked by

---

1 As formulated in the official website <www.forsvaret.dk/FKO/eng/ Defence+Agreement> 'In general total defence encompasses the utilisation of all resources in order to maintain an organised, functional society and to protect the population and the national assets. The threats to be countered by total defence cut across national borders and the domestic administrative domains of various public authorities. As a result, threat containment demands joint solutions and close coordination among the accountable international and national authorities.'

internal coherence, political consensus and common identity – in essence, political stability. Denmark is probably among the most organised countries in the world, a flourishing civil society demonstrated by its high number of organisations such as political parties, trade unions, cultural groups, hobby/sports clubs, and grass-roots networks. Political stability, however, is in danger of being weakened by the growing population of immigrants and refugees and the accompanying politicisation of this issue. Despite its vulnerability Denmark has decided not to defend itself in the traditional way (Udenrigsministeriet, 2003). Why?

One could ask whether vulnerability matters in an era where everybody – even the sole superpower – is, in fact, vulnerable. The future is unpredictable: the threats are new and unknown, referred to by the former Secretary of Defence Rumsfeld as 'unknown unknowns'.[2] Does it matter in an international world order where conventional military threats are diminishing and where great power wars seem unlikely to occur? How is Denmark operating in the new international world order as concerns defence? What are the choices for Denmark regarding possibilities and restraints for its military forces in terms of denationalisation, professionalisation, and privatisation and militarising the foreign policy?

In order to cope with these questions we have to assess and analyse the international setting.

The Six Revolutions of Globalisation

Two trends affect the vulnerability of small states like Denmark: globalisation and fragmentation.[3] The fundamental transformation in the organisation of world affairs, the change from bipolarity to unipolarity as a consequence of the end of the cold war, has allowed these two trends to emerge. Globalisation is increasingly demonstrated in what could be characterised as six revolutionary developments (Heurlin, 2006). The revolution in international affairs, the revolution in economic affairs, the revolution in technological affairs, the revolution in regulatory affairs, the revolution in societal affairs, and finally the revolution in military affairs. Fragmentation is manifested in processes opposing and negating these six revolutionary developments. As a general observation, Denmark is an integral part of globalisation, scoring high on all six revolutionary trends.

Revolution in international affairs has to do with the fact that the basic international organisation of the international system has been transformed from bipolarity to unipolarity. This implies that the unipole, the United States, is able to pursue its vital interests – a situation where in urgent security terms all the other states only have the option of either to align with the sole superpower, or become marginalised or stigmatised (Hansen, 2000). This also is supporting the trend whereby almost all states, at least on the surface, are aiming at a *single set* of international and global norms comprising democracy, market economy, human rights, personal freedom and the rule of law. This is completely different from the bipolar cold war world. At the

---

2   See note 8.

3   See Hansen, Birthe & Bertel Heurlin (eds) (2000), *The New World Order: Contrasting Theories* (London: McMillan), especially the chapter by James Rosenau.

same time, the fragmentation trend is to oppose these norms, because they are seen as Western, not global norms.

Revolution in economic affairs refers to the present situation that the economic and financial sphere has become global, and independent of time and space. Trillions of dollars change hands in seconds. For the first time in history we have a functioning and growing world market as concerns production, capital and services. Here, the fragmentation trend emphasises national economic self-reliance and opposes the globalisation of the market.

Revolution in technological affairs concerns new dimensions regarding knowledge, information and human relations. Time and space are on the verge of disappearing due to new information technology and nanotechnologies. The fragmentation trend in turn is aiming at distorting or limiting these technological developments.

Revolution in regulatory affairs has to do with the disappearance of common goods such as the sea and the oceans, the air, space and the new dimension – cyberspace. It is all about survival and sustainability of the globe. One cannot, for example, fish what and where one likes; pollution and other environmental issues are threatening; space is overloaded; international regulation is necessary, and nations are generally inclined to co-operate. This goes also for the increasing politicisation of human security, for example food security, consumer security, security for child labour, trafficking, and slavery. Fragmentation, on the other hand and using all means, will try to avoid the inevitable demand for global regulation.

Revolution in societal affairs alludes to global changes in the perception of man as a political, economic and social actor. Democracy, market economy, individual freedom all enable the single individual to have influence through personal action such as voting, by participating, by buying, consuming and investing. This implies a new and important role for the individual. Also the individualisation of the soldier, avoidance of human casualties and flat organisational structures are all included in this revolution. Conversely, the fragmentation trend will emphasise collective identity by means of hyper-nationalism, religious or ethnic fundamentalism, and by minimising individual freedom and responsibility.

Finally, there is the revolution in military affairs which is related to the ongoing broadening of the concept of national security following the disappearance of traditional threats and the emergence of new ones. As a consequence, the military forces have to consider new roles, a new organisation, strategies, equipment and not least new kinds of war.[4] The key words are 'knowledge', 'contra 'mass' and 'leaner but meaner armed forces'. Fragmentation trends are aiming at thwarting and obstructing this revolution by asymmetric countermeasures.

---

4   See Heurlin, Bertel et al. (eds) (2003), *The New Roles of Military Forces*, Copenhagen, Danish Institute for International Studies.

The Impact of Global Revolutionary Changes on Denmark

There is no doubt that the revolutions mentioned above are having an increasing impact on a growing number of countries, not least on a country like Denmark. Based on empirical observations concerning IT and transnational processes and activities, Denmark may be regarded as one of the most globalised countries.

Generally, the notion of vulnerability has to be assessed in new ways. Vulnerability and non-safety are not necessarily negative conditions. Due to globalisation (meaning global political norms, the increasing role of the individual as an actor, ever widening economic and trade relations, global industries and business, as well as the worldwide spread of technological developments), no one – be this an individual or any kind of unit – can be safe and invulnerable. Freedom and individualism foster the lack of general safety and security, but at the same time they increase mutual dependence and mutual responsibility. Eventually, the focus will not only be on security of individual units but will also include the much bigger issue of the survival of the globe – spaceship Earth – which is threatened by ecological overstretch and by overall political, economic, ethnic and social fragmentation. This also means that the narrow, fragmentation-oriented internal political invulnerability will receive less attention in the future. Consequently, Denmark's national strategy will not just aim at material gains, but at creating and exploiting knowledge. Likewise, the defence of Denmark will not be geared towards protecting the country from conventional attacks or invasions, but to maintain, defend and develop a safer world order that reflects the new global values and norms (as these are also Danish values and norms). A farewell will have to be said to large mobilisation forces based on conscription, while expeditionary units based on the principles of revolution in military affairs will emerge in their stead. Denmark certainly stands before the most comprehensive transformation of its military forces in modern times.

Why this shift? As alluded to above, Denmark seems to be fairly responsive to developments and trends in the regional and global setting in order to avoid international marginalisation. But why exactly choose military tools?

Only recently, a Danish officer suggested a complete shut-down of the Danish armed forces. A couple of years ago a former Danish minister of defence declared that had it not been for the civil wars in former Yugoslavia in the 1990s, Danish defence would have ceased to exist (Heurlin, 2004b). Among other responses to the challenges of the present global environment, one could suggest increasing other international activities than armed intervention, specifically peacekeeping by police-forces, technical assistance to developing countries or failed states, international assistance to environmental projects, and to projects aiming at creating peace and stability, not least through programmes supporting democracy, law and order, and civil society, in Denmark referred to as the 'MIFRESTA' , an acronym for Environment, Peace and Stability. What is crucial is that Denmark has chosen to do both – military as well as civilian development-related international activism (Heurlin, 2001).

Militarising Danish Foreign Policy as Part of Denationalisation of the Armed Forces

The fact that Denmark has chosen specifically to emphasise its armed forces as part of its foreign policy since the end of the cold war can be explained in the following way.

The main priority for a country in a globalised world is to avoid being marginalised or isolated. The globalisation process had already begun during the cold war period, but globalisation experienced the most promising conditions for development after the era of the East–West bipolarity had ended. As mentioned earlier, after 1991 the new world order seemed to be based on just one vision – democracy, market economy, human rights, personal freedom, and the rule of law.

During the cold war, NATO secured survival for a Denmark that was located in a rather critical geographic position. It was then a frontline state – extremely close to the Iron Curtain. In terms of security policy, Denmark was able to be a free-rider, i.e. secure under NATO's nuclear umbrella, and keeping its defence close to NATO standards by benefiting from NATO's technological advances. The probability for real fighting was very low. Military forces were considered as merely symbolic, having a deterrent role in a kind of virtual war (Danish Institute for International Studies, 2005a; Heurlin, 2004b).

After the cold war, and with plans for NATO's enlargement, Denmark suddenly lost its frontline status. It was feared that the nation would become marginalised. How could Denmark re-position itself in the new world order? One could emphasise the soft security efforts – technical assistance to developing countries, including specific support for the new independent states in the Baltic region. But Denmark was looking for new and more spectacular responses to the sea of changes in world politics after the cold war.

It was now seen as important to deal with the new soft and hard security policy issues that were emerging as a consequence of the globalisation process. The issues included international crime, internal and transnational ethnic problems, environmental challenges, human trade, and hyper-nationalism. The response was a broad spectrum of efforts, most notably among them the emphasis on new roles of military forces. Crisis management, peacekeeping, peacemaking and peace-enforcement, or so-called humanitarian intervention missions, stood at the forefront. In fact, this was the first step in the post-cold war militarising of Danish foreign policy.

One can thus distinguish between three phases of Danish defence policy: the cold war symbolic–virtual war-like hard defence policy, the post-cold war soft/sharp defence policy manifested in military actions, and finally the post-9/11 defence policy manifested in sheer war (Iraq and Afghanistan).

While Denmark could be characterised as a *'defensive, non-provocative actor'*[5] during the cold war, it can be claimed that in the post-cold war period Denmark has

---

5   See Heurlin, 2001.

emerged as a '*civilian/military offensive actor*', and since 9/11 could be considered as a '*strategic offensive actor*'.[6]

These shifts in status have to be viewed against the background whereby in the cold war Denmark was a security political actor with very limited scope for manoeuvre on the one hand, and free-riding tendencies on the other. Often referred to as a NATO-footnote country, not supporting the nuclear rearmament in the official NATO-statements, Denmark was stigmatised by the introduction of the term 'Denmarkisation', referring to a country being protected but not willing to pay the price (Heurlin, 1983). Denmark pursued a double policy, seeking protection in NATO and at the same time playing a non–provocative game towards the USSR; in other words, acting as a defensive non-provocative actor.

In the new open international setting after the cold war, Denmark saw new possibilities in conducting an active, offensive defence policy based primarily on UN – Chapter 7 engagements (meaning military support for peacekeeping and peacemaking missions in accordance with Chapter 7 of the UN Charter).[7] It is interesting that the military intervention in Kosovo not was not referred to as a 'war'. German Chancellor Schröder, for instance, called it 'a political action with military means in order to establish peace'. Denmark acted then as a 'civilian/military offensive actor', preferring to regulate the conflicts of other people with as limited military means as possible.

After 9/11, Denmark changed its agenda again becoming an active participant in the Afghanistan war, and later in the Iraq war. It was argued that these wars were directed against states not complying with US-security demands, states that also were considered rogue states harbouring terrorists and developing weapons of mass destruction (WMD). Moreover, they were directed against non-state actors using terror as weapons, against 'the known unknowns, and the unknown unknowns'.[8] Denmark then became what the Danish scholar, Sten Rynning, has termed a 'strategic offensive actor', an actor willing to use armed forces as appropriate means in the confrontation with forces hostile to the New World order.[9]

As the post-cold war 'civilian/military offensive actor' Denmark has militarised its foreign policy basically in two ways. First, by participating in offensive, intervening military actions, taking their point of departure in international organisations as the UN and NATO. Indeed, in 1993 it was decided to establish a Danish international brigade for use in future UN as well as in NATO operations. Military use by the EU was prohibited political territory for Denmark due to fact that defence policy was one of the opt-outs from the Maastricht Treaty, to which Danish voters had only agreed with reservations in the 1993 referendum, a year after the infamous

---

6   See Rynning, Steen (2003) 'Danish Security Policy after 11 September', in *Danish Foreign Policy Yearbook 2003*, Copenhagen: Danish Institute for International Studies, **24**.

7   Ibid.

8   In February 2002 U.S. Secretary of Defence Donald Rumsfeld stated, 'There are known knowns; there are things we know we know. We also know there are known unknowns; that is to say there are some things we do not know. But there are also unknown unknowns – the ones we don't know we don't know'. Citation from *Foreign Policy*, January–February 2004, 47.

9   See Rynning 2003, p. 24.

'no' to the Maastricht Treaty in 1992 (Petersen, 2004). Thus, Danish participation in international missions was restricted to those recommended by the UN and NATO. Denmark participated in the UN-supported war against Iraq in 1991, in the internal Balkan wars in the mid-1990s, and as part of the NATO campaign against Serbia in Kosovo in 1999, among others.

The second issue over which Denmark proved the 'militarisation of its foreign policy' was offering military-diplomatic support to the Baltic countries and Poland. The aim was to assist the transformation processes in these countries, in particular the restructuring and rebuilding of their defence organisations and armed forces in order to meet NATO standards. In other words, Denmark emerged as an advocate of Estonia, Latvia, Lithuania and Poland in their military integration process with NATO. This was done effectively, through training and education of these countries' military personnel and civilians in Denmark, through participation in Danish exercises, and the integration of Baltic troops in Danish military units operating under NATO or UN mandate in the Balkan area. Furthermore, Copenhagen delivered military equipment to those countries. Demark was also very active in the set up of a Baltic Defence College in Estonia by establishing a joint Baltic Peacekeeping Battalion (BALTBAT), and the Nordic–Polish Brigade. Notably, the Baltic Defence College was headed by a Danish Brigadier General until recently. Also the establishment of the Polish, German, and Danish Multinational Corps was based on a Danish initiative (Forsvarskommissionen, 1997).

It was 9/11 that initiated Denmark's most recent transformation from a 'civilian/ military offensive actor' to a 'strategic offensive actor'. Danish security policy now implied a will to go to war against forces hostile to the present world order. This change was manifested in two ways: participation in interventionist and expeditionary, warfare and an ever closer co-operation with the superpower – the United States. In terms of diplomacy, Denmark, together with the NATO partners, adopted an Article V declaration immediately after 9/11, stating that the terrorist attack on the United States was considered an attack against all allies. The Danish Prime Minister, Poul Nyrup Rasmussen, declared that 9/11 'was a ruthless attack on everything we represent: individual freedom, safety for many, and our collective security – everything that sustains the concept of democracy. [...] Our future is common – our security is also that of NATO and the United States'. (Rynning, 2003: 28).

In connection with the Iraq war, Denmark whole-heartedly supported the political line of the United States and United Kingdom. Furthermore, Denmark has warmly supported the new NATO initiative to establish a response force that is able to undertake offensive action on a global scale. This was endorsed by the Alliance at the Prague summit meeting in November 2002. Since then Denmark has closely followed US strategy in Iraq, Afghanistan and in the global war on terror. After 9/11, Denmark's diplomatic initiatives have been followed up by direct war efforts. Denmark contributed to the Afghan war (and the war against terrorism) with airlift, fighters, Special Forces, and staff-work. A submarine and Danish land forces have contributed in the Iraq conflict. At the 2006 NATO-summit in Riga, the Danish defence minister, Søren Gade, even openly criticised the larger NATO members such as Germany, for saving its forces for operating in the heavy and dangerous areas in Afghanistan, while together with the British, Danish troops were carrying out missions at the sharp end. Denmark was also positive towards the upgrading of the Thule radar by the United States in connection with the American endeavour to establish the beginning of an operative missile defence system as from 2005 (Kristensen, 2005). In 2006, the Danish government even expressed willingness to participate in a future European missile system (Nielsen, 2006). Denmark has truly become a strategic player in the closest collaboration with the United States, presupposing a comprehensive, if not revolutionary transformation of the Danish defence (Heurlin, 2005).

The Danish vision – primarily as a function of the new position as a strategic offensive actor – is now close to sharing the US idea as to how armed forces have to be transformed (Boot, 2006; Heurlin, 2003b; Kagan, 2006; Rasmussen, 2006). In connection with the United States Joint Forces Command, NATO has set up an Allied Command Transformation in Norfolk (USA) on the same level of command as ACO, Allied Command Operation (the former ACE, Allied Command Europe). This change has been supported by Denmark. Copenhagen is also following NATO's recommendations on revolutionary changes in structure and content of the military forces of member states.

Transformation and Decision-Making

Over the last 15 years, two Danish comprehensive defence commissions – each lasting around 2 years (1988–89 and 1997–98) and comprising politicians, military personnel and experts – have thought deeply about military and security issues, and come up with two impressive 3 volume reports (Heurlin, 2004b).

Significantly, neither of the commissions seriously considered technological developments, since it was perceived that high-tech equipment, research and development would rapidly consume the limited Danish defence budget. Since 9/11 this attitude has changed. Now, transformation and technology are on the agenda. But no defence commission was set up in the context of a changed security environment after 9/11. Instead of a small group of experts and civil servants, the so-called the 'Bruun-group' was established in 2003. Its task was to deliver a report within months on the new security policy conditions affecting Danish defence policy.

The traditional aim of Denmark's security policy of upholding the nation's sovereignty, and to foster international peace and security, including preventing conflicts and war, activities for peacekeeping and peacemaking, and efforts to promote stability, were now expanded to include meeting direct and indirect threats against Danish territory and Danish citizens. The Bruun Group suggested an increased capacity for total defence (including anti-terror activities) and for swiftly deployable military capacities. The planning ought to be capacity-based (following the US strategy). Regarding international operations, the main aim should be to concentrate on a capacity to rapidly deploy for short and focused war efforts rather than offering a long presence in conflict areas with low intensity warfare. Denmark should hence participate in military actions early on in the conflict and contribute to limiting the conflict and its direct results. Consequently, Denmark would become a more visible actor in international affairs.[10] Still, as was suggested, Denmark should also be in the possession of a certain capacity for stabilising and restructuring activities. Conscription plays a crucial role in the evolving Danish defence policy. The Bruun-report emphasised that conscription was a necessity in the cold war context and with it the strategy of defence based on general mobilisation. Now, however, the training and education of conscripts that focuses on territorial defence was considered to have lost its relevance. But there was nevertheless a need for defence personnel to be responsible for Denmark's total defence (homeland security). How could this be done? One possibility was to continue with some form of conscription in order to meet the needs of homeland defence. In fact, it could be a system that supports the recruiting of professional soldiers from a pool of conscripts.

Conscription in Denmark has a long tradition. It is considered part of a democratic culture going back to Denmark's first democratic constitution of 1849. This constitution states that it is the duty of all men capable of bearing arms to contribute to the defence of their country. The principle of conscription has never been seriously challenged. It was only in connection with the report from the defence commission of 1997 when the small but influential social-liberal party (*Radikale Venstre*) – then in government coalition with the Social Democrats – insisted on the suspension of conscription. However, this did not happen. Indeed, despite the general tendency in Europe to abolish conscription, it was decided to keep the system which had served Denmark so well during the cold war.

Clearly, the politicians are not ready to abandon the so-called the 'Danish model'. (Heurlin, 2007a). The drafting of men then has been kept for democratic and recruitment reasons, yet with a view of increasing the professionalism of troops. The Danish Chief of Defence stated: 'Denmark has a professional defence based upon conscription.' Conscription has thus been justified as militarily reasonable and democratically sound.

The arguments of the past and the present are that the individual draftee in the military is a representative of the rest of the society, and within the society a representative of the military. The military is democratically firmly anchored in society, and society is firmly anchored in the military. A defence based upon flexible mobilisation preparedness, as conscription constitutes is, so it is claimed, also a valuable tool for crisis management (Heurlin, 2000b: 111).

The combination of conscription and professional forces has been regarded as the best of all worlds, even if in truth the democratic principles have never been fully met. Indeed, the draft has always been decided by a lottery since less than 30 per cent of young men have had to serve. Moreover, the call-up has only affected the male population. This method, it was believed, secured the necessary intake of new recruits and the maintenance of the necessary military competence. At the end of 1990s there was clearly no readiness in the political and military constituency to give up conscription, the disadvantage being the costs (Hækkerup 2002). A professional army could simply not be funded within the limits set by the budget. Today, in 2006, the situation is different. Now, centre and left-wing parties are in fact seriously

---

10 See Bruun-report, 41, <www.forsvaret.dk>.

considering suspending conscription. Some youth organisations (those of right-wing parties) even have professional armed forces on their agenda.

The Defence Command Plan

How then has the Danish Armed Forces reacted to the challenges outlined in the Bruun-report? Surprisingly, the Danish Defence Command has taken the initiative and acted offensively. Having participated in producing the Bruun-report, the Defence Command was ready to spearhead the movement towards change. Immediately after the publication of the report in August 2003, the Command presented its own proposal for renewing the Danish defence. The Command sought to sell to the politicians a new 5-year defence agreement. This was regarded as such a revolutionary proposal that the politicians could not refuse.

This proposal included a basic transformation of Danish defence from territorial defence to expeditionary forces, characterised as leaner, but meaner. The rationale was the following: Globalisation means increased vulnerability; revolution in military affairs is a fact; and war is again a real alternative as part of security policy means. The short-hand picture of threats refers to: No actual conventional military threat against Danish territory; new asymmetric and unforeseeable threats; and finally, indirect threats. This implied that territorial defence and total mobilisation defence should be eliminated. Instead, the emphasis would be upon two efforts: first internationally deployable military capabilities, and second, a homeland defence, including the ability to respond to terror activities.

The deployable capabilities were intended to affect two categories of brigades: one unit consisting of professional personnel, as a rapid response force fully deployable, i.e. with available lift capacity and solidly sustainable, with continuous logistical support. The other category of brigade would be lighter, primarily involved with peacemaking, peacekeeping, restructuring tasks. Potentially it could be a brigade which can include of voluntary conscripts.

Conscription was the biggest issue. The Defence Command's plan proposed an entirely new kind of conscription which encompassed defence as well as homeland security, and was limited to three months (later 4 months). It could be interpreted as a compromise attempting to appease the parties still supporting conscription and the parties opting for a suspension. One rationale behind this proposal was the need for personnel to fulfil the obligations of homeland defence and to have a necessary recruitment body for professional soldiers.

The problem was, however, to make ends and means meet. The Danish government had put forward a very ambitious objective: to be a reliable international military actor. Danish defence should be a serious actor in Danish foreign and security policy; and Danish defence should be able to participate at the sharp end of international military interventions. The aim was to be at the forefront of the 'first-in – first-out concept.' The Danish defence was to be able to double the amount of internationally deployed soldiers from around 1,000 men to more than 2,000. Further, the home guard, currently consisting of 60,000 volunteers, was intended to be considerably reduced. In March 2004 the government presented its draft for a 5-year defence arrangement based on the Defence Command Plan to the political parties, including the opposition. In June, the new defence agreement became a reality. It was accepted by most of the parties in the parliament, and heavy debates were avoided.

The Denationalisation Case

All in all, the trend that the Danish armed forces are in a process of denationalisation can be confirmed. This is demonstrated in two ways. First, the traditional military defence of the national territory has disappeared. The dimensions, the structure and the organisation of the Danish military are now determined not by domestic needs, but by vital global security needs, mostly identified by the international community, e.g. the UN Security Council. Second, partly as a consequence of the fact that the military has to reinvent itself in global terms and thus transform itself, the national aspect is disappearing. This process can be seen as part of what we called the societal revolution whereby the individual, more markedly than hitherto, has become an active actor politically, economically, citizen-like, including a military actor. The soldier has become an individual, professional, independent, knowledgeable, responsible military actor not fighting for national survival. He/she is a still a national citizen, but also an individual and a global person. Add to this the trend of 'demilitarisation of the military', implying the demand for the ability and possibility for close cooperation with civil authorities and volunteer civil organisations aiming at aid and development. In this connection, the state-attached and related foundations are weakened. Also the taking over or outsourcing to private firms or corporations of activities normally associated with the activities of the armed forces is a demarcation of denationalisation of the military.

How do these developments influence the structure, organisation and priorities of the Danish defence? As stated, significant changes took place as a consequence of the Defence Plan 2005–2009 (Nørby, 2006). Basically the aim is to reverse the present overall distribution of the structure from 60 per cent command and support structure to 40 per cent, leaving the 60 per cent to the operational structure. This has to be done in order to live up to the political goal of having 2,000 soldiers constantly on international missions alternatively to be able to deploy a full brigade for a shorter period at short notice. On the other hand, the new defence also lives up to the mantra of leaner but meaner armed forces: fewer soldiers in general. The total is now around 21,000 (IISS, 2007), and foreseen as part of the abolishment of the territorial forces based on mobilisation. But the agreement also implies doubling the amount of operational combat-ready soldiers who will have better and more advanced equipment. All this has to be done within a fixed defence budget. The military has been forced to prioritise in order to get the best equipment for the internationally deployable forces. The entire submarine capacity – a proud part of the Danish armed forces – was given up. Also the minelayers were abolished. The same goes for the recently upgraded HAWK air defence system. The number of fighter airplanes was reduced to 48, and the navy – though modernised – experienced a significant reduction in the size of the fleet. Further, the total number of tanks was reduced as the older Leopard types were scrapped. On the other hand, the personal equipment of the individual soldier has been upgraded; procurement of new artillery howitzers is under reconsideration, and a decision taken to produce mere infantry fighting vehicles. As regards the air force, new helicopters were introduced and four new Hercules C 130 J were bought for transport purposes; three new Challenger-air planes are now in operation. The navy, now with a fleet of forty vessels – half of the previous number was upgraded as the new units were considerably bigger, meaner and immediately more usable for international operations. Two large support ships and two frigate-like so-called combat patrol ships, are now an important part of the naval capacity. Further, ten minor new multi-role patrol vessels are to be introduced. The strategic sealift has also been enlarged.

It is manifest that all Danish military services have been transformed according to the presumed and predicted needs in international operations far from Danish shores. Global interventions and activities are now the main initiators and architects of the Danish armed forces. But what about the total defence forces, partly built upon the new kind of conscription? Total defence has to do with assuring the security of Danish society, its citizens and its facilities against terror and other threats. To strengthen homeland security, an expanded concept of 'total defence' is foreseen, making use of the military draft. Increased cooperation and integration between the armed forces and other national security authorities is considered necessary. The 'Danish model' regarding conscription is as follows. The Danish political establishment has not been ready to fully give up conscription for introducing an all-volunteer force, as we have seen in many European nations, not least France, and more recently Romania and Latvia. The reason has generally not been associated with the concept of the nation and national identity: the argument has mainly been to establish a broad and well-educated pool of primarily young men,[11] hoping that some will sign up to a contract in the armed forces. The point of departure is the event, the Day of Defence, when the examination by the draft board and the following lottery for serving the 4-month conscription takes place. In the last examination for the draft, the lottery process was not important as a sufficient number of volunteers signed up.

The conscription service is of a new kind. One will not be trained as soldier – four months is certainly not enough to train a person to be able to fight in the deployable armed forces, ready for first-in – first-out missions. The four months intensive training will produce not a soldier, but a 'total defence person': this means a citizen in uniform with kind of rudimentary training in policing, rescuing, fire fighting, first aid, patrolling and in protecting and securing people. The total defence person can handle a weapon and may defend him or herself. But he or she is certainly not able to fight in a regular war. Five thousand individuals from the year's class will be drafted or taken in voluntarily. But why exactly 5,000? The plan is that around 20 per cent of each class will sign up for a contract to continue the real soldering training of 8 months. Also, in case of an extensive catastrophe, the general objective is to support fire brigades, police and emergency management units with 5,000 persons from the armed forces for a period of seven days and nights. This number of total defence personnel is based on a worst-case scenario such as an attack on

---

11 Women are not compelled be examined by the draft board, but are more than welcome to join their male companions in the basic and subsequent training.

Copenhagen airport or the Copenhagen metro, major accidents or environmental disasters. Being able to mobilise total personnel of 5,000 at any time requires a pool of 15,000. This number is to be achieved by introducing a three-year mobilisation period after the 4-month conscription period. This relatively short time ensures that troops are fresh and recently trained; no retraining is needed. In connection with the concept of denationalisation of defence is that the military forces active in these cases of catastrophe are under civilian, not military, command. Another indication of denationalisation has to do with the individualisation and globalisation of the single soldier. As mentioned, this concerns the revolution of societal affairs and the revolution of military affairs. Also, this new position and role is reflected in the way in which soldiers, according to advertising, are recruited (Joennini, 2005). In the commercials and official advertising, no reference is made to defending the nation. What is emphasised is first, the individual development and experience attached to the profession of the soldier; second, the evident possibility to 'make a difference' in order to enhance global and international security, stability and development.

A renewed endeavour to strengthen the cooperation between civil and military activities in international operations also seems to have an impact on the denationalisation trend. Civil–military cooperation in international operations in itself can be considered as an indication of lack of any involvement national supreme interest. 'Fighting for the Fatherland' is normally a matter of survival, a matter of life and death where there will be no doubt about who are the enemies, who are the invaders and violators of national sovereignty and survival. In that case – defence of the nation – civil–military relations as part of the general as well as of the narrower military strategy, is irrelevant. Civil–military relations are part of international interventions occupied with regime change, failed states, crimes against humanity, nation building.

Denmark has politically and practically been in the forefront in the matter of civil-military (CIMIC) relations. It was one of the initiators of establishing a CIMIC doctrine for NATO. CIMIC is a military tool to secure the best relations with the civil population in a zone of conflict. It is part of the operation to have smaller units comprising of specifically-trained personnel. Their vehicles can have the inscription CIMIC with large letters. A new initiative, also introduced by the Denmark is the so-called *concerted planning and action* of civil and military activities in international operations, the acronym being *CPA*. The main aim of CPA is coordination of deployment of troops with the deployment of civilian personnel including personnel from NGOs. The overall purpose is to stabilise and normalise the conditions in the area of conflict. There is a direct line between improving the social and economic situation in an area and the improvement felt in the security situation. It is not the intention that soldiers shall be relief workers; the military is not trying to take over the role of the NGOs. As emphasised by the Danish minister of defence: 'Soldiers have their core skills as well as the NGOs have theirs. And as a rule, civilian organisations should conduct the humanitarian and reconstructions efforts.'[12] The inclusion of the strategic planning for Concerted Planning and Action of Civil and Military Activities was presented at the November 2006 Riga NATO summit as part of the so-called

---

12 Speech by Søren Gade, Denmark June 2005.

Effects-Based Approach Operations. CPA should improve the following issue areas (NATO unclassified, Nov. 2006): optimise planning and conduct of NATO operations and missions, develop NATO's cooperation with other international actors on an equal basis (mentioned were EU, other international organisations and NGOs, UN, and other nations), and ensuring a more coherent approach to the definition of end-states. As demonstrated, CIMIC and CPA can be considered as an additional indication of the denationalisation of the Danish defence.

The Privatisation Case

The last issue to be mentioned is the increasing use of outsourcing and privatisation in the Danish armed forces. Compared to the US, where comprehensive parts of military activities in international missions and assignments have been privatised, primarily activities related to maintenance, strategic and tactical air lift and transport, securing personnel and organisational safety etc., the Danish military is only in the initial phase. But important parts of military operations and organisation are increasingly handed over to civil firms and corporations. This has primarily to do with chartering transport airlift and large shipping transport to the normally remote areas of international military operations. Generally, the Danish Defence organisation has received the emerging political and economic pressure to intensify privatisation, outsourcing – including invitation to submit tenders, in an open and positive way, expressing no monopoly-like restraints to suggestions coming from the political community.

Privatisation also deals with the defence industry. In the Nordic countries, the defence industry has traditionally been state owned. Kongsberg in Norway, Saab in Sweden and Patria in Finland are still under close financial control of the state. Denmark is the exception. The defence industry in Denmark is growing, but compared to the other Nordic countries, is still marginal. The Danish defence industry is mainly confined to high-tech niche-products and to shipbuilding. Production has always been completely privately owned.

Similar to most industrialised nations, Denmark is experiencing increased privatisation of public enterprises, increased outsourcing of well-defined and separate issue areas from public as well as private companies. This is supported by the increased application of 'New Public Management', a process which implies principles of management from the private business sector to be applied to public enterprises, including more nationally sensitive activities. To the military, this general development raises the question of how to handle the issues involving vital national interests, up to the notion of sovereignty. According to the analysis above, the denationalisation process suggests that vital interests and national sovereignty are having a decreasing impact on missions and structure of the armed forces. There still are, however, reminiscences of the debate on sovereignty. An example is the general claim from traditional discourses, that changes have occurred concerning vital societal functions guaranteed to operate during time of crisis: communication, supply, infrastructure. According to these claims, these functions are required to be managed by state-owned agencies and by loyal, long-term employed civil servants who, for example, were not allowed to go on strike. With the vital functions privatised, outsourced or managed according to private business-like procedures how, it is argued, can Denmark ensure its sovereignty and vital interests during time of crisis? Ownership in foreign hands, for example, could easily threaten or obstruct vital societal interests.[13]

Debates in keeping with these lines are nevertheless extremely seldom. The Danish defence organisation seems to acknowledge its new position and role in the present society in the same way as Danish society seems to have accepted the armed forces in its new main function as deployable forces for international missions, only marginally attached to vital national interests, involving the notion of sovereignty.

As mentioned above, privatisation and outsourcing in the Danish military primarily takes place inside the sector dealing with transport of personnel and equipment, the administrative sector and non-military supply sector. As concerns lift by air or by sea, the Danish armed forces have long-term contracts with large private enterprises such as DFDS Transport A/S (De Forenede Dampskibs Selskaber) for ship transport, and international leasing firms for Antonov transport airplanes. Often, non-traditional methods are used, one example being the process of transporting equipment for Danish forces to be stationed in southern Afghanistan in February 2006. DFDS was hired together with a Pakistani transport firm to take care of this mission. From the harbour of Karachi in Pakistan the equipment – a total of 400 containers – was to be transferred to the new camp in southern Afghanistan, a distance of 1,000 kilometres.[14] Due to the temporary closure of the Danish Embassy in Pakistan (the 'cartoon crisis'), the permit to transport military equipment through Pakistan came at the very last minute, and there was no permission for Danish military personnel to disembark. Therefore the lorries from the private firm had to be taken on board the DFDS ship in order to take over the containers and the military lorries. The containers were deliberately made to appear very old and damaged, and the military vehicles were covered by tarpaulins. This strange transport unit, managed and driven by Afghan and Pakistani chauffeurs and protected by private security personnel, loaded with Danish military equipment but without Danish soldiers, succeeded in its difficult mission in spite of being attacked by Taliban forces.

This example demonstrates that under the banner of improvisation and flexibility the Danish armed forces are willing to use private firms and outsourcing to a very high degree even at the sharp end of sensitive military missions.[15]

Another critical dimension of privatisation and outsourcing is IT and economic management. Here the Danish defence has experienced mixed outcomes. In the late 1990s, DeMars, the management and resource supervising system of the Danish defence, was introduced. This happened to be the most expensive and demanding public system ever. IBM was responsible for the project that in some ways created more problems than it solved. During the spring of 2004, in the blind auction for the IT-systems – now split in two parts, the SAP-system, deMars and the IT-operation

---

13 *Politiken*, 25 April 2005, section 2, p. 5.

14 A 20-foot container is supposed to contain what an average soldier needs as concerns equipment, ammunition, and general supplies for a period of one month.

15 Articles by Christian Brøndum in *Berlingske Tidende*, June 20 2006, section 1, p. 7.

part covering 15,000 PC-units and 800 servers – Siemens Business Service won the contract for the ensuing four years. The IT-part, however, became an internal part of the Danish defence organisation, structured as a concern. The external offers were more than 40 per cent more expensive than the do-it-yourself model, the reason being the specific security requirements, and the fact that the defence internal salaries were lower. Thus, in some cases 'in-sourcing' is the better solution for the defence.[16]

A specific dimension as concerns the relationship between the military and the private sector has to do with the use of volunteers in the armed forces. The organisation Interforce was established in 1999 with the aim of developing and improving cooperation between the armed forces, and private and public enterprises. The cooperation should increase the general understanding in the civil sector for the tasks and missions assigned to the military. This has mainly to do with personnel of the reserve willing to participate in international operations while still employed in private and public companies. This also applies for the voluntary personnel belonging to the home guard.

Following increased recognition of the fact that the armed forces may be able to win the military missions but not to win the peace, the government – as stated – introduced the concept of 'concerted planning and action' (CPA) in international missions. CPA aims at a close planning and cooperation between military missions and the necessary civil reconstruction, stabilising and development. Concerted action is different from CIMIC, which is a military discipline. The concept is considerably wider, broader and incorporates military and civil efforts in an equal and concerted manner. In Denmark, the concerted action, coordinated by the Ministry of Foreign Affairs, involves units from the armed forces, the Military Intelligence, the Civil Defence, the Police, Danish relief organisations, and not least from the Danish industry and business world.[17] As part of these efforts, from 2004–2005, the Danish Defence began training and educating of the so-called 'Functional Specialists', initially recruited from the Military. These specialists have civil skills, qualifying them to act as advisers and project leaders for the military forces.

Conclusions

For many years, Danish defence forces faced the continuous problem of a structure too large for a decreasing number of soldiers. Another important on-going challenge was the lack of resources used for research and development, high–tech equipment and operations, while salaries, pensions and general maintenance continued to be at a high level. The most crucial political challenge for Denmark is, however, how to deal with the new security threats and changing international conditions especially after 9/11, and how to participate in the international responses to these threats – responses that take the form of military interventions based on ad hoc coalitions. Also, how should Copenhagen respond to the revolution in military affairs, meaning new wars, new strategies, and new equipment?

---

16 Articles in *Computer World* January 21, 2005, *Perspektiv* section, p. 12, and 21 April, section 1, p. 4.

17 *Interforce News*, 21 March, 2005, article by Commander Torben Ørting Jørgensen.

Denmark is on its way to undertake the largest transformation in its military forces in modern times. Very ambitious political visions have been presented, and likewise plans for how to reorganise, modernise and transform the forces have been put forward for implementation. The sheer basic organisation is affected: the aim is streamlining, rationalising and securing cohesion. The military services will merge in some organisational functions. Changes in personnel – how to transform the conscript-based forces into fully professional armed forces, how to include the volunteer personnel (the home guard) in the force – are also at stake. The same is the case with equipment. At present, it has been argued, there is too much surplus equipment, and there is too little of that which is vital for the new role the Danish defence is planning to play, namely the role of a 'strategic-offensive actor'.

This is where significant choices have to be made: where to prioritise, where to cut down, where to specialise within a budget that is limited and with no prospect for being increased. Will Denmark be able to be at the forefront of intervention warfare? Will Denmark be able to undertake the demanding transformation that is necessary? Many questions remain regarding Denmark's responses to the ongoing Revolution in Military Affairs (RMA). The answers will indicate where Denmark will stand in the future.

RMA is crucial (McNaugher, 2007). It also includes asymmetric warfare and politically correct wars supported by a large part of the international society. It favours professional military forces. So does the Revolution in Technological Affairs which gives the individual soldier an unprecedented killing capacity, denouncing the concept of mass armies. The same goes for Revolution in Economic Affairs as well as for Revolution in Societal Affairs as the globalisation of the economy puts enormous pressure on the effective use of resources for military purposes, and as expeditionary forces have more to do with professional fighting as an individual than with defending the national sovereignty. Finally, the Revolution in International Affairs, as the superior heading, is favouring professionalism: a unipolar international structure supporting global norms as democracy, market economy, human rights, personal freedom, and the rule of law will point in the direction of wars fought by professional soldiers.

These observations form the background for the main argument of this chapter – that the Danish armed forces can be characterised as subject to a process of denationalisation. This is a process deliberately chosen by successive Danish governments. As a consequence of Denmark's general political and geopolitical position after the cold war, one way to avoid international marginalisation in the new world order was to militarise the foreign policy, i.e. to use Danish military forces as a foreign policy tool, as part of a global activism.

Due to the above-mentioned six revolutionary developments, denationalisation was the logical solution to the future of Danish armed forces. Faced with an international environment without any possible conventional military threats, the only usable choice for the Danish military was in international operations. In this way international operations initiated by instability and conflicts in the global security environment became an important point of departure for the design of Danish armed forces, and a stimulus for how defence matters were to be prioritised in the long term. Already now, this can be demonstrated in the choice of equipment, hardware, software, training, and organisation of the forces. Further, the denationalisation is deeply rooted in the new role of the individual as a political and military actor. Civil–military relations and increasing privatisation and outsourcing are trends in the same direction. There are some minor deviations: the fact that Denmark wants to avoid the traditional military specialisation – as it is opting for solid, compact units which are sustainable and immediately deployable. Add to this the fact that Denmark is dependent on NATO; that is, dependent on the general military and operational needs formulated in the organisation (Asmus 2004). But Denmark is also more than willing to participate in 'coalitions of the willing and capable' outside the NATO framework. As expressed by an influential general in the Danish defence community: 'Danish defence is more and other things than NATO'.[18]

One more dimension: As a consequence of precisely the denationalisation of the armed forces – implying no national supreme interest involved in keeping a military force – a domestic political interest of broader scope evolves, namely the question of where, how, and when to intervene internationally? An increased domestic policy angle is added: Democratisation of decision-making in the use of armed forces.

We may thus conclude that the new Danish defence is being denationalised to a degree never seen hitherto.

References

Asmus, R. D. (2002), *Opening NATO's Door: How the Alliance remade itself for a new Era* (New York: Columbia UP).

—— (2004), 'The Atlantic Alliance at a New Crossroads: What does it mean for Denmark and Northern Europe' in Carlsen, P. and Mouritzen, H. (eds) *Danish Foreign Policy Yearbook 2004* (Copenhagen: Danish Institute for International Studies) 25–48.

Bailes, A. J. K. et al. (eds) (2006), *The Nordic Countries and the European Security and Defence Policy*, SIPRI. (Oxford: Oxford University Press).

Boot, M. (2006), *War Made New: Technology, Warfare, and the Course of History* (New York: Gotham Books).

Buzan, B. et al. (1998), *Security: A new Framework for Analysis* (Boulder Colorado: Lynne Rienner Publishers).

Clemmesen, M. (2003a), 'Dansk forsvar på vej fra fortiden' [Danish Defence on its way from the Past], *Udenrigs*, **3**, 33–45.

——(2003b), 'De danske væbnede styrker. En skitse fra sidelinien' [The Danish Armed Forces], *Militært Tidsskrift*, **2**, <www.bdcol.ee/publications/otherarticles>.

—— red. (2005), 'Festskrift. Forsvarsakademiets 175. årsdag' [Homage Volume: The 175th Anniversary for The Royal Danish Defence College] (Copenhagen, Forsvarsakademiet).

Dansk Institut for Internationale Studier (2005a), *Danmark under den kolde krig* [Denmark During the Cold War] bind 1–4. (Copenhagen: DIIS).

---

18 Per Ludvigsen, Forsvarsakademiet: *Festskrift*. FAKs 175. årsdag. 2005, 58.

—— (2005b), *Nye trusler og militær magtanvendelse* [New Threats and the Use of Military Power] (Copenhagen: DIIS).

—— (2005c), *Danish Foreign Policy Yearbook* (Copenhagen: DIIS).

Dörfer, I. (forthcoming), 'Sveriges forsvarspolitik' [Sweden's Defence Policy] in Heurlin, B. et al. (eds) *De Nordiske Landes Forsvarspolitik* [The Nordic Nations' Defence Policies].

Forsvarets Oplysnings og Velfærdstjeneste (2005a), *Dansk Forsvar og Kosovokonflikten 1999–2005* [Danish Defence and the Kosovo Conflict] (Copenhagen: FOV).

—— (2005b), *Det danske Flyvevåben – nu og i fremtiden* [The Danish Air Force – Now and in the Future] (Copenhagen: FOV).

—— (2004), *Det nye NATO. Fra integreret alliance til fleksibel Koalition* [The New NATO] (Copenhagen: FOV)

Forsvarskomissionen af 1997 [Defence Commission of 1997] <www.forsvaret.dk>.

Hansen, B. and Heurlin, B. (2000), *The New World Order. Contrasting Theories* (London: MacMillan).

Hansen, B. (2000), 'The Unipolar World Order and its Dynamics' in Hansen, B. and Heurlin, B. (eds) *The New World Order. Contrasting Theories* (London: MacMillan) 112–133.

Heurlin, B. (1997), *Dansk Forsvarspolitik: En ny verden – en ny forsvarspolitik* [Danish Defence Policy] (Copenhagen: DUPI).

—— (2000), 'A New World Order: The Vitual War and Virtual Peace' in Hansen, B. and Heurlin, B. (eds) *The New World Order. Contrasting Theories*, (London: MacMillan) 167–196.

—— (2001), *Global, Regional, and National Security* (Copenhagen: DUPI).

—— and Rasmussen, M. V. (eds) (2003a), *Challenges and Capabilities: NATO in the 21ˢᵗ Century* (Copenhagen: Danish Institute for International Studies).

—— et al. (eds) (2003b), *New Roles of Military Forces: Global and Local Implications of the Revolution in Military Affairs* (Copenhagen: Danish Institute for International Studies).

—— (2003c), *Forsvarets linjeofficersuddannelser* [The Education of Officers] (Copenhagen: Danmarks Evalueringsinstitut).

—— (2004a), 'Revolution in Danish Military Affairs? Professionalisation and Network Centric Warfare' in Readman, Kristina Spohr, *Building Sustainable and Effective Military Capabilities. NATO Science Series: Science & Technology Policy*, **45**, 109–122. (Amsterdam: IOS Press 2004).

—— (2004b), *Riget, magten og militæret. Dansk forsvars- og sikkerhedspolitik under Forsvarskommissionerne af 1988 og af 1997* [The Kingdom, the Power and the Military. Defence and Security] (Aarhus: Aarhus Universitetsforlag).

—— (2005a), *USA som militærmagt* [The United States as a Military Power] (Copenhagen: Danish Institute for International Studies).

—— (2005b), 'The Future of US-European Relations' in Elletson, H. (ed.) *The New Security Environment and its Implications for Procurement* (Henley-on-Thames, UK: The New Security Programme, Centre for Defence and International Security Studies).

—— and Rynning, Steen (eds) (2005), *Missile Defence. International, Regional and National Implications Cass Series: Contemporary Security Studies* (London: Routledge).

—— and Rynning, Steen (eds) (2006), *Det 21. århundredes trusler* [The Threats of the 21st Century] (Copenhagen: Danish Institute for International Studies).

—— (forthcoming), 'The New Danish Model: Limited Conscription and Deployable Professionals', in Williams Cindy, *Building Military Capacities: Transforming Military Personnel Policies in Europe and North America* (Boston, Mass.: MIT-Press).

—— (ed.) (forthcoming), *De nordiske landes Forsvarspolitik* [Defence Policy of the Nordic Countries].

Hækkerup, H. (2002), *På skansen* [On the Fort] (Copenhagen: Lindhardt og Ringhof).

International Institute for Strategic Studies, IISS (2007), 'The Military Balance 2007' (London: Routledge).

Joenniemi, P. (2005), *Farewell to Conscription: The Case of Denmark.* (Copenhagen: Danish Institute for International Studies).

Kagan, F. W. (2006), *Finding the Target: The Transformation of American Military Policy* (New York: Encounter Books).

Kristensen, K.S. (2005), 'Negotiating base rights for missile defence: the case of Thule Air Base in Greenland' in Heurlin, B. and Rynning, S. (eds) *Missile Defence. International, Regional and National Implications* (New York: Routledge) 183–203.

McNaugher, T. L. (2007), 'The Real Meaning of Military Transformation' in *Foreign Affairs*, **86**(1) 2007: 140–147.

Møller, L. (2001), *Operation Bøllebank. Soldater i Krig* [Operation Beat the Rowdies. Soldiers at War] (Copenhagen: Høst og Søn).

—— (2004), 'Vi er amatører, men er vi også glade?' [We Are Happy Amateurs] in *Militært Tidsskrift, December 2004*, 740–754.

Nielsen, O. B. (2006), 'Dansk Interesse for USA's missilskjold' [Danish Interest for Missile Defence] in *Berlingske Tidende*, 11 October 2006.

Nielsen, R. R. (2001), *Den europæiske forsvarsdimension Baggrund og Perspektiver* [The European Defence Dimension] (Copenhagen: DUPI).

Nørby, S. (2006), 'Det danske forsvar' [Danish Defence] (Copenhagen: Aschehoug).

Nørgaard, K. (2006), *Tillidens teknologi* [The Technology of Trust] (Copenhagen: Forsvarsakademiet).

Petersen, N. (2004), *Europæisk og globalt engagement 1973–2003 bind 6, Dansk Udenrigspolitisk Historie* [European and Global Engagement 1973–2003, Vol. 6, The History of Danish Foerign Policy]. (Copenhagen: Gyldendal).

Rasmussen, M. V. (2003), *Nye Krige* [New Wars] (Copenhagen: FOV).

—— (2005), 'Camp Eden: The Defence Agreement, Military Power and Danish Values' in Carlsen, P. and Mouritzen H. (eds) *Danish Foreign Policy Yearbook 2005* (Copenhagen: Danish Institute for International Studies).

—— (2006), *The Risk Society at War Terror Technology and Strategy in the Twenty-First Century* (Cambridge: Cambridge University Press).

Rynning, S. (2003), 'Denmark as a Strategic Actor?' in Carlsen, Per & Hans Mouritzen, *Danish Foreign Policy Yearbook 2003* (Copenhagen: Danish Institute for International Studies).

—— (2005), *NATO renewed: The Power and Purpose of Transatlantic Cooperation* (London: MacMillan).

Udenrigsministeriet (2003), De sikkerhedspolitiske vilkår for dansk forsvarspolitik [Security Policy Conditions for Danish Defence Policy] (Copenhagen: Udenrigsministeriet [Danish MFA]).

Chapter 8

A New Swedish Defence for a Brave New World

Jan Joel Andersson

Swedish defence and defence policy have undergone dramatic changes since the end of the cold war. Although Sweden's long-standing policy of military non-alignment remains in place officially, international crisis management and peacekeeping missions abroad have replaced the country's traditional focus on national territorial defence in practice. Indeed, Sweden is a key participant in the European Security and Defence Policy (ESDP) and one of the most active member states in NATO's Euro-Atlantic Partnership Council and Partnership for Peace (PFP). Currently, Swedish troops are participating in fifteen international missions abroad under EU, NATO or UN command. A further indication of Sweden's commitment to international crisis management missions is its decision to assume leadership of one of the EU new battlegroups – The Nordic Battlegroup – in 2008. In addition, Sweden has replaced a long-standing tradition of independent advanced weapons systems development and production with a policy prioritising international armaments cooperation and the pursuit of cross-border defence industry mergers and acquisitions.

Although Sweden was rather late in acknowledging the effects of the end of the cold war on its defence posture, the shift that eventually occurred was quite dramatic. In 1996, for example, the Swedish government officially stated that direct military threats to its borders were 'improbable,' and it was therefore unlikely that Swedish Armed Forces would be required to be able to counter an armed attack for some years to come.[1] The lack of a perceived military threat to Sweden in combination with budgetary pressures consequently led to massive cuts in the country's armed forces and the military establishment more generally. At the height of the cold war, the Swedish military was capable of mobilising a total force of some 800,000 troops, fielding one of the largest and most sophisticated air forces in the world and deploying some 20 submarines in the Baltic Sea. Today, in contrast, Sweden's territorial defence establishment has largely been dismantled and many support privatised functions. Although universal male conscription remains the law of the land, the reality is that fewer than one in five Swedish 19-year-olds will be called upon to do military service. At the same time, however, the Swedish troops that do exist have never been better equipped nor have they been better trained for

---

1   See, for example, Swedish government bill *Totalförsvar i förnyelse*, Parliamnetary Proposition 1995/1996:12, 1 January 2006.

demanding international crisis management missions abroad. How did such far-reaching change occur?

This chapter examines the nature of the shift towards internationalisation and privatisation that has taken place in Swedish defence and defence policy since the end of the cold war. It is divided into two parts. In the first part, I describe the shift from national defence to international crisis management with regard to military non-alignment, the demise of universal male conscription and the outsourcing of support functions. In the second part, I look at the Swedish defence industry sector and discuss how such a large and largely state-owned sector became privatised and internationalised so rapidly.

From Passive Neutrality to Active International Engagement

The fall of the Berlin Wall and the end of the cold war allowed Sweden to rethink its defence posture. During the fifteen years since the end of the cold war, the Swedish government has presented a series of comprehensive defence bills outlining a reformed defence policy and armed forces. In these government bills, the transformation of Swedish defence policy can be traced from territorial defence based on military non-alignment and a domestic defence industry, to a defence policy focused on international missions under the command of international organisations such as the UN, the EU and NATO, and backed by a privatised and internationalised armaments sector.

For analytical purposes, Sweden's post-cold war defence policy can be divided into three periods. The first, immediately following the fall of the Berlin Wall, was marked by guarded optimism of the developments in international relations but combined with concern of 'Russia's permanent geopolitical interests' requiring a strong territorial defence and continued military non-alignment.[2] The second period begins in the mid-1990s and is characterised by a considerable change in outlook. Although Russia remains a concern, the end of the cold war is now fully recognised, allowing for large defence reductions (but with certain caveats) as well as the adoption of a widened concept of security to include civilian crises.[3] The third period begins in 1999–2000 and is marked by globalisation and that international missions take precedence above regional concerns and national territorial defence.[4]

---

2 Swedish government bill, *Om totalförsvarets utveckling till och med budgetåret 1996/97 samt anslag för budgetåret 1992/93*, Proposition Prop. 1991/92: 102, 1 January 1992.

3 Swedish government bill, *Totalförsvar i förnyelse*, Proposition Prop 1995/96: 12, 1 January 2006; Försvarskommissionen [Defence Commission], *Omvärldsförändring och svensk säkerhetspolitik*, Departementsserien Ds 1996: 51 (Stockholm: Ministry of Defence); Swedish government official report, *Ett säkrare samhälle*, Huvudbetänkande, Statens offentliga utredningar (SOU) SOU 1995: 19 (Stockholm: Ministry of Defence).

4 Swedish government bill, *Förändrad omvärld – omdanat försvar*, Proposition Prop. 1998/99: 74, 4 March 1999; Swedish government bill, *Det nya försvaret*, Proposition Prop. 1999/2000: 30, 18 November 1999; Swedish government bill, *Fortsatt förnyelse av totalförsvaret*, Proposition Prop. 2001/02: 10, 26 September 2001; Swedish government bill,

Traditional threats, including Russian aggression, are seen as highly unlikely and that the risk of military attack from another state against Sweden improbable for the foreseeable future (at least ten years), allowing for a fundamental transformation of Swedish defence policy and armed forces.[5]

A new Swedish defence

The Swedish defence is currently undergoing a dramatic process of transformation. As a result of the end of the cold war and the emerging common approach in Europe to security, Sweden is reorganising its defence policy, armed forces and defence industry (Britz, 2004; Eriksson, 2006; Wedin, 2006). The goal is to create smaller, more focused and mission-oriented armed forces capable of rapid deployment for both national and international missions (Swedish Armed Forces, 2006a: 4). The Swedish defence industry, in turn, has been privatised and integrated into the international defence industry through joint ventures, mergers and acquisitions (Andersson, 2004). This process began in the mid-1990s but has accelerated during the last few years. The current Swedish military defence organisation is a fraction of its cold war level but better trained and more active then ever before. International missions are today a priority for the Swedish armed forces and Swedish military units are currently deployed under EU, NATO or UN command in the Balkans, Central Asia and Africa (Swedish Armed Forces, 2006a). The Swedish armed forces are also among the best equipped in the world today. Evidence of this fact is that the United States, in order to train with the best, is currently leasing a Swedish Navy submarine with crew to function as opposing force to US Navy carrier groups training in the Pacific Ocean (Andersson, 2006b; *Navy Newsstand*, 2005).

The post-cold war development of Sweden's defence policy is similar to that of many other European countries. Although Sweden's traditional policy of military non-alignment officially remains in place, it has all but lost meaning in a post-cold war world focused less on domestic territorial defence and more on international crises and conflict management (Agrell, 2000: 271). The official policy of military non-alignment has certainly not prevented Sweden from being a very active member in the development of the EU's European Security and Defence Policy (ESDP), or

---

Vårt framtida försvar, Proposition Prop. 2004/05: 5, 24 September 2004; Försvarskommissionen [Defence Commission], *Förändrad omvärld - omdanat försvar*, Departementsserien Ds 1999: 2, 12 January 1999 (Stockholm: Ministry of Defence); Försvarskommissionen [Defence Commission], *Gränsöverskridande sårbarhet - gemensam säkerhet*, Departementsserien Ds 2001: 14, 2 March 2001 (Stockholm: Ministry of Defence); Försvarskommissionen [Defence Commission], *Säkrare grannskap - osäker värld*, Departementsserien Ds 2003: 8, 27 February 2003 (Stockholm: Ministry of Defence); Försvarskommissionen [Defence Commission], *Vårt militära försvar - vilja och vägval*, Departementsserien Ds 2003: 34, 3 juni 2003 (Stockholm: Ministry of Defence); Försvarskommissionen [Defence Commission], *Försvar för en ny tid*, Departementsserien Ds 2004: 30, 1 June 2004 (Stockholm: Ministry of Defence).

5   Swedish government bill, *Det nya försvaret*, Proposition 1999/2000: 30, 18 November 1999; Swedish government bill, *Vårt framtida försvar*, Proposition 2004/05: 5, 24 September 2004; Försvarskommissionen [Defence Commission], *Säkrare grannskap – osäker värld*, Departementsserien 2003: 8, 27 February 2003 (Stockholm: Ministry of Defence).

participating in NATO-led operations in the Balkans or in Afghanistan (Andersson, 2005; Bailes et al., 2006). Sweden has contributed troops to all of the EU military missions. In particular, the deployment in 2003 of Special Forces soldiers in Operation Artemis in Africa, the first independent military EU operation outside Europe was a clear sign of Sweden's commitment to EU military crisis management.[6] Another sign of this commitment is Sweden's role as Framework Nation for one of the EU's newly formed rapid reaction forces, the Nordic Battlegroup (NBG). An EU battlegroup is a battalion-sized rapid reaction force available at ten days notice for crisis management missions around the world. Since 2007, two such EU battlegroups are on stand-by at any given time. The Nordic Battlegroup will be on stand-by during the first half of 2008 and includes forces from Sweden, Finland, Norway and Estonia (Andersson, 2006a; Nordic Battlegroup, 2007).

Sweden is also a member of NATO's Partnership for Peace (PFP). As perhaps the most active PFP-country, Sweden has rapidly adopted and applied NATO-standards in equipment and training and is today one of the most NATO-compatible countries in Europe.[7] Sweden is also participating in NATO's military operations. Currently, Sweden contributes 440 troops to the NATO-led Kosovo Force (KFOR) in Kosovo, and 248 Swedish soldiers serve in the NATO-led International Security Assistance Force (ISAF) in Afghanistan (Swedish Armed Forces, 2006a). In fact, more Swedish troops currently serve under NATO command than under EU or UN command.[8] Further cooperation with NATO has been announced by the newly-elected Swedish government and will most likely lead to Swedish participation in the NATO-led naval operation Active Endeavour in the Mediterranean Sea and possibly also in NATO's Rapid Reaction Response Force (NRF) (Odenberg, 2007; Swedish Armed Forces, 2007). Moreover, Sweden has agreed to join fifteen NATO member countries to collectively buy and operate C-17 strategic transport aircraft (NATO, 2006; Swedish Armed Forces, 2007).[9] While the current Conservative-led Swedish government is clearly more positive towards NATO-membership than previous Social Democratic-led governments, the defence minister has announced that a membership in NATO is not on the agenda during the government's present term in office (Odenberg, 2006: 4). However, due to Sweden's active contribution to NATO operations and ambitious transformation of its armed forces Sweden is frequently given access to information and consultations that is normally only extended to member countries.[10] Sweden's increasingly close relationship with NATO was further underlined in a series of remarks and interviews given by senior US government officials in 2005 and 2006.

---

6   On Operation Artemis, see United Nations 2005, and Ulriksen et al., 2004.

7   For example, U.S. Under-Secretary of State, Nicholas Burns, stated in an interview in May 2005, that no other country had been more involved in NATO's PFP than Sweden and that 'Sweden is the leader' (Burns, 2005).

8   As of January 2007.

9   The planes will form a 'Strategic Airlift Capability' for NATO at Ramstein Air Force Base in Germany and used for airlift purposes which may be purely national in character but could also be allocated for NATO operations or for UN, EU, or other international purposes (e.g., humanitarian airlift and disaster relief) if a country so decides (NATO, 2006). See, http://www.nato.int/issues/strategic-lift-air-sac/index.html.

10   Interview with senior officials at NATO.

In these statements Sweden was singled out as one of five leading partner countries to NATO in the world and that Sweden would be welcomed to join the organisation overnight if it ever sought to do so (Burns, 2005, 2006).[11]

The transformation of the Swedish armed forces

The Swedish armed forces is a single national authority answerable to parliament and the government. The head of the Swedish armed forces is the Supreme Commander who is the only four star general/admiral in the services.[12] The deputy head of the Swedish armed forces is the Director-General, who is a civilian. The armed forces headquarters in Stockholm includes the Joint Forces Command, land, naval and air forces and the territorial defence forces. Organised according to NATO standard (J1-J10), the Joint Forces Command is responsible for the conduct of operations on Swedish territory as well as international missions such as NATO-led PFP operations. The responsibility for maintaining territorial integrity rests with the operational commander at the armed forces headquarters but it is the armed forces training establishments which provide the operational readiness units, including air and naval units, security teams, soldiers on standby contracts and national home guard units. All the logistics and support services for the armed forces in both war and peacetime are the responsibility of the armed forces Logistics Unit (FMLOG) (Vienna Document, 2006: 18).[13]

At the height of the cold war, Sweden had the capacity to mobilise some 800,000 men in a field army of more than 30 brigades, an air force larger than those of Great Britain and France, and a navy capable of sending some 20 submarines into the Baltic Sea.[14] In 2007, the operational organisation of the Swedish armed forces consists of 47,000 men and women, including civilian personnel (Swedish Armed Forces, 2006a: 11). The majority of units in the operational organisation have a preparedness and training time of one year. Fully mobilised, the Swedish armed forces, including the national home guard could, in theory, comprise approximately 200,000 men and women.[15] However, the majority of these units and troops would require a preparedness and training time of at least five years (Vienna Document, 2006: 12). The core of the operational land forces is organised around two active brigade command and control elements and eight mechanised battalions equipped

---

11 The other four countries are Finland, Australia, Japan and South Korea. See, Burns 2006a, 2006b. In an interview in May 2005, Nicholas Burns stated that 'if Sweden applied for NATO membership it would probably take about 24 hours to decide by unanimous consent that we'd want Sweden in. But it's up to Sweden to decide that. If Sweden chooses partnership, then that's fine with us too, because we're working so closely together' (Burns, 2005).

12 While the King of Sweden also hold's the rank of four star general/admiral in all of the armed services, he has no command authority over or function in the armed forces.

13 For more information on the organisation of the Swedish armed forces, see http://www.mil.se/.

14 For figures, see *The Military Balance*, IISS, various years.

15 The National Home Guard is a voluntary organisation but forms a part of the Army and Navy. In 2006, there were 42,000 Home Guard soldiers organised in 69 battalions throughout the country. For more information, see http://www.hemvarnet.mil.se.

with Leopard II main battle tanks, CV90 infantry fighting vehicles, and tracked and wheeled armoured personnel carriers. Two of the mechanised battalions will be specifically geared for international missions. The navy consists of seven surface warships, nine mine counter-measures ships, four submarines and one battalion of marine infantry. The combat component of the air force consists of 140 SAAB JAS-39 swing role fighters organised in four squadrons (Vienna Document, 2006, Annex 3).[16]

Table 8.1   Strength of the Swedish Armed Forces

Year	1975	1995	2004	2008 (plan)
Field Army brigades	31	16	4	2
Air Force combat squadrons	40	16	8	4
Navy surface combatants	70	24	17	7
Navy submarines	20	9	7	4
Career Officers (approximately)	16,000	16,000	12,000	10,000
Conscripts conducting basic military training per year (approximately)	47,000	30,000	16,000	9,000

Sources: Swedish Ministry of Defence, Swedish Armed Forces

As a consequence of the end of the cold war, the view of the Swedish parliament and government over the past decade has been that the risk of an armed attack on Sweden by another state is improbable in the medium term. Accordingly, the armed forces and their capability to undertake major operations in a five to ten year perspective have been sharply reduced. Although national territorial defence is currently re-emerging as an issue of political debate, everyday focus of the military is on international crises and conflict management operations in collaboration with the EU, NATO or the UN.[17]

International crises and conflicts tend to arise with little warning and quickly cross international borders. If any response is to be successful, rapid deployment of international forces is often necessary. Operational rapid reaction units are therefore in much demand by the international community. Such units must be capable of deploying at home or abroad with little preparation time and able to carry out a wide range of missions in all kinds of operational settings. Since 1999, the main mission of the Swedish armed forces has therefore been to transform itself from a large cold war territorial defence organisation at low readiness to a much smaller organisation

---

16 Eventually, the Swedish Air Force will be reduced to 100 JAS-39C/D Gripen Fighters (Armed Forces, 2007).

17 See, for example, remarks by General Håkan Syrén, the Supreme Commander of the Swedish Armed Forces, at *Folk och Försvars'* annual conference 14 januari 2007.

capable of establishing and maintaining operational units at high states of readiness.[18] The transformation of the Swedish armed forces is meant to ensure that Sweden can make an active contribution to the development of a joint EU crisis management capability as well as to other international missions under UN or NATO command (Swedish Armed Forces, 2006a: 4–5). The transformation of the Swedish armed forces is also meant to cut costs and increase efficiency by streamlining support function, outsourcing non-military activities to private suppliers and by employing civilian management expertise.[19]

Over the years, some 100,000 Swedish soldiers have served on international missions around the world. Most of these have been UN peacekeeping operations in which Sweden has participated since 1956 (Utlandsstyrkan, 2006). However, it is Sweden's more recent membership in the EU and close cooperation with NATO which provide the main reasons for the internationalisation of the Swedish armed forces. Sweden's commitments to these organisations mean that the Swedish armed forces must be able to contribute to preventing and managing crises and conducting peace operations on a global basis. This requires the capability to undertake the full range of missions from confidence building and conflict prevention to humanitarian, peacekeeping and peace enforcement operations. Today, some units need to be on standby for immediate deployment on missions both at home and abroad. Other units are placed on call but with longer reaction times (Swedish Armed Forces, 2006a: 10). In recent years, around 1,000 Swedish troops have served abroad annually. The long-term goal of the Swedish government is to raise the number of soldiers in international missions to 2,000 (Odenberg, 2007: 5). Currently, Sweden has declared around 15 military units and a number of specialist capabilities for inclusion in various international force catalogues that can be called upon by organisations such as the EU, UN and NATO for international missions. The Swedish units in these lists include a mechanised battalion, an engineer company, a ranger platoon, a corvette unit, a naval mine clearing unit, fighter/reconnaissance aircraft, transport aircraft and a Chemical, Biological, Radiological and Nuclear (CBRN) counter-measure unit. The most recent Swedish unit to be included in the international force catalogues is an independent mechanised infantry company (IA 06) on call at ten days' notice for international deployment (Swedish Armed Forces, 2006a: 15). However, the most important component of the transformation and internationalisation efforts of the Swedish armed forces is the decision to assume leadership of the EU Nordic Battlegroup. This rapid reaction force will include troops from Finland, Estonia and Norway. Although the Nordic Battlegroup represents only a small part of the Swedish armed forces, its formation is a major driver for change within many areas of the Swedish defence and defence policy including training, control and command, recruitment and logistics, and international coordination and planning (Andersson, 2006a; Syrén, 2007: 2).

---

18 See, Swedish government bill, *Det nya försvaret*, Proposition 1999/2000: 30, 18 November 1999.

19 Swedish government bill, *Vissa ledningsfrågor inom det militära försvaret m. m.*, Proposition 2000/01: 113, 22 March 2001.

The Nordic battlegroup

The capability to deploy military forces on short notice during crises is an essential aspect of the European Security and Defence Policy (ESDP). The European Union battlegroup concept lies at the centre of this capability. An EU battlegroup consists of a battalion-size force package of around 1,500 troops, complete with combat support and logistics units as well as the necessary air and naval components, ready for rapid deployment around the world. The EU's ambition is to be able to launch a battlegroup operation within five days after approval by the Council. Once the decision has been made, troops should be on the ground implementing their mission within ten days. To date, the EU Member States have agreed to the establishment of fifteen battlegroups. Every six months, two of these will be on stand-by to deploy within 5–10 days. Full operational capability is to be reached in 2007. At that time, the EU should be able to undertake the simultaneous or near-simultaneous launch of two concurrent single battalion-size rapid response operations. The battlegroups will be capable of managing the full range of response tasks, including humanitarian assistance, traditional peacekeeping and peacemaking by force. In support of the ESDP, Sweden, Finland, Norway and Estonia have agreed to establish a joint Nordic Battlegroup (NBG) under Swedish leadership, which will be on standby during the period 1 January – 30 June 2008 (Quille, 2004; Andersson, 2006a).

A battlegroup is considered by the EU to be 'the minimum military effective, credible, rapidly deployable, coherent force package capable of acting alone, or for the initial phase of larger operations' (European Union 2004). This battalion-size formation should be flexible enough to rapidly undertake combat operations in distant crisis areas and in extremely demanding environments, including mountain regions, desert and jungle settings for at least 30 days but should be able to operate up to 120 days if re-supplied appropriately. While its limited size and the need for reserve forces should be taken into account, a battlegroup is expected to be capable of performing the full range of tasks outlined in the Treaty on European Union (Article 17.2) and those identified in the European Security Strategy, including high intensity combat in a crisis management situation (European Union, 2004). During the Military Capabilities Conference in Brussels on 22 November 2004, Sweden, Finland and Norway declared that they would establish a multinational battlegroup based on the EU battlegroup concept: the Nordic Battlegroup (NBG) (Declaration 2004).[20] Estonia joined the Nordic Battlegroup shortly thereafter (Memorandum of Understanding, 2005).

In accordance with the EU battlegroup concept, the Nordic Battlegroup consists of a mechanised infantry battalion with attached tactical and strategic support units. The core of the battalion is formed by two light companies equipped with splinter-protected wheeled vehicles and one heavy company equipped with Hägglunds CV9040 tracked infantry combat vehicles armed with 40 mm automatic cannon. Combat Support Units drawn from a 'menu' of capabilities will complement the core battalion. These capabilities include fire support (mortars, armour), engineers,

---

20 EU and Norway signed an agreement establishing a framework for the participation of Norway in EU crisis management operations in Brussels on 3 December 2004.

air defence, helicopters, ISTAR, CIS-support, CBRN and force protection. The exact combination of combat support will depend on the type of mission in question. In addition, logistics, medical services, military police and civil-military cooperation (CIMIC) personnel will provide combat service support as needed. In order to enable the battlegroup to rapidly deploy to its area of operation, the Nordic Battlegroup will also possess pre-identified strategic air and sealift resources, tactical air transport and close air support, logistics and Special Forces units (Nordic Battlegroup 2007). As the Framework nation for the Nordic Battlegroup, Sweden has assumed overall responsibility for coordinating planning, preparation and training. Sweden will also contribute the majority of troops to the battlegroup and Swedes will form its core battalion. In total, the Swedish contingent will number around 1,100 personnel (Andersson, 2006a: 37–38; Vienna Document, 2006: 8–9).[21]

Any EU request to deploy the Nordic Battlegroup will follow the EU decision-making procedure. The final decision to deploy the Nordic Battlegroup, however, will be made by consensus among the participating governments of Sweden, Finland, Norway and Estonia. To enable rapid deployment of the Nordic Battlegroup, all four participating countries must make the decision to participate simultaneously at the national level. In times of emerging international crises that could result in an EU request to deploy the Nordic Battlegroup, the four participating governments have therefore agreed to engage in regular consultations shortly before, and during a stand-by period. As the Framework nation of the Battlegroup, Sweden will lead these consultations (Memorandum of Understanding 2005, Section 8). In case the Nordic Battlegroup is deployed during its first stand-by period from 1 January to 30 June 2008, it will be led by an EU-appointed Operation Commander with support from the British Multinational Operational Headquarters (OHQ) located in Northwood in the north-west London suburbs. Since the Command and Control system within the EU is still under development, the British OHQ in Northwood was pre-identified and selected for the Nordic Battlegroup in order to ensure the presence of a trained and tested chain of command in time for the Nordic Battlegroup's stand-by period. Approximately twenty Nordic officers will be seconded to the British OHQ in Northwood, and operational planning will be coordinated between Sweden, Finland, Norway, Estonia, Britain and the EU Military Staff in Brussels.[22] Although each national contingent in the Nordic Battlegroup will remain under the full command

---

21 Finland's contribution to the NBG will consist of around 200 soldiers forming combat support elements, such as a heavy mortar platoon, a platoon-sized Chemical Biological Radiological and Nuclear (CBRN) detection detachment and a unit in the joint Swedish-Finnish intelligence ISTAR Company. Finland will also provide certain combat service support elements, such as logistics and military police. Norway will contribute another 200 personnel serving in support functions such as medical services, logistics and strategic lift. Estonia, in turn, will provide an infantry platoon of 40–50 troops for force protection. All four countries will provide staff personnel to Operation Headquarters as well as Forward Headquarters.

22 Once the EU has developed a more advanced Command and Control system, any battlegroup may be commanded by any OHQ at any given time. At present, however, a system of prearranged relationships between a specific OHQ and a specific Battlegroup will be the usual course of action.

of its government, participating governments in the Nordic Battlegroup have agreed to delegate operational control of the contingent to the Operation Commander for the duration of the operation (Memorandum of Understanding, 2005: Section 11).

Negotiations over the distribution of positions between Sweden and the other three countries in the HQs and the coordination of other questions has been carried out within a pre-existing framework for cooperation known as the Nordic Coordinated Arrangement for Peace Support (NORDCAPS). This framework encompasses both political and military issues (Sjöden, 2004: 60). Whenever possible, the formation and training of the Nordic Battlegroup has relied upon existing Nordic channels such as NORDCAPS, and overall coordination of defence policy and military issues for the NBG have been conducted by national representatives in the NORDCAPS Steering Group and Military Co-ordination Group (Memorandum of Understanding, 2005: Section 9). As the Framework nation, Sweden has a leading role in designing and coordinating training activities for the Nordic Battlegroup. However, Finnish participation in another EU Battlegroup (with Germany and The Netherlands) and Norwegian experience with NATO's Response Force (NRF) concept have provided valuable input into planning for the Nordic Battlegroup. While Nordic military cooperation has been growing over the past few years, the establishment of a joint Nordic Battlegroup serves to further increase military cooperation among countries in the region (Andersson, 2006a: 41; Declaration, 2004).

From conscripts to contracts

In peacetime, the Swedish armed forces consist of officers, reserve officers, civilian employees and conscript soldiers in basic or refresher training. In 2006, there were around 10,000 officers, 12,000 reserve officers, and 7,000 civilians employed in the Swedish armed forces. In addition, 10,000 conscript soldiers were in basic military training (Vienna Document, 2006: 12–13; Swedish Armed Forces, 2006a: 17). The manning of the Swedish armed forces wartime organisation is based on a conscription and mobilisation system that complements the permanently employed cadre of professional officers. Compulsory military service was introduced in Sweden in 1901, and all Swedish males between the ages of 19 and 47 are liable for military service. Women may undertake military service on a voluntary basis. During the cold war era, almost all men were called up for military service. However, the policy for recruitment of both officers and conscripts is changing. The transformation from a large cold war territorial defence army to a smaller, more flexible and mobile operational defence organisation no longer requires large numbers of conscript soldiers. In 1975, the total number of conscripts conducing military service was 47,000. Of the 55,000 young men eligible for conscription in 2005, only 10,000 were called up for basic military training (National Service Administration, 2006: 11). The number of conscripts called up for basic military training will continue to decrease to an average of around 8500 per year (Swedish Armed Forces, 2006a: 17). Given the Swedish government's goal of keeping 2,000 troops abroad annually in international missions, there is a need to mainly select and train conscripts who are later prepared to volunteer for international service. Recruitment has therefore generally shifted towards finding the most motivated conscripts rather than those most fit for service. Since less than one in five young men are being called up for military service, there is a growing political awareness that the present system of conscription has to be reformed.[23]

The shift from territorial defence to international missions also affects recruitment and training. Serving in international missions abroad used to be on a strictly volunteer basis for career officers and conscript soldiers alike. Today, career officers employed in the Swedish armed forces since 2004 can no longer refuse to serve in international missions.[24] While international service remains strictly voluntary for conscript soldiers, basic military training has changed in order to increase the number of volunteers. Commencing in 2006, the majority of conscripts now serve two semesters of basic military training for a total of 11 months after which they are invited to serve a third voluntary optional semester preparing for international missions. At the end of the third semester, the conscript may accept employment in the Swedish armed forces for up to two years as a 'readiness soldier' in a standing unit on call for national and international missions at short notice. The first such readiness unit, a mechanised infantry company consisting of contracted 'readiness soldiers' who have just completed their third optional semester of basic military training, was commissioned on 9 October 2006 (Swedish Armed Forces, 2006b). The 151 officers and men of the IA 06 company will be ready for immediate national or international deployment providing the first standing army unit in modern Swedish military history.[25] Similarly to the mechanised readiness company IA 06, the Swedish core battalion of the Nordic Battlegroup will consist of contracted 'readiness soldiers' (Nordic Battlegroup, 2007: 26).

Privatising and outsourcing

The dramatic down-sizing of the Swedish armed forces and its shift from territorial defence to international missions has led to major changes in logistics that include privatisation and outsourcing of non-essential support services. In a major overhaul of how to organise maintenance and support for the transformed armed forces, the Swedish government ordered the creation of a new unit for logistics in March 2001.[26] The new unit, The Swedish armed forces Logistics Organisation [Försvarsmaktens logistik – FMLOG], was to merge all the armed forces' existing logistics and support services, including mechanical shops and aircraft maintenance centres, and be responsible for providing all support services to the armed forces in peacetime and wartime, and for national and international missions. By concentrating all maintenance and support operations in a single organisation, it was believed that

---

23 For example, see recent statements by *Folkpartiet* (the Liberal party).

24 See, Swedish government bill, *Tjänstgöring i utlandsstyrkan inom Försvarsmakten*, Proposition 2002/03: 26, 23 January 2003.

25 IA 06 was deployed to Kosovo in February 2007 to reinforce the Swedish battalion serving with the KFOR. See http://www.mil.se/index.php?lang=S&c=news&id=35765<br% 20/.

26 Swedish government bill, *Vissa ledningsfrågor inom det militära försvaret m. m.*, Proposition Prop. 2000/01: 113, 22 March 2001.

services would be more efficient and cost effective. In addition to concentrating production activities, cutting back on administration and reducing the number of different locations, the new FMLOG was also to make greater use of civilian suppliers and outsourcing services whenever private actors could offer competitive prices. Outsourcing activities to private companies at lower prices would not only cut costs but also allow the armed forces to focus on core missions. Consequently, in the new organisation many of the military officers were to be replaced by civilian experts.[27]

FMLOG was formally activated on 1 January 2002 and was organised in three divisions: Supply, Technical, and Support Divisions.[28] With activities spanning the entire country and with 6,000 employees of which the majority were civilians, FMLOG became overnight the largest 'unit' in the Swedish armed forces. The aim was to make FMLOG a modern logistics organisation drawing on civilian industrial standar and knowledge. Although FMLOG continued to be an integral part of the armed forces and commanded by a general officer, the government resolved that a civilian with extensive experience from the business world would be its deputy head.[29] Reforming logistics, however, turned out to be a difficult challenge. Despite the grand visions of uniting all logistics functions under one command, responsibility remained fractured in practice.[30] Lack of clear directives from the Military Headquarters (HKV) led to competition and infighting between FMLOG and the Defence Materiel Administration (FMV), among others. These organisational difficulties led to the resignation of the first civilian deputy head of FMLOG just one year after his appointment (*Logistik Nytt*, 2003b: 27). Nevertheless, despite initial difficulties, FMLOG has managed to increase efficiency and productivity. Privatisation and outsourcing have contributed to these results. Today, food services, janitorial services and the stockpiling of spare parts, have mostly been outsourced to private companies. Among the first services to be outsourced to private actors were food services.

In an experiment in 2001, two military restaurants at the regiments in Strängnäs and Skövde were taken over by private companies. While the two companies faced initial problems with both staff and maintaining quality, the outsourcing of food services eventually led to increased quality in the military restaurants and greater flexibility in food services during field exercises (*Logistik Nytt*, 2003a: 8–10). The

---

27 See Swedish government bill, *Vissa ledningsfrågor inom det militära försvaret m. m.*, Proposition Prop. 2000/01: 113, 22 March 2001, p. 13.

28 FMLOG is responsible for maintenance and support to units, staffs and schools within the Armed Forces. FMLOG deals with stores, transport, workshops, reserve materiel handling, IT support, military catering and restaurants, procurement, finance and salaries, personnel support, travel administration, expeditions, printing and copying, cleaning, etc. Its activities are financed out of revenue and are demand-driven. FMLOG supports all branches of the Swedish Armed Forces. See http://www.fmlog.mil.se/.

29 The first deputy head of FMLOG was a former CEO with 20 years experience in the civilian IT, telecomm and logistics industry. See interview with Mats Herdenfeldt in *Logistik Nytt* 2002b, 4–5.

30 See for example the evaluation of FMLOG in 2005 (Swedish government Official Report, 2005), 26–27.

successful experiment led to the stated goal that all food services in the Swedish armed forces should be considered for outsourcing by 1 January 2009. Another service to be outsourced early was janitorial services. By 2003, almost all janitorial services for the armed forces had been outsourced. One company, Sodexho, dominates the market and outsourcing janitorial services to Sodexho was estimated to save the armed forces SEK 25 million per year. Moreover, in a major evaluation of customer satisfaction, 69 per cent of respondents in the armed forces were satisfied with Sodexho's cleaning services (*Logistik Nytt*, 2003b: 19). In a somewhat more complicated deal, the stockpiling of spare parts for the armed forces was outsourced to private firms in 2005. The deal included responsibility for maintaining spare parts and reserve materiel supply system for the armed forces centrally and at the various garrisons around the country. SAAB AerotechTelub, a technology service consultancy and a subsidiary of the aircraft manufacturer SAAB, submitted the winning bid and took over the responsibility for stockpiling and supplying spare parts for the armed forces in October 2005 for an initial contract period of five years with the possibility of an extension for an additional three years (*Logistik Nytt*, 2005a: 11).

The outsourcing of services such as food, cleaning and stockpiling of spare parts is one aspect of streamlining logistics. However, an even more challenging aspect of logistics and the outsourcing to private actors is the provision of services to military units in international operations. Under what conditions can private civilian contractors be sent abroad into potential combat zones? Recent experience from the wars in Iraq and Afghanistan demonstrates that there are no longer any 'safe' rear areas behind the front lines where civilians can move around in relative safety. In modern asymmetrical warfare it is increasingly difficult to distinguish enemies from friends and where terms such as 'Three Block War' dominate; how far can a private civilian contractor be expected to go? The reliance on private contractors to supply food services and transportation in Iraq led to shortages when civilian truck drivers simply refused to work due to dangerous conditions. As a consequence of the challenges experienced primarily by American and British reliance on private contractors in combat zones, the move in Sweden towards privatising and outsourcing logistics and support for international missions has been delayed. Currently, there is little political pressure on the Swedish armed forces to outsource services to private providers concerning international missions.[31]

Arguably, the Swedish armed forces have been completely transformed since the end of the cold war. The size of the Swedish military today is a fraction of its cold war level but more active then ever before. Swedish military units are currently deployed under EU, NATO or UN command in Kosovo, Afghanistan and Liberia, among other places. While international peacekeeping missions used to be frowned upon by many in the armed forces as paid vacations for those without further career prospects, participation in international missions today is a potentially deadly affair, deep in the jungles of Africa or in the mountains of Afghanistan, but quite necessary for a successful military career.[32] The Swedish armed forces are also among the best

---

31 Interview with two members of the Swedish Parliament, January 2007.

32 An increasing share of new company commanders has had experience from service in the Balkans or elsewhere.

equipped in the world. Some of today's most advanced combat vehicles, fighter jets, surveillance systems, and warships are of Swedish design and origin. The Swedish-led EU Battlegroup to be set up in 2008 will hold its own in comparison with those of the great powers in terms of equipment (Andersson, 2006a). However, while these weapons systems may be designed and produced in Sweden they are no longer products of a 'Swedish' defence industry. In fact, the defence industry in Sweden is largely privatised and internationally owned and controlled. It is to this fact we now turn.

From Government Arsenals to Privatised International Companies

Sweden has a long tradition of armaments production. The iron works, cannon foundries, and rifle factories established in Sweden in the 16th Century by immigrant Germans and Walloons led to a thriving armaments industry. For more than 150 years, from the early 17th to the late 18th centuries, Sweden was one of the world's leading arms exporters and dominated the international trade in cast-iron cannons (Krause, 1992: 42). The tradition of large-scale armaments production was resumed in Sweden before and during World War II. Difficulties in importing arms as Europe prepared for war in the late 1930s led to a rapidly expanding Swedish defence industry sector. By the end of World War II, Sweden was one of the major arms producers in the world, in part because many other countries' defence industries had been destroyed. The strength of the Swedish defence industry was also one of the key foundations for the discussions of a Scandinavian defence union between Sweden, Denmark and Norway in 1948 (Agrell, 2000: 104). When Norway and Denmark chose to join NATO, Sweden decided to continue its military non-alignment policy which in turn required a high degree of self-sufficiency in arms production.

While it was impossible for Sweden to produce all types of weapons, domestic arms production during the cold war included advanced jet fighters, guided missiles, surface combatants and submarines as well as main battle tanks, armoured vehicles, heavy artillery, anti-aircraft guns and small arms (Harlow, 1967b: 68–74). Almost all armaments were produced by government-owned factories or by private companies with close ties to the Swedish government. Most of the arms production was for domestic needs. With a wartime military organisation of 800,000 men, a very large air force and a significant navy, the Swedish armed forces constituted a considerable domestic home market for the Swedish defence industry (Andersson and Stenquist, 1988: 22–23). Although official Swedish government policy stated that the domestic defence industry would not be supported if required equipment could be obtained more cheaply from abroad, the Swedish government did not want to risk ruining a strategic industry dependent on government orders. The relationship between government and defence industry was thus close and mutually supportive (Harlow, 1967b: 69). At times, the defence industry increased production at short notice to meet unexpected government demands. For example, in the early 1950s the aircraft producer, SAAB, cancelled its production of a civilian airliner in order to meet the Swedish air force's urgent need for more fighter jets (Andersson, 1989). At other times, the Swedish government supported the defence industry by placing orders for armaments that the military did not need nor want.

The Swedish defence industry also exported arms to other countries (Hagelin, 1985; Andersson and Stenquist, 1988). Examples include the export of fighter jets to Finland, Denmark and Austria (SAAB), artillery to India (Bofors), tracked all-terrain vehicles to more than 40 countries (Hägglunds), and the famous *Carl-Gustaf* light anti-tank weapon around the world (FFV). Although foreign sales were important, arms exports were less crucial to the Swedish defence industry than for defence industries in many other countries. Every major weapon system developed by the Swedish defence industry during the cold war was tailored and designed for the Swedish armed forces and export sales were thus a bonus rather then a condition for production. For example, SAAB rarely exported any of its fighter jets but lived rather well on its orders from the Swedish Air Force. Similarly, Bofors did not sell any of its 'S' model main battle tank beyond the 300 ordered by the Swedish Army (Harlow, 1967b: 68–69; Andersson and Stenquist, 1988: 22–23).

However, by the 1980s it became increasingly clear that the Swedish defence industry was facing difficulties. The drop in domestic defence spending after the end of the cold war in combination with rising research and development costs and increased competition in the international export markets led to a crisis in the Swedish defence industry sector. With a rapidly diminishing domestic market, Swedish defence companies looked to increase their international exports. But with little export experience the Swedish defence industry, was unable to compete successfully in the international arms market (Dörfer, 1983; Andersson and Stenquist, 1988). In the early 1990s, it became increasingly evident that the breadth and independence of the Swedish defence industry could not be maintained at previous levels (Hagelin, 1992: 185).

Faced with a growing crisis in the defence industry the Swedish government concluded that the defence industry had to be restructured and rationalised even if this restructuring in certain cases could lead to partial foreign ownership of Swedish defence companies. The Government also acknowledged that cooperation with the international defence industry had to be accepted and supported as long as it furthered central Swedish interests and general foreign policy goals.[33] In the mid-1990s, the Swedish government actively encouraged the Swedish defence industry to find international solutions to the challenge of rapidly shrinking domestic demand. Through privatisation, new laws on domestic ownership structures, and subsidised export promotion, the government enabled the defence industry to restructure on an international level. However, the initiative and the details on how the restructuring should take place were left to the industry itself to decide.[34]

---

33 See Swedish government bill, *Om totalförsvarets utveckling till och med budgetåret 1996/97 samt anslag för budgetåret 1992/93*, Proposition Prop. 1991/92: 102, 1 January 1992; Riksdagen [Swedish Parliament], *Försvarsutskottets betänkanden och yttranden 1991/92: FöU12*.

34 Accordingly, when it was announced that the Swedish armoured vehicle producer Hägglunds Vehicle AB would be sold to the British company Alvis in 1997, the Swedish government did not intervene. Similarly, the Swedish government had no objections to the

During the cold war, the Swedish government brought together military-run arsenals into large entities producing everything from small arms to sophisticated telecommunications systems. These entities were turned into state-owned companies in the early 1990s in an effort to increase efficiency and productivity. The largest of these entities, *Försvarets Fabriksverk* (FFV), was incorporated as FFV AB in 1991. Less then a year later, FFV AB merged with another government owned company, Celsius AB.[35] By merging FFV and Celsius, the government brought together most of Sweden's state-owned ordnance, shipbuilding, electronics and aerospace companies into one single company. The new company, Celsius Industries, accounted for some 50 per cent of Sweden's total armaments production which gave it a pivotal role in the restructuring of the defence industry sector. After a series of consolidations and divestures, Celsius Industries was successfully listed on the Stockholm stock exchange in 1993. Three-quarters of Celsius' shares were openly traded while the Swedish government retained effective control of the company through its holding of 25 per cent vote-controlling 'A' shares, equal to 62 per cent of the voting rights (Bitzinger, 2003: 53–54). In 1999, the government put its remaining shares in Celsius on the market. By that time, Celsius was a profitable company with a turnover of SEK 14.3 billion and nearly 11,000 employees. With the merger of FFV and Celsius in the 1991, the Swedish defence industry had in effect been consolidated into two major groups. The other major defence industry group consisted of SAAB and other companies controlled by the Wallenberg family.

SAAB can trace its origins back to the 1936 government defence bill in which it was decided that Sweden should become self-sufficient in aeroplane production. As a result, SAAB was founded in 1937. In 1939, the Wallenberg family became a major shareholder in the company. By the end of the war, SAAB had become the main producer of military aircraft in Sweden. Military aircraft production continued during the cold war years and SAAB developed a highly successful series of jet fighters. The J-29 Tunnan, A/J-32 Lansen, J-35 Draken and A/J/S-37 Viggen fighters could all compete with the very best in the world (Andersson, 1989). In 1987, SAAB celebrated its 50th anniversary by rolling out the first test aircraft of its most recent jet fighter, the JAS-39 Gripen. The Gripen was the world's first 4th generation fighter jet and had been conceived by the Swedish Air Force as a replacement for its ageing fighters in the 1990s and beyond (Ahlgren et al., 2005). However, spiralling costs and the sudden end of the cold war threatened the whole project and the survival of SAAB as an independent aircraft producer. The company was saved by the Swedish government's decision in 1992 to order a second batch of 110 Gripen fighter jets – for a total of 140 aircraft. The order was placed after considerable pressure from

takeover of the naval shipbuilder Kockums AB by HDW of Germany in 1999. In fact, the internationalisation of the Swedish defence industry was made possible by the government and reflected a change in strategy on how to maintain armoured vehicle and submarine technology expertise in the country.

35 Celsius AB had been founded as Svenska Varv AB in 1977 as a result of a series of mergers in the shipbuilding industry. The company had been created to manage and restructure the crisis-stricken Swedish shipyards industry into a competitive industry able to survive without state-support. Svenska Varv was renamed Celsius in 1987 and in 1991 was given control of the shares in FFV by the government.

industry on the government to save Sweden's largest industrial project even though the cold war was over.[36]

SAAB was delisted from the Stockholm stock exchange in 1991 and became a subsidiary of the Wallenberg company, Investor. In 1995, SAAB was broken up and underwent considerable restructuring in which the automobile division was sold to the American company General Motors and civilian aircraft production shut down. Strengthened by the Swedish government's decision in 1997 to order a third batch of 64 Gripen fighters for a grand total of 204 aircraft, SAAB was reintroduced on the Stockholm stock exchange in 1998.[37]

By the end of the 1990s, the Swedish defence industry had been restructured, slimmed down, and largely privatised. While both Celsius and SAAB were large companies in a domestic and Scandinavian context, they were small and increasingly isolated in the larger reorganisation of the European defence industry taking place on the continent.[38] In a final major push to further restructure the defence industry sector, the Swedish government put up its remaining shares in Celsius on the stock market in 1999. In the following year, SAAB acquired Celsius and became Sweden's dominant defence company. The merger between Celsius and SAAB in 2000 effectively privatised the Swedish defence industry. With 18,000 employees and annual sales of $2.2 billion, the new company, renamed SAAB Technologies, controlled 80 per cent of all arms production in Sweden (Leijonhufvud, 1999; Bitzinger, 2003). In a further consolidation of the Swedish defence industry, SAAB acquired the majority share of the radar and sensor equipment producer Ericsson Microwave Systems from the telecom company Ericsson in June 2006.

The consolidation and privatisation of the Swedish defence industry in the 1990s and early 2000s was dramatic and far-reaching. However, an equally important change was the internationalisation of the Swedish defence industry. Realising that the country could no longer afford to sustain a national defence industry to the same extent it had in the past, Swedish authorities began to openly admit in the 1990s that autarky in armaments production was no longer financially or technically possible.[39] International collaboration and cross-border acquisitions and mergers would have to become more prevalent. The first Swedish defence company to be sold to an international buyer was the armoured vehicle producer, Hägglunds, in 1997. The deal was one of the very first cross-border acquisitions of a major defence industry platform producer in Europe, but the Swedish government did not object to the sale of Hägglunds to the British defence industry company Alvis. (Andersson, 2000: 13). Only a year later, in 1998, the British aerospace company BAE Systems became

---

36 Gripen was developed by an industrial consortium consisting of SAAB, Ericsson Microwave Systems, Volvo Aero Corporation, SAAB Avionics, and FFV Aerotech. A joint venture company, Gripen International, has been set up by Saab and BAE Systems to market the Gripen for export markets. BAE Systems is building the main landing gear unit and wing attachment unit. Ahlgren, Linnér and Wigert 2005, p. 53–54.

37 On 7 May 1998, the board of investor decided to distribute 44.8 per cent of Saab AB's share capital, equivalent to 29 per cent of the voting rights, to Investor's shareholders.

38 For an analysis of this process, see Schmitt 2000.

39 See interviews with Sweden's Supreme Commander and National Armaments Director quoted in Bitzinger 2003.

the largest shareholder in SAAB following its acquisition of a 35 per cent stake from Investor AB (Hagelin 1998).[40] In 1999, the Swedish submarine producer, Kockums, was sold to its German rival submarine builder HDW (Andersson 2004).

Today, all the principal Swedish defence companies have major foreign ownership. British, American, German, French and Norwegian interests dominate (Association of Swedish Defence Industries 2006). The changing ownership structure and internationalisation of the Swedish defence industry is a result of a larger and quite dramatic restructuring of the European and international defence industry (Schmitt 2000, 2003). For example, in 2004, the British multinational defence company, BAE Systems, acquired its domestic British rival firm Alvis to form a large Land Systems company of which Hägglunds is now part. A year later, in 2005, BAE Systems American subsidiary, BAE Systems Inc., bought its American rival company United Defence. United Defence had earlier acquired Swedish gunmaker Bofors Weapons Systems. As a result, BAE Systems became owner of both Hägglunds and Bofors. These two Swedish-based companies were then brought into a holding company called BAE Systems AB but run by BAE Systems American subsidiary based in the United States (Association of Swedish Defence Industries 2006).

A smaller defence also requires a smaller defence material establishment. As a result of the cuts in the armed forces there has been increasing pressure on developing public–private partnerships within areas such as logistics, training, defence research, arms procurement and maintenance. The objective of these public–private partnerships is to allow the military to focus its resources and energy on its primary task of 'armed combat' by drawing on the expertise and efficiency in the private sector (Swedish Armed Forces 2007). The goal is to form long-term contracts with selected partners in the private sector in a variety of sectors. For example, one goal is for the armed forces to outsource the servicing of military equipment and for industry to assume life-long responsibilities for maintenance, upgrades and finally disposal. While there are grandiose plans for these public–private partnerships (some of which have been realised), there are still many uncertainties regarding long-term effects on costs and the division of labour and responsibilities (Britz 2004, 173; Swedish Defence Material Administration 2005, 6).

Conclusion

In the fifteen years that have passed since the end of the cold war, Sweden's defence policy and armed forces have undergone a dramatic transformation. An inward-looking defence policy based on territorial defence and focused on military non-alignment and universal male conscription has been transformed into an outward-looking, holistic defence policy based on a broad security concept and focused on international missions in collaboration with the EU and NATO. While military non-alignment and universal male conscription remain important in theory, both

---

40 From January 2005, BAE has reduced its shareholding to 20 per cent of SAAB, which it views as a long term interest. Investor AB also maintains a 20 per cent share (Association of Swedish Defence Industries 2006).

policies have been abandoned in practice. Today, Sweden is one of the most active member states in the EU when it comes to promoting a greater role for the Union in crisis management activities, and it has participated with troops in all of the EU military missions. Moreover, Sweden has assumed leadership of one of the EU battlegroups – The Nordic Battlegroup. In addition, Sweden is one of the most active partnership countries in NATO and has participated fully in NATO-led missions in Bosnia, Kosovo, and most recently, Afghanistan. As one of five especially close NATO partners, Sweden would be welcomed immediately into NATO if it were to express a wish to join. Meanwhile, Sweden's large and once domestically controlled defence industry has been successively privatised and internationalised. Indeed, the transformation of Sweden's defence and defence policy continues at a rapid pace. In the autumn of 2006, a newly elected Swedish government announced that it would increase the defence budget and allocate more money for international missions. In February 2007, the Swedish armed forces submitted a plan of action for 2008 – one that strongly reflects developments within the EU European Security and Defence Policy (ESDP) as well as Sweden's cooperation with NATO (Swedish Armed Forces, 2007). As the plan's emphasis on recruitment shows, rising demands for more rapid reaction forces and the Swedish government's goal of increasing the country's contribution to international missions means that considerably larger numbers of troops must be raised for international service in the coming years. Although the plan makes clear that conscription should remain the basis for Swedish armed forces' national missions and territorial defence in case of war, the Supreme Commander has also requested that the government allow Swedish soldiers to enlist in the armed forces for a period of three-and-a-half years for primarily international missions. The armed forces action plan further recommends that these same soldiers be allowed to re-enlist for a subsequent period of three-and-a-half years with a maximum of seven years of service. In addition to their role in international missions that, according to the action plan, these enlisted troops would also serve as a standing rapid reaction force for use in national missions should the need arise. Finally, the Supreme Commander has requested that the government also reintroduce the class of Non-Commissioned Officer in the armed forces in order to allow for a higher degree of specialisation and an increased focus on unit training (Swedish Armed Forces, 2007: 38–41, Attachment, 4).[41] If the Swedish government should decide to follow these requests and recommendations, Sweden will soon possess what is in effect a professional army and standing forces available for immediate deployment in rapid reaction missions under the command of the EU, NATO or the UN. This would indeed mark the emergence of a new Swedish defence – one capable of responding more quickly and more effectively to the exigencies of a brave new world.

---

41 The Swedish armed forces is rather unique in that it has only one officer class in contrast to most other armed forces which have officers and non-commissioned officers.

References

Agrell, W. (2000), *Fred och fruktan. Sveriges säkerhetspolitiska historia 1918–2000* [Peace and fear. Sweden's security policy history 1918–2000] (Lund: Historiska Media).

Andersson, B and Stenquist, B. (1988), *Vapensmugglarna* [The Gunrunners] (Stockholm: Författarförlaget).

Andersson, H. G. (1989), *SAAB Aircraft* (London: Putnam).

Andersson, J. J. (2000), 'Cold war Dinosaurs or Hi-Tech Arms Provides?' *Occasional papers 23* (Paris: Institute of Security Studies).

—— (2004), 'Försvarindustrin och den svenska försvarspolitiken' [The Defence industry and the Swedish defence policy] *Kungliga Krigsvetenskapsakademiens Handlingar och Tidskrift*, **208**(4) 45–55.

—— (2006a), Armed and Ready? The EU Battlegroup Concept and the Nordic Battlegroup (Stockholm: SIEPS).

—— (2006b), 'Från försvarsindustri till högteknologi' [From defence industry to high technology] in *Exportkontroll i tiden*.

—— (ed.) (2005), *Sverige och Europas försvar* [Sweden and the defence of Europe] (Stockholm: Utrikespolitiska Institutet).

Andrén, N. and Möller, Y. (1990), *Från Undén till Palme. Svensk utrikespolitik efter andra världskriget* [From Undén to Palme. Swedish foreign policy after WWII] (Stockholm: Nordstedts).

Association of Swedish Defence Industries (2006), 'Försvarsindustrin i Sverige' [The defence industry in Sweden] Available at <http://www. defind. se/statistik. html>. Accessed 7 December 2006.

Bailes, A. et al. (eds.) (2006), *The Nordic Countries and the European Security and Defence Policy* (Oxford: Oxford University Press).

Bitzinger, R. A. (2003), *Towards a Brave New Arms Industry*, Adelphi Paper 356 (Oxford: Oxford University Press).

Britz, M. (2004), *The Europeanization of Defence Industry Policy*. Stockholm Studies in Politics 103. Department of Political Science, Stockholm University. October, 2004.

Brzoska, M. and Lock, P. (eds.) (1992), *SIPRI, Restructuring of Arms Production in Western Europe* (Oxford: Oxford University Press).

Burns, R. Nicholas (2005), Interview by Dagens Nyheter, 24 May 2005, Transcript available at <http://italy.usembassy.gov/viewer/article.asp?article=/file2005_05/alia/a5053009.htm>.

—— (2006a), 'Riga and Beyond' remarks by R Nicholas Burns, Under Secretary for Political Affairs to the Welt-am-Sonntag Budeswehr Forum, Berlin, Germany, 23 October, 2006. Available at <http://www.state.gov/p/us/rm/2006/75422.htm>.

—— (2006b), Remarks to the American Council on Germany by R Nicholas Burns, Under Secretary for Political Affairs, Washington, DC, 27 November 2006, available at <http://www.state.gov/p/us/rm/2006/77003.htm>.

Cramér, P. (1989), *Neutralitetsbegreppet. Den permanenta neutralitetens utveckling* [The Concept of neutrality. The Development of the permanent neutrality] (Stockholm: Nordstedts Juridik).

Declaration (2004), Declaration by Sweden and Finland and Norway on the Establishment of a Joint EU Battlegroup of 22 November 2004, available at <http://odin.dep. no/fd/norsk/aktuelt/nyheter/010051-990085/dok-bn.html>.

Dörfer, I. (1983), *Arms Deal: The Sellling of the F16* (new York. Praeger).

Eriksson, A. (2006), *Europeanization and Governance in Defence Policy: The Example of Sweden*, Stockholm Studies in Politics 117, Department of Political Science, Stockholm University.

European Union (2004), Declaration on European military capabilities, EU Military capability commitment conference. Brussels, 22 November 2004.

Exportkontroll i tiden [Contemporary export controll] (2006) (Stockholm: ISP).

Hagelin, B. (1985), *Kulorna rullar. Ekonomi och politik kring svensk militär export* [Economics and politics and Swedish military exports] (Stockholm: Ordfront).

—— (1990), Neutrality and Foreign Military Sales (Boulder, CO: Westview Press)

—— (1992), 'Sweden's search for military technology', in Brzorska and Lock (eds).

—— (1998), 'Saab, British Aerospace and the JAS 39 Gripen Aircraft Joint Venture', *European Security*, 7(4) 91–117.

Harlow, C. J. E. (1967a), *The European Armaments Base: A Survey. Part 1: Economic Aspects of Defence Procurement* (London: IISS).

——(1967b), *The European Armaments Base: A Survey. Part 2: National Procurement Policies* (London: IISS).

Krause, K. (1992), *Arms and the State: Patterns of Militray Production and Trade* (Cambridge: Cambridge University Press).

Lemne, M. and Sohlman, S. (2004), *FMV:s Initiativ, förslag och avtryck i omvärlden 1996-2003* [Initiatives, proposals and imprints of the Swedish Defence Material Administration 1996-2003] (Stockholm: FMV).

Leijonhufvud, S. (1999), 'Saabs köp av Celsius skapar högteknologisk plattform' [SAAB's acquisition of Celsius creates high technology platform company] *Svenska Dagbladet*, 17 November 1999, p. 41.

Memorandum of Understanding (2005), Memorandum of Understanding between the Ministry of defence of the Republic of Estonia and the Ministry of Defence of the Republic of Finland and the Ministry of Defence of the Kingdom of Norway and the Government of the Kingdom of Sweden concerning the principles for the establishment and operation of a multinational battlegroup to be made available to the European Union, 23 May 2005.

Navy Newsstand (2005), 'Swedish Submarine Continues to Play Important Role in Joint Training' (Story Number: NNS051220-05, Release Date: 12 December 2005).

National Service Administration (2006), *Årsredovisning 2005* (Karlstad: National Service Administration).

Nordic Battlegroup (2006), (Stockholm: Swedish armed forces).

Odenberg, M. (2007), Våra viktigaste framtidsfrågor [Our most important questions for the future], Speech by Minister for Defence Mikael Odenberg at Folk och Försvars annual conference, Sälen 14 January 2007 (available at <http://www. folkochforsvar. se/images/Rikskonferensen2007_Tal/vara_framsta_utmaningar. Pdf>).

Quille, G. (2004), 'Battle Groups to strengthen EU military crisis management'. *European Security Review*, no. 22, April.

Sjöden, A. (2005). Fakta: Ledning Battle Group [Facts: Battlegroup command and control]. *Insats & Försvar*, no. 3.

Svensk försvarsindustri (1982), *Svensk försvarsindustri* [Swedish defence industry] FOA rapport C10200-MF (Stockholm: FOA).

Swedish Armed Forces (2005), *Försvarsmaktens Grundsyn Logistik Förhandsutgåva* [Armed Forces' basic view on logistics] (Stockholm: Försvarsmakten).

—— (2006a), *The Facts 2006–2007* (Stockholm: Swedish Armed Forces)

—— (2006b), 'IA 06 är redo...' [IA 06 is ready...] Published 22 oktober 2006 (available at <http://www. p7.mil.se/index.php?lang=S&c=news&id=34400>).

—— (2007), *Försvarsmaktens budgetunderlag för år 2008 med särskilda redovisningar* [Armed Forces' budget plans for 2008] (BU 08/SR) (Stockholm: Swedish Armed Forces).

Swedish Defence Material Administration (2005), *FMV Årsredovisning* [Annual report] (Stockholm: FMV).

Syrén, H. (2007), Insatser nu och utmaningar 2008 [Missions now and challenges for 2008]. Speech by Supreme Commander General Håkan Syrén, at Folk och Försvars' annual conference, Sälen 14 January 2007 (available at <http://www. folkochforsvar.se/images/Rikskonferensen2007_Tal/obsalenfinal2007. pdf>).

The Military Balance (various years) (London: International Institute for Strategic Studies).

Ulriksen, S., Gourlay, C. and Mace, C. (2004), Operation Artemis: The Shape of Things to Come? *International Peacekeeping*, **11**(3) Autumn.

United Nations (2004), Operation Artemis: The Lessons of the Interim Emergency Multinational Force, United Nations Peacekeeping Best Practices Unit, Military Division, October 2004 (available at <http://www.peacekeepingbestpractices. unlb.org/pbpu/library/Artemis.pdf>).

Utlandsstyrkan [The International force] (2006), (Stockholm: Bokförlaget Arena).

Vienna Document (2006), Vienna Document, Annual Exchange of information on defence planning 2006, The Kingdom of Sweden, valid as of 15 March 2006.

Wedin, L. (2006), 'The impact of EU capability targets and operational demands on defence concepts and planning: the case of Sweden', in *The Nordic Countries and the European Security and Defence Policy* (Oxford: Oxford University Press).

Chapter 9

Modernising the Finnish Defence – Combining Tradition with Cost-efficiency and Internationalisation

Anu Sallinen

The White Paper on Finnish Security and Defence Policy from 2004 states that Finland maintains and develops its defence capability as a militarily non-allied country and monitors the changes in its security environment. Finland's primary objective in its security and defence policy remains the promotion of security and stability in Northern Europe (see Finnish Security and Defence Policy, 2004).

Corresponding with tradition, Finland's future defence is to be based on a modern territorial defence system, general conscription and military non-alignment. The current defence system is estimated to meet the challenges and requirements of both traditional national defence and the wider concepts of threats. Nevertheless, the ongoing modernisation of the defence forces' organisational structure and defence materiel must take into consideration changes in security environment, developing technology and international cooperation, and in the near future also the tight national fiscal policy in the public sector in general.

Like its western neighbours, the Finnish defence forces are going through profound organisational changes. The size of the peacetime organisation is being reduced, and even the strength of the wartime troops is also being decreased. Forces will be more mobile, better equipped, and the whole defence system will fulfil the requirements of network-centric warfare.[1] But unlike the other Nordic countries and the UK, the basic concept and the primary task of the Finnish defence forces' remains the same: being able to respond to all military crises and threats against Finland using primarily national resources. The requirement for a strong public will to defend the nation is emphasised and is considered to be one of the basic preconditions for a credible defence capability. It is considered to be highly important that the will to defend the country and a positive attitude towards the defence forces will be maintained and

---

1   Network-centric warfare (NCW), commonly also called as the network-centric operations (NCO) is an emerging theory of war that seeks to translate an information advantage into a competitive war-fighting advantage through the robust networking of well-informed geographically dispersed forces allowing new forms of organisational behaviour. *See:* Finnish Security and Defence Policy, Government Report 6/2004; Kuusisto R, Rantapelkonen J. (eds) (2005), *Struggling to Understand Information War*.

promoted by increasing the ways and means by which citizens can participate in voluntary defence activities.

Various forms of international cooperation have also had impact on Finnish defence. At the international level, crisis management serves as an example. Finland has been an active participant in peacekeeping missions and in different kinds of contemporary crisis management operations. This is an important part of Finnish defence policy and vital for developing the preparedness of the defence forces. Crisis management capabilities are developed solely according to NATO standards and forms. But in Finland, unlike the other Nordic countries, there has not been any strong need or will to use the defence forces as an active tool in security policy, the primary task being the defence of the sovereignty and territory of the country. Even more importantly, the capability requirements for international operations do not direct the development of defence forces in the same way as in the neighbouring countries.

Both due to the increasing budgetary constraints and the need to focus resources on core functions and processes, the defence forces have developed public–private partnerships as a part of the organisational change. Public–private partnership, or as it is referred to in Finland, *The strategic partnership initiative*, is based on a vision where the future defence forces exist as a logistic system with the longest-term possible integration with the rest of the public sector and with private business, and where the structure does not need to be changed in different stages of readiness. The objective of the *strategic partnership initiative* is to focus the resources of the defence forces in its core functions and processes and to identify, develop and implement new ways to arrange its various support activities. The intention is to facilitate the delivery of such support services in cooperation with strategic partners from both public and private sectors.

In this chapter the nature of Finnish defence and its past and the future will be examined. The Finnish defence is going through changes which will form the ground for the future defence in the next decennium and is required to focus on core activities, on-going structural changes and international capabilities. Therefore, the important affects of internationalisation and denationalisation processes will be analysed. Based on the analysis the conclusions are presented in the context of denationalisation process.

The Development of Independent National Defence

Early independence and pre-Cold War

In the aftermath of the 1917 Russian revolution, two independent armed groups were established in Finland – the Civil Guard and the Red Guards. After independence, the government had to choose which group would form the basis for Finland's official armed forces. A separate primitive military committee had been created in the autumn 1917 for the future armed forces, chaired by Lieutenant General C. G. E. Mannerheim. He was authorised to create and lead the forces in Finland.

The Civil Guard had a centralised command structure and represented the ideology of the government and for this reason was considered to be more suitable to form the basis for the armed forces. Civil war, which had broken out in January 1918, ended in May with victory for the government troops, the Civil Guard – led by General Mannerheim (Finland: Ministry of Defence 2003).

After the end of the civil war the *Whites*[2] started to argue about the direction of Finland's foreign policy and how the armed forces should be organised. The Jaeger movement, together with the activists, put pressure on President Svinhufvud in favour of strong German influence. An important episode in Finnish history and in the history of the defence forces – and also one of the first visible expressions of the desire for independence – was the Jaeger movement. It set off for Germany to obtain military training for the independence struggle. The idea of armed opposition originated first with university students. Germany agreed to provide military training for 200 volunteer Finns. Military training under the guise of a scout camps was begun in Lockstedt near Hamburg on 25 February 1915. When Finland declared its independence on 6 December 1917, the Jaegers wanted to return to Finland. The civil war had broken out in Finland, during which most of the Jaegers fought on the side of the government troops.[3]

German experts arrived in Finland already in early June, and they reorganised the command system of the armed forces according the German system, established the position of Commander-in-chief of the Finnish Army, and presented the new defence planning system. The German surrender in the autumn of 1918 changed the political scene across Europe including Finland. Since then, the highest military command – wartime excluded – has been exercised by the head of state (The Finnish Defence Forces, 2003).[4]

---

2   The Civil Guard was also called The Whites (valkoiset), led by the Senate of Vaasa representing the Senate of Finland formed by the bourgeois parties. The Whites were supported by the German Empire and Swedish volunteers. See Ministry of Foreign Affairs, *Main outlines of Finnish History, The Indepent Republic,* <http://virtual.finland.fi/netcomm/ news/showarticle.asp?intNWSAID=25909#inde>.

3   Altogether 1,900 Finns received military training of which some 600 Jaegers continued to serve in the newly formed Finnish Army after the civil war. They were instrumental in forming, training and equipping the National Defence Force. For a period of 33 years the Commander of the Finnish Defence forces was a Jaeger. In September 1915, this training was expanded to include a whole battalion and the Royal Prussian Jaeger Battalion No. 27 comprised of Finns was formed in May 1916. In order for the battalion to gain combat experience, it was sent to the eastern front in the Kurzeme region of Latvia. See Embassy of Finland in Latvia, *History – The Finnish Jaeger Movement,* <http://www.finland.lv/doc/en/ embassy/jaeger.html>.

4   A considerable amount of Russian field army equipment was left in Finland by the Russians after the Civil War and after the Russian troops had left the country. After the end of the First World War, Finland supplemented its arsenal by buying guns and ammunition from army surplus stocks in Europe. Finland also bought, among other things, 32 light 6 tonne Renault tanks and in 1919, 32 planes. See The Finnish defence forces, *German leading the armed forces,* <http://www.mil.fi/perustietoa/esittely/historia/index_4_en.dsp>.

Securing Finland's independence and territorial integrity gradually became the prime objective of the national defence by the 1930s. Another central principle was that Finland was to remain neutral in disputes between other countries. At that time it was thought that the only way to be sure of preventing territorial violations was for the enemy to believe that Finland was capable of protecting itself. However, financial resources restricted the development of materiel readiness. Training was improved in an attempt to make up for the materiel deficiencies (The Finnish Defence Forces, 2003).[5]

In August 1939, Germany and the Soviet Union signed a non-aggression pact which included a secret protocol relegating Finland to the Soviet sphere of interest. When Finland refused to allow the Soviet Union to build military bases on its territory, the latter revoked the non-aggression pact of 1932 and attacked Finland on November 30, 1939. The 'Winter War' ended in a peace treaty drawn up in Moscow on March 13, 1940, giving south-eastern Finland to the Soviet Union. When Germany invaded the Soviet Union in the summer of 1941, Finland entered the war as a co-belligerent with Germany. The 'Continuation War' ended in armistice in September 1944. The terms of the armistice were confirmed in the Paris Peace Treaty of 1947 (The Finnish Defence Forces, 2003).[6]

The Cold War era

After the Second World War, Finland had to re-assess the basis of its national security. New considerations included the Paris Peace Treaty and also the Treaty of Friendship, Cooperation and Mutual Assistance with the Soviet Union, the lessons of Finland's wartime experience, and the technical and tactical advances in warfare.

In the 1950s and 1960s, several changes were made: an organisational restructuring conducted in 1952 aimed to get all troops geographically under a unified leadership; the brigade became the basic unit in the army and in 1957 the defence council was established. New garrisons were established in the countryside in the 1960s. Also the defence forces' arms and equipment were modernised in the 1950s and 1960s (The Finnish Defence Forces, 2003).[7]

---

5 By 1924, 168 concrete bunkers had been built on the Karelian Isthmus. This fortification work was interrupted but then continued in 1932, and by the time the Winter War broke out in 1939, 221 bunkers had been completed. Older bunkers were also repaired and improved. *See*: The Finnish defence forces, *Aiming for territorial integrity*, <http://www.mil.fi/perustietoa/esittely/historia/index_6_en.dsp>.

6 According to the terms, Finland was obliged to pay the Soviet Union 300 million dollars in war reparations. The size of Finland's armed forces also had to be reduced. The strength of the army was limited to 34,000 men. The naval strength was limited to 4,500 men, with a maximum displacement of 10,000 tonnes for the vessels. The air force strength was limited to 3,000 men and 60 fighter planes. All bombers and submarines had to be scrapped. *See*: *The Finnish Defence Forces, Finland attacks*, <http://www.mil.fi/perustietoa/esittely/historia/index_8_en.dsp>.

7 Assault rifles and new light machine guns had been designed to replace the outmoded rifles, light machine guns and the submachine guns. Aged tanks were replaced with tanks bought from Russia and Britain. A new 122 mm heavy cannon designed in cooperation with

Finland's defence was becoming more closely integrated with national security policy in the mid-1960s. The Finnish defence doctrine was beginning to focus more on the prevention of war and crises. It was considered necessary to extend defence systems to cover the entire country, emphasising regional defence. In 1966, the defence forces thus adopted a system of military provinces. In 1970, the first parliamentary defence committee was established, and the 1974 Act on the Defence Forces incorporated many of the committee's recommendations. The tasks, which the defence establishment had been fulfilling for 55 years, were now made statutory. At the same time, the name was changed from the Finnish Armed Forces to the Finnish Defence Forces to underline of the nature of the armed forces. Troops were designed only for the defence of the country.

New operational and tactical provisions were developed in the 1970s. As the number of men of conscription age declined, changes were made in the composition and location of military units in the late 1980s. Old military units were closed or merged with other units. Amendments to the Conscription Act changed the duration of conscription and the age and times of year at which conscripts started their compulsory military service (The Finnish Defence Forces, 2003).[8]

The post-Cold War era

A major shift in geo-politics took place in 1989–90. This is most commonly referred to as the end of the Cold War. The post-Cold War era brought new options and challenges for the Nordic region. For Finland it meant that due to this development in world politics, the position of the Finnish defence forces changed considerably in 1990 when the government decided that the restrictions stated in the Paris Peace Treaty concerning Finnish sovereignty – with the exception of a ban on atomic weapons – were no longer relevant. Finland could now decide on the number of the troops, vessel tonnage, number of aeroplanes and the type of missiles.

During the Cold War, Finland's international position was characterised by its policy of neutrality and by its special relationship with the Soviet Union. At the same time, Finnish neutrality was more instrumental than ideological. Due to demands both by Finns themselves and from abroad in connection in maintaining its status, this policy led to a cautious attitude towards Western political and economic cooperation (Tiilikainen, 2006).

In the early 1990s, the Nordic countries rethought their institutional choices and strategic affiliations. During that period, Finland did not hesitate to change the official description of its defence policy from *neutral* to *military non-aligned*. In 1992, Finland applied for membership of the EU and became member in 1995 (Bailes,

---

Tampella supplemented Finland's field artillery arsenal. The number of navy vessels was reduced after the war (to 1,500 tonnes), but when decisions to buy more were made in 1955, the tonnage was quadrupled in ten years. The air force got its first flight of new-generation fighter planes (MiG-21 interceptors) between 1963 and 1965. See The Finnish defence forces, *After the war*, <http://www.mil.fi/perustietoa/esittely/historia/index_9_en.dsp>.

8   See: The Finnish Defence Forces, *From defence establishment to Defence Forces*, <http://www.mil.fi/perustietoa/esittely/historia/index_10_en.dsp>.

2006). For the first time Finland could decide on its own security policy freely and purely based on its own incentives. Still, we have to remember that Finland's motives behind the EU membership clearly included an interest in the EU's ability to provide security for Finland in case of external security threat (ibid.).

In the case of defence forces, the latest, larger structural changes were initiated with the White Paper on Finnish Security and Defence Policy that was completed in the spring of 1997. As in the neighbouring countries, the changes in the security environment affected the defence forces first in the late 1990s. Contemporary reforms are carried out according to the latest White Paper which was published in autumn 2004 (see Finnish Security and Defence Policy, 2004). These reforms are presented below.

Key issues in Finnish modernisation of defence

The doctrine of a credible national defence forms the basis for Finnish defence policy. The most important goal of contemporary reform is to preserve the capability for a credible national defence in the coming decades. The aim is to do this by maintaining the deterrent threshold for use of force against the country which is high enough to outweigh the perceived benefits of attack. The primary goal of Finland's defence remains to guarantee the country's independence and to safeguard its sovereignty as a militarily non-allied country. Finnish national defence aims at being able to respond to all military crises and threats by using first and foremost national resources. A strong will to defend the country is also considered to be a central precondition for achieving a credible national defence, and is promoted by general conscription and voluntary defence activities (Finland: Ministry of Defence, 2006).

As a part of the doctrine of credible national defence, Finland's defence is based on general conscription and on a modern territorial defence system. It is estimated that the current defence system, as such, still meets the challenges and requirements of both national defence and the changing security environment in a cost-effective manner, even though the modernisation of the defence forces' organisation and defence materiel takes into consideration changes in security environment as well as in warfare, developing technology and international cooperation (see Finnish Security and Defence Policy, 2004).

The defence forces are obliged by law to solve the following tasks: surveillance and safeguarding of territorial integrity, defence of the country – including its legal system and the living conditions of its people – maintenance of military defensive readiness, military training, support for voluntary defence training, executive assistance to other authorities, participation in emergency and rescue operations, and participation in international crisis management. In brief, the primary tasks of the future defence forces can be divided into three categories: military defence of Finland, support of other national authorities (internal security), and participation in international military crisis management. The key issues in Finnish modernisation of defence can be founded on these tasks.

Military defence

The defence forces must be prepared to prevent and, if necessary, repel any use of military force against Finland. The likelihood of the use of military force against Finland is considered very low, as it is in its neighbouring countries. However, according to the assessments, a significant and qualitatively improving military capability remains in Finland's neighbouring areas (Finland: Ministry of Defence, 2005). Moreover, the probability of military force being used against Finland may increase as a part of global conflict. Therefore, the defence structure is to be maintained and developed on a long-term basis.

The crisis and threat scenarios that are used in contemporary defence planning (see Finnish Security and Defence Policy, 2004) are:

- a regional crisis that may have effects on Finland
- political, economic and military pressure, which may include a threat of using military force and its restricted use
- use of military force in the form of a strategic strike or an attack beginning with a strategic strike aimed at seizing territory.

In addition to threat scenarios, Finland's defence planning primarily takes into account external security threats and the consequent requirements regarding the capabilities of the defence forces, and available resources. The capability to prevent, and if needed, limit any use of asymmetric warfare against society is also included in defence planning in cooperation with other national authorities.

The development of a credible defence system requires intensified concentration on core functions and further restructuring of the defence forces. The basic premise of territorial defence remains. As long as resources can be allocated for the required military capabilities, the development of the defence system does not signify compromising the defence of the territory of entire nation (Finland: Ministry of Defence, 2006).

The military command system will be retained at national, regional and local levels, but the tasks and roles of the different headquarters is to be reviewed, and the defence staff reorganised based on international equivalents. A common intelligence, surveillance and command and control system covering all services, and fulfilling the requirements of network-centric warfare, will be created for the defence forces in order to enhance capability. This system will improve command arrangements, enable the common real-time situation picture to be communicated to every service and further the creation of sufficient communication links. The system will be interoperable with those of international partners and enhance Finnish international defence capability (see Finnish Security and Defence Policy, 2004).

The defence capability will be based on peacetime troops in various stages of readiness as well as on wartime troops which will be mobilised when necessary. Wartime troops are divided into regional and operational forces. During the first years of the new millennium, the strength of the wartime forces has dropped from some 435,000 troops to approximately 350,000. There will be approximately 250,000 troops in the regional forces and 100,000 troops in the operational forces by the end of 2008 (see Finnish Security and Defence Policy, 2004). The regional forces, to which the new local defence troops also belong, will be used to protect vital military and civilian infrastructures, and to control areas in the country which are deemed to be crucial for the defence of the nation.

With a decisive political census, general conscription is seen to form the core of the Finnish defence. Conscription is maintained, even if the number of wartime troops is decreased. General conscription is considered to guarantee the training and mobilisation of the necessary number of troops for the defence of entire country. The average age of operational troops can be kept suitably low as well, and the sufficiency of troops in the reserve can be guaranteed. A sufficiently large reserve is also seen as necessary for the allocation of personnel to positions essential to the vital functions of society. The general conscription is first and foremost a cost-effective way to implement the defence of the entire territory of the nation as well as to carry out the other tasks of the defence forces.

The national service training system, which also forms the basis for the conscript service, is currently being developed to form an entity comprising call-up, conscript training, refresher training, voluntary exercises run by the defence forces, and voluntary defence training. The competence acquired during the compulsory national service will be taken into account more widely in the national education system (see Finnish Security and Defence Policy, 2004).

The overall aim of the structural measures in the defence forces is not only to rationalise, but also to create monetary savings of 50 million euros per year to be allocated to development projects. This will require permanent savings in personnel and real estate expenditures. The rising costs of acquisition and maintenance of defence materiel will force the defence forces to put increasing emphasis on cost-efficient action. The defence budget will remain at approximately 2.2 billion euros per year. The share of defence budget of GDP has varied during the last 12 years from 1.66 per cent in 1994, with a defence budget of 1.5 billion euros, to 1.22 per cent in 2001 with a defence budget of 1.65 billion euros. Currently, the share is 1.43 per cent (Finland: Ministry of Defence, 2006).[9]

It seems that for economic reasons Finland is being forced to reduce the future number of wartime troops. According to estimates, the number of the troops will be further reduced to 250,000 during the next decade (Kaskeala, 2006a.) This may affect the principle of territorial defence in a longer perspective. This remains to be seen. The next White Paper on Finnish Security and Defence Policy, which is to be published in the autumn of 2008, has to draw guidelines for these issues as well. So far, the basis of the trinity of Finnish Defence is clear cut: *military non-alignment* will be kept, *territorial defence* will form the basis for military defence, and the *general conscription* will be further developed.

---

9 See Ministry of Defence, *Division of Defence Spending*, <http://www.defmin.fi/ ?l=en&s=120>.

Support of other national authorities

Territorial defence in 2010 places a clearer focus on defending strategic targets and the vital functions of society. At the same time many of the wide-ranging security threats are interlinked, difficult to predict and multifaceted, and may arise with little or no warning. Preparedness for wide-ranging security threats is considered as the Finnish defence system is being developed. As an essential part of the preparedness to prevent or limit any use of force or any means of asymmetric warfare against society, further cooperation with other authorities is also included in defence planning. The defence forces' expertise, equipment, infrastructure and situational awareness information can be used to defend society in adequate ways – which at the same time provides the defence forces with information and expertise for the development of its own activities (Finland: Ministry of Defence, 2006).

The 2001 White Paper on Finnish Security and Defence Policy paid particular attention to the cross-border threats. In accordance with the report, the Government embarked on a project to define the areas vital to the functioning of society and to draft action and development plans. This government resolution and the related strategy, *Strategy for Securing the Functions Vital to Society*, defined society's vital functions and established targets and development policies that would guide each administrative branch of the government in dealing with its strategic tasks in all situations. An updated version of the strategy was published in the autumn of 2006. An important part of the process was the enhancement of defence forces' options for support to other national authorities – both in peacetime and in the different levels of security situations.[10]

Furthermore, the preparedness to support other countries' authorities as required by the European Union solidarity clause has also been taken into account in contemporary defence planning (see Finnish Security and Defence Policy, 2004). The clause requires the Union and its members to provide assistance to any Member State that is victim of a terrorist attack, or natural or man-made disaster. Assistance can be given by all available means, including military resources. Still, each Member State itself decides on the content and scope of the aid it will supply. It remains to be seen whether the clause will ever be fully applied due to the EU member states failure to approve the new Constitutional Treaty.

Participation in international military crises management

Participation in international crisis management operations is an important part of Finnish defence policy and is considered to support the development of the

---

10 The different levels of security situations are defined in *The Strategy for Securing the Functions Vital to Society 2006*. The Strategy describes the threats that jeopardise the vital functions and their stability. There are altogether nine threat scenarios, including 61 associated special situations. A competent ministry has been assigned to each special situation for the purposes of preparedness and situation control. Supporting ministries are also designated, if required. *See, The Strategy for Securing the Functions Vital to Society 2006*, Ministry of Defence of Finland, <http://www.defmin.fi/?l=en&s=335>.

preparedness of the defence forces. Capabilities for international cooperation and military crisis management are to be developed in accordance with the country's international obligations and the requirements of future operations. Currently, increasing attention is given to the development of rapid reaction capabilities for the use of the EU rapid reaction forces. Attention is also given to central requirements in international crisis management as well as to maintaining Finnish competence in high technology, quality, and professional know-how. Specialisation requires developing the materiel standard of international readiness units, and a closer commitment of specialist personnel to international duties.

The national political guidance combined with the EU capability requirements set the framework for the deployment of troops. Then, in order to ensure international military cooperation, the defence forces' operational and material interoperability is developed according to NATO standards and norms, certification procedures, and exercises. Technical interoperability programs began in 1995 when Finland joined NATO's Planning and Review Process. In addition to fulfilling the goals of international crisis management, the interoperability/partnership goals (IO/PG) has helped to fill the gaps needed for joint operations of Finnish key forces. In the coming years Finland will establish a capability for participating in more demanding crisis management operations. This will include further improvement of the capabilities of interoperability and force protection against wide-ranging security threats (Kerttunen et al., 2005; Santavuori, 2006).

Legislation concerning peacekeeping operations was revised in spring 2006 to provide a closer reflection of the new reality of crisis management. The revision was needed to allow Finnish participation in *inter alia* EU-mandated operations and to fully operate in rapid reaction forces operations. Previously, only mandates from the UN or the OSCE[11] were accepted as grounds for participation (see Finnish Security and Defence Policy 2004; Finland: Ministry of Defence of, 2006).

The international framework of Finnish defence

The threat of a conventional war has receded, particularly in Europe. At the same time national security remains linked to the wider international environment. After years of uncertainty, the security environment of the new millennium has slowly started to form. The wider spectrum of threats to comprehensive security has started to reflect on the external and internal security of European countries to an increasing degree. More traditional threats are combined with new types of risks, necessitating that the provision of security must include not only military means, but also numerous other sectors both at the national and international level. Threats such as international terrorism, organised crime, epidemics, natural disasters and the vulnerability of critical infrastructure have changed our concept of security (Martelius and Sallinen, 2006). Each country remains responsible for the security of its citizens, but effective international cooperation and the strengthening of the international legal order have become increasingly essential.

---

11 Organization for Security and Co-Operation in Europe.

The EU context

Rapid changes in the external environment mean that countries have to frame their security and defence policy in a wider context. Global security problems are shaping the objectives and opportunities of both single countries and international organisations. The European Union serves as an excellent example. Integration and enlargement of the EU has provided Europe with unprecedented stability and strength. Through its partnership and neighbourhood policies, the EU also helps to create sustainable stability in areas adjacent to the community. By strengthening its external capabilities, the EU aims to improve global security.

The major decision to take a direct role in military crisis management and to establish own military institutions as well as defence capability goals was made at the Helsinki European Council of December 1999. Steps had been taken before (Treaty of Maastricht in 1992, WEU operations as EU's policy goals and Treaty of Amsterdam in 1997, EU's full political responsibility for such operations and considering WEU as a tool), but the Helsinki European Council decisions formed the ground for the current work (Bailes et al., 2006).

During the last few years, the European Union has made great progress in its efforts to forge a common foreign and security policy (CFSP) and an European Security and Defence Policy (ESDP). Progress has been fast even if the member states failed to pass the new Constitutional Treaty. The EU has had the advantage of being able to combine a broad range of security-enhancing instruments for preventing and settling crises: political, humanitarian, development policy and economic instruments as well as military and civilian crisis management measures. As part of its common foreign and security policy, the European Union is currently building a capability for independent military crisis management. The goal is to play a more comprehensive role in international relations.

The challenges of globalisation, the cross-border nature of security threats and threats imposed by weak states (not least the security situation in the Balkans in the 1990s) have worked as catalysts for the emerging ESDP. Similarly, growing expectations towards the EU as the largest supplier of development assistance in the world and major player in global trade policy have furthered its development. Strengthening external capacity has been of great value for EU's credibility both inside the Union and towards third parties. The European Security Strategy adopted in December 2003 was a milestone in guiding and strengthening the Union as a global actor that would enable the Union to make a more coherent and efficient use of an extensive range of instruments for promoting its common values and security.

The Nordic countries, and especially Finland, Denmark and Norway, can be viewed as being united by a 'small-country' tradition, which has meant that national sovereignty has had a prominent position in their political values (Tiilikainen, 2006). During the Cold War, Finland's international position was characterised by its policy of neutrality and by its special relationship with the Soviet Union. The collapse of the Cold War system, including the Soviet Union, and the Swedish decision to join the European Union sometime later, provided ground for a change in Finnish policy. The reorientation proved to be comprehensive as Finland renounced its former policy of neutrality and replaced it with a firm commitment to European integration.

What was left from the former doctrine of neutrality was re-formulated as a policy of military non-alignment. This did not, however, prevent Finland from taking part in the development of ESDP, nor increased cooperation with the NATO Partnership for Peace cooperation (ibid.).

In total, the changes taken by Finland in 1994–95 were less dramatic than might be thought. It was more a question of the Finnish security policy instruments being adapted to new political conditions. Finland has traditionally been very pragmatic in its defence and security policy, which meant that Finnish EU-membership had clear security implications from the beginning. Finland's line of action is based on a credible national defence, the functioning of society, a consistent foreign policy as well as a strong international position and an active participation as a member of the EU. Finland is working with the other member countries to strengthen the European Union as a security community and as an international actor. The Union's coherence, solidarity, and common commitments in this area will serve to enhance Finland's security. The central goal here is to participate in the Union's growing cooperation on military and civilian capabilities and in the creation of new capability goals, especially to improve the quality of the capabilities.

Currently, Finland is supporting the creation of independent crisis management capability for the European Union and is in favour of further strengthening that capability. Closer cooperation between the EU and NATO serves as an important basis for the build-up and use of this capability. All in all, during its Presidency, Finland placed great value on good relations and seamless cooperation with third parties such as the UN, the African Union, the OSCE, and last but not least, NATO.

From the Finnish point of view, the European Defence Agency (EDA) is an essential actor in future EU cooperation and integration, helping the Member States to identify common needs and promoting collaboration to provide common solutions in the area of capabilities. Future work will focus on three major strategies: The Capability Development Plan, an European Research and Technology strategy, and an European Defence Technological and Industrial Base strategy. These strategies will be built on '*the Long-Term Vision of ESDP Capability and Capacity Needs*' work which was endorsed at the Levi ministerial meeting in Finland in October 2006 (Finland: Ministry of Defence, 2006).

In the context of the EU it is important to mention the Finnish EU presidency which commenced on 1 July 2006. The guiding principle for the Finnish presidency was to further enhance the EU as a credible and coherent global actor. Finland had interesting challenges related to the ESDP during its presidency. In the field of *operations,* the main goals for the Finnish presidency were the assessment of ongoing operations (ALTHEA operation in Bosnia & Herzegovina and EUFOR RD operation in the Democratic Republic of Congo being purely military crisis management operations), managing possible future operations (Kosovo and Lebanon serving as examples, even though the latter operates under UNIFIL mandate), and preparations for future challenges. Close *coordination between military and civilian crisis management activities* (Finland: Ministry of Defence 2006) was of high priority as well.

The ongoing *capabilities work*, a third key issue, was to produce capabilities for future operations. During Finland's previous EU presidency in 1999, the *Helsinki*

Headline Goal was initiated, and since then much work has been done to further develop military capabilities. The special focus of the Headline Goal was to improve EU rapid reaction capability by developing the Battle Group concept. The key objective was to enable deployment in order to start implementing missions within 10 days of the decision to launch an operation. Full operational capability to launch two rapid response operations simultaneously was to be achieved as from January 2007. A historical milestone in itself, and of special importance to Finland, is that the German–Dutch–Finnish battle group, along with the French-Belgian group, will be the first on stand-by readiness. It is argued that the battle group concept represents a turning point for the Finnish crisis management tradition, and the nature of the groups is something new and very different compared to traditional peacekeeping and military crisis management (Finland: Ministry of Defence, 2006: 8; Kerttunen et al., 2005).

NATO

The Euro-Atlantic Partnership Council (EAPC) and Partnership for Peace (PfP) provide the framework for Finland's cooperation with NATO (Salo, 2006).[12] The EAPC and the PfP cooperation provide Finland with an opportunity to cooperate in security policy-making, participate in crisis management tasks in NATO-led operations, and improve national capabilities and interoperability through the NATO Planning and Review Process (PARP). Finland also participates in exercises and in civil emergency planning cooperation.

For Finland, the most important and concrete element of the PfP is crisis management cooperation (Hagelstam and Sallinen, 2005).[13] Finland offers the same troops for operations led by NATO, the EU or the UN. The PARP process has helped Finland make its military forces more interoperable with the alliance and through Partnership Goals, Finland has enhanced its national crisis management capabilities. PARP is considered to support Finnish national defence as well. The development of interoperability means focusing on advanced technology. The key areas are command and control, communications and intelligence (Salo, 2006).

Finland has been an active participant in PfP, and follows NATO's transformation and developments of PfP closely. In order to strengthen the military dimension of the PfP, the development of the Operational Capabilities Concept (OCC) has become an important element. The OCC refocuses existing PfP tools and introduces new

---

12 Finland has been member of EAPC since May 1997 and taken part into the Partnership for Peace Program (PfP) since 1994. Finland has also been observer in the North Atlantic Cooperation Council since 1992. See: Tietoja *Suomen kokonaismaanpuolustuksesta*, 2006; interview with Adviser Krista Salo, European Crisis Management Branch, International Division, Defence Staff, 5 September 2006.

13 Finland has been, or is currently involved in NATO-led ground operations (IFOR/ SFOR in Bosnia, KFOR in Kosovo, and ISAF in Afghanistan). Finland has also been twice responsible for the coordination and command of KFOR brigade C in Kosovo directly under the KFOR Commander. See Hagelstam and Sallinen 2005, *Homeland Security in Finland in Protecting the Homeland: European Approaches to Societal Security – Implications for The United States*.

mechanisms and elements, making a more detailed evaluation of military capabilities possible. Through the OCC evaluations, NATO can be certain that the partnership forces can fully cooperate with the allies. The importance of the OCC will be emphasised when NATO allows PfP countries to take part in its own exercises and plans their entry into more demanding operations (ibid.).

In February 2004, the Ministry of Defence published a report on the effects of a possible membership in a military alliance on the development of the Finnish defence system and to the defence administration (Finland: Ministry of Defence, 2004). During recent years, there has been a lively discussion on whether or not Finland should join NATO. The thematic discussion has been especially vigorous during both parliamentary and presidential elections. In this sense Finland differs from its neighbour, Sweden, where no security policy-related discussion has played a part in the latest elections. Parliamentary elections were held in Finland in March 2007 and the next White Book on Security and Defence Policy is to be published in the autumn of 2008. It is too early to speculate whether Finland is willing to change its attitude towards military alignment after these elections and in the next White Paper. The membership question is politically sensitive, but in practical terms it would be very easy – interoperability of the Finnish defence forces is already high. Finnish non-alignment and neutrality have always been more pragmatic than a matter of principle.

Participation in international crises management

Taking into account the EU troop requirements, the performance requirements of the PfP planning and assessment process and Nordic crisis management cooperation are used to develop Finland's international crisis management capacity. Finland also contributes to the development and implementation of the EU's resource and materiel cooperation.

The need for more diverse and demanding crisis management missions in the international operating environment is evident. Contemporary crisis management demands greater flexibility, faster response and continuous adjustment to the changing security situation. Crisis management requires swift decision-making at all levels as well as sufficient military resources on higher readiness than previously. In the last few years, Finland has participated in two or three crisis management operations simultaneously. Participation in more traditional military crisis management and peacekeeping operations will remain at the present level (Finland: Ministry of Defence, 2006).[14]

The development of EU rapid response capabilities is a milestone in the field of military crisis management. As described above, self-sufficient battle groups are being established as a part of the development of a rapid deployment capability within the wider framework of the EU desire to add a military dimension to its

---

14 In December 2006, Finland was participating in 11 operations with some 850 troops. In addition to this some 160 soldiers are in readiness in the EUBG (EU Battlegroup) in early 2007. See The Finnish Defence Forces, *Operaatiot*, http://www.mil.fi/rauhanturvaaja/operaatiot/.

otherwise wide range of security political tools. Finland will take part in two groups: the German–Dutch–Finnish group that will be on readiness for the first time in early 2007, with approximately 160 troops; and the Nordic Battle group that will be on readiness in early 2008 – with approximately 200 troops (Finland: Ministry of Defence, 2006;[15] Kerttunen et al., 2005). During the Finnish EU presidency work towards full operational capability of the battle groups will be completed. In addition, new initiatives on the maritime and air dimensions of rapid response capability are taken forward (Finland: Ministry of Defence, 2006).

However, it is important to note that in the Finnish defence system, participation in international crisis management is primarily to support the development and the credibility of national defence. The development and training of forces for international deployment is based on national troop production. (Troop production is a commonly used term in this context.) International training is given in designated military units. All troops, which are trained for international tasks, are primarily trained for national defence tasks. Most of the capabilities used in international crisis management operations simultaneously belong to those reserved for national defence. Only materiel with special requirements is procured separately. Even the battle group contributions are seen to enhance this overall goal. In many cases internal political factors have outweighed the external pressure for change. In practice, this means that the idea of a national defence is so deep-rooted that many politicians are not ready to give the mandate for the defence forces to act based purely on criteria set by the international operations and crisis management.[16] It is also considered that our resources are so limited that we need to combine the elements of national and international actions.

In addition to more demanding crisis management operations and capabilities, Finland may face a growing pressure to increase its contribution to international operations. This will put greater pressure on the Finnish system where national requirements direct the tasks and the future development of the defence forces. Enhanced international cooperation is a double-edged sword; it guarantees greater security, but it also increases national dependence on partners and greater responsibility for common security. Countries must be able to bind themselves to collective engagements and adjust national modes of operation and ambitions to international cooperation. At the same time, the rising overall costs and especially the cost development of defence materiel commits the defence forces to make a choice between enhanced international cooperation and development of national capabilities. It is clear that these elements do not necessarily compete, but neither are synergies automatic.

All in all, binding responsibilities and restrictive realities lead to the ultimate question: What incentives does Finland (and other countries) have behind its

---

15 See Ministry of Defence, *EU Battlegroups*, http://www.defmin.fi/?l=en&s=90.

16 President Halonen and Minister of Foreign Affairs Tuomioja speak frequently in international solidarity and about the problems caused by globalisation. This way of thinking reflects strongly also on Finnish Security and Defence Policy and underlines the desire for keeping international crisis management as a balanced part of an otherwise strong national defence.

international engagements? Do we want to test national capabilities in an international environment and/ or bring international know-how to Finnish defence forces as we have done so far? Or do we maybe have a wider political agenda for participation in the future? An answer to these questions is very important. Finland's incentive behind the participation in international operations is an interesting combination of binding responsibilities due to international engagements, bearing responsibility for international security situation and of a peacekeeping tradition. The participation in the battle groups concept will effect this tradition of policy-making, although we do not know how at the present time. There has not been a common discussion concerning the future incentives. As for its neighbouring countries, Finland wants to safeguard shared democratic values and to further democratic development in the world. But as stated, Finland takes part in the international operations first and foremost due to the need for common responsibility in crisis situations, secondly due to the fact that different crises may affect Finnish security directly or indirectly, and thirdly due to fact that the Finnish defence forces gain valuable know-how. At the same time the international credibility remains high (Kaskeala, 2006b).

Defence materiel procurement

The availability of sufficient and up-to-date military equipment is an essential part of defence capability. International defence materiel cooperation is one of the means to achieve this end, and may cover the whole life cycle of defence materiel, ranging from research and development to the eventual discharge of materiel. The aim is to gain technological and economic benefits by avoiding duplication of efforts and achieving an economies of scale. Defence materiel procurement is regulated by national legislation and the European Union regulations concerning public procurement. In compliance with the Finnish defence administration's general principles of procurement, the operational preconditions for domestic defence materiel industry must be safeguarded and central questions concerning international cooperation must be taken into account: invitations for tender are primarily aimed at the other EU countries and Nordic countries. Procured materiel must also fulfil the requirements of interoperability, and possible European cooperation has to be taken into account in the procurement process.

The domestic know-how in various fields of the defence industry is of great importance to national defence and military supply of security (Finland: Ministry of Defence 2006). When the Finnish defence forces make large purchases of defence material from foreign suppliers, industrial participation (formerly offset deals) is required. Supply contracts are usually subject to the condition of offset when the value of the procurement exceeds 10 million euros. Industrial participation is designed to safeguard domestic security of supply. The aim is to involve the industry in materiel and technology projects already at the planning stage.

On a national level, the Finnish defence industry must manage three essential areas of competence. These are: 1) the assemblage, maintenance and repair of large, technologically complex systems, 2) the management of information systems technology and systems integration, and 3) availability (and if necessary, manufacture) of critical components and spare parts (Finland: Ministry of Defence 2006).[17]

Finland participates in international defence materiel cooperation both bilaterally and multilaterally. Bilateral cooperation extends to the fields of research, development, production, maintenance, quality assurance and procurement. Finland is also involved in various multilateral forums, including:

- The European Defence Agency (EDA)
- Nordic Defence Materiel Cooperation (NORDAC)
- NATO's Partnership for Peace (PfP)
- NATO Maintenance and Supply Agency (Finland acts as an observer)
- NATO Munitions Safety Information Analysis Centre (MSIAC) (Finland: Ministry of Defence 2006).

The European Defence Agency has rapidly developed into an important actor in the field of European defence capabilities. Finland has adopted an active role in the EDA together with Sweden. A new era for defence procurement in the European Union began on 1 July 2006 with the introduction of a regime designed to increase transparency and competition in the European Defence Equipment Market. The idea of the European Defence Equipment Market was to broaden business opportunities for defence companies and strengthen the global competitiveness of European industry. European countries have committed themselves to procure defence equipment from each other if the offer is the best available instead of automatically contracting with a national supplier. Limited defence budgets, and the fact that European countries have to integrate their defence business if they are to sustain a globally competitive defence technological and industrial base in Europe, have forced countries to cooperate. This is also a major step for Finland (European Defence Agency 2006).

As an example of the Nordic Defence Materiel Cooperation, Finland, Sweden and Norway have made a joint purchase of NH 90 multi-role helicopters from joint European NH industries. The countries based their decisions to purchase this model on a recommendation made by the Nordic Standard Helicopter Program Office. NH 90 was estimated to best fulfil common and national requirements, and would be the most suitable for the three Nordic nations. The common selection also forms a basis for further cooperation in logistics and training, and for possible cooperation regarding crisis management. The need for tactical transport aircraft, and especially transport helicopters (NH 90), is in evidence especially in the context of Nordic Battle Group and forms a basis for future cooperation. Another objective is to secure the participation of relevant Nordic industry in the manufacturing and assembly of the helicopters as well as to gain know-how on sophisticated technology (Finland: Ministry of Defence 2006).[18]

---

17 See Ministry of Defence, *Defence materiel industry and industrial participation*, http://www.defmin.fi/?l=en&s=150.

18 The process has been delayed at the moment. The manufacturer has not been able to deliver the helicopters in the frame of the original timetable. *See*: Ministry of Defence, *Defence Materiel Procurement*, http://www.defmin.fi/index.phtml?l=en&s=133.

Public–Private Partnership in the Finnish Defence Forces

Cooperation between the defence forces and civil society is both old and familiar, but remains controversial to some extent (Solstrand, 2005). Traditionally, the defence forces have been self-sufficient in many respects. The new millennium with its changed security environment, new security threats, high-tech weapon systems and limited financial resources has changed the culture of the defence forces, brought new tasks and added pressure to increase the cost-effective use of these limited resources. This development has also emphasised the need for closer cooperation with other parts of society. In addition, the common need for rationalisation of public services – 'more value for money' thinking – has affected the defence forces.

The foundation for the public–private partnership in defence forces was laid down in 2002 when the Ministry of Defence launched the *Strategic Partnership Initiative* (SPI). The initial aims of the initiative were to direct, coordinate and evaluate seven different areas of development and pilot projects linked to these areas (Finland: Ministry of Defence, 2003).[19]

The basic idea is that the Finnish defence forces comprise a multi-divisional concern with a *raison d'être* to prepare for a crisis, but normally operating under peacetime conditions. The most significant expenses of the concern, in addition to salaries and wages, comprise materiel administration including maintenance and repairs, telecom and data communications (the defence forces being one of the largest telecom operators in the country), different manufacturing activities, logistics, and real estate and facilities management.

The SPI is based on a vision where the future defence forces exist as a logistical system with the longest-term-possible integration with the rest of the public sector and with private business, and where the structure does not need to be changed with increasing stages of readiness. The vision emphasises features such as openness, transparency, flexibility and dynamism – with the defence forces as an actor in the modern, networked information society. The objective of the SPI is to focus the resources of the defence forces on core functions and processes, and to identify, develop and implement new ways to arrange its support activities. Concurrently, the fine line between the core functions and support elements is diminishing every day.

The strategic partnership was chosen to be the goal for cooperation between the defence forces and its civilian co-partners right from the beginning. There has been discussion both nationally and internationally how we should define the concept of strategic partnership. In the Finnish context, strategic partnership is defined as a long-term cooperative business relationship between the client (the national defence forces) and the service provider. Cooperation is to be founded upon mutual trust, with characteristics such as continuity, broad in-depth exchange of information between the partners, and common goals of development. *A unique feature of strategic partnerships in the defence forces is the always-present aspect of preparation for*

---

19 First initiatives were made in the areas of food services, clothing services, health care, facilities managements, salaries, transportation services and maintenance services. See The Finnish Defence Forces, *Puolustushallinnon kumppanuusohjelma*, http://tietokannat.mil.fi/kumppanuusohjelma/.

a crisis. The main goal is that a strategic partnership is a cooperative relationship that continues unchanged during times of crisis with the defence forces remaining closely networked with the rest of society as part of the concept of total defence (Finland: Ministry of Defence 2006).

The latest White Paper on Defence and Security Policy states that partnership arrangements with service providers will form part of the defence forces' controlled restructuring. In future, necessary support functions and services are to be procured from specialist providers under long-term contracts. A reassessment of the need for efficiency and practicality of various support functions will be part of this process. This reassessment is part of a new development and rationalisation programme based on the latest White Paper. The intention is to facilitate the delivery of support services partly or wholly in cooperation with strategic partners from both public and private sectors. The aim is to create a service centre network which can be linked to equivalent systems in other parts of public services. Service centres are service concentrations inside the defence forces. As an example, the following areas of support services have been, or are currently, subject to such rationalisation initiatives:

- Food services: Creation of service centres in the beginning of 1.1.2006. A service centre leads 24 military restaurants. First partnerships created with civilian food provider, Amica Ravintolat Oy, in Reserve Officers School and in Kotka Coastal Area in 1.1.2005 with a three year contract.
- Clothing: Currently there are three clothing centres which are responsible for repair and washing services. In addition to this normal equipment storage is maintained. The basis for clothing services is strategic partnerships.
- Facilities management: Facilities management project will be further developed. As a part of this work the defence forces have given up ownership of real estates and land areas, and they are now owned partly by state and partly by private companies. An important role inside the concept is given to the defence forces' Materiel Command.
- Information technology: The strategic partnership initiative's goal is to structure the defence forces' information technology services as a centralised entity. The defence forces new command and control system is firmly linked to this entity.
- Health care: Creation of a strategic partnership with the public health services in the areas of special health care and medical supplies from 1.1.2006. The central military hospital was closed down as a part of this process. Military health care will also provide the basic health care in the future. It will also concentrate on research, development and training duties.
- Financial (including salaries) and personnel management: Creation of a service centre as of 1.3.2005. Provides concentrated financial and personnel management services for entire defence forces. In future this service centre may be linked to the equivalent systems in other parts of public services.
- Materiel functions: Currently ongoing negotiations on strategic partnership which is supposed to activate on 1.1.2008. The concrete goal for savings is 10 to 20 per cent (Miettinen, 2006).

The concrete goals for the strategic partnerships and service centre networks in general are increased cost effectiveness and concrete monetary savings of up to 15 – 25 per cent. As already mentioned, another aim is the integration of the defence forces with the rest of society to an extent where the structure does not need to be changed in a crisis. In the long term, the goal is to ensure that through strategic partnerships, society – including the private sector – takes part in the development of high quality support functions. So far, further experiences are limited due to the project's novelty. In the areas where strategic partnerships are chosen, expectations of clear benefits of the use of external entrepreneurs are very high (Miettinen, 2006).

Also relevant to an efficient strategic partnership are optimally shared workloads and shared risk assessments. As a result partners can specialise on their core functions. Other import factors are:

- cost-effective production of core functions
- improved working processes and high-quality goods and services
- structural flexibility and allocation of human resources to the core functions.

The need for successful networking in different forms has become increasingly evident both at national and international levels. New competence emerges in the interplay between partners where information capital can be incorporated. Self-learning is not enough. Information capital has become the most significant factor in competition while also being the key factor for the new competence.

It is essential for the defence forces to know how to act as customer. The defence forces need personnel with the required skills for purchasing and knowledge of competitive tools. Own processes and cost structure must be clear and comparable. At the same time it is necessary that the command is engaged in the processes. If needed, organisational changes together with necessary amendments to the existing norms should be carried out without disincentives.

A well-planned and executed strategic partnership is becoming a key element for success and competitiveness. At the same time such partnerships represent a clear doctrinal change for the defence forces. Suddenly, their role has changed from that of a service producer to that of a customer. In some cases it has even given up its old ownership role totally, and has become purely a user of the services, facilities services serving as an example. This process as a whole may be painful and demanding. The organisation must be ready for setbacks in some areas. The reforms demand much from the organisation and its personnel, and it takes years before it can be judged whether the rationalisation processes have worked and the strategic partnerships have achieved the goals.

Conclusions

In this chapter, I have summarised the history and the modernisation process of Finnish defence with the purpose of describing the effects of internationalisation and privatisation. Based on this, I would argue that the denationalisation process has not affected Finnish defence as much as its western neighbours. In fact, there is not even a proper Finnish translation for the word 'denationalisation!' Denationalisation has clearly taken place, for example in the forms of growing interoperability, but at the same time Finnish defence remains a unique combination of a strong traditional national defence system and new challenges, close cooperation with the EU and with NATO, though with the latter as a non-allied partner. In this process, history has had a deep impact on Finnish defence and its current nature.

The Finnish Defence is a strongly national enterprise and the Finnish defence system as a whole maintains strong national characteristics. As previously mentioned, the central trinity of Finnish defence is still clear: *military non-alignment*; *territorial defence* and *general conscription*. Nevertheless, the privatisation process has also come a long way at the national level, even though it is mainly concentrated on service and support elements and driven primarily by the principle of cost-effectiveness. This development supports the idea of a denationalisation of defence: the state does not retain the ultimate control over all of the elements alone, and which may affect the use of military force.

In the coming years, two main questions are required be answered – strongly guiding the direction of Finnish defence – whether Finland will join NATO, or continue on the current track of non-alignment; and the size of future defence budgets. All in all, the development of a credible defence system requires increased concentration on core functions and further restructuring of the defence forces. This is mainly due to the increasing complexity of threats and the operating environment, the expansion of international cooperation, the rapid advancement and rising cost of technology, and demographic trends in Finland. Even if the objective should be to keep the nature of the Finnish defence very 'national', it is evident that the system will be increasingly affected by external factors and actors arising from developments in technology and changes in warfare, the operating environment and international commitments together with restrictions set by budgetary constraints. These factors will further the denationalisation process of the Finnish defence in the coming years.

References

Literature

Bailes, A. J. K. et al. (eds) (2006), *The Nordic Countries and The European Security and Defence Policy* (New York: Oxford University Press).
—— and Tiilikainen, T. (2005), *The Nordic Countries and the EU-NATO Relationship* in *The Nordic Countries and The European Security and Defence* [The Nordic Countries and The European Security and Defence Policy] in Bailes, A. J. K. et al. (eds).
Finnish Security and Defence Policy 2004, Government Report 6/2004.
Hagelstam, A. and Sallinen, A. (2005), *Homeland Security in Finland* [Protecting the Homeland: European Approaches to Societal Security – Implications For The United States] in Hamilton, D. et al. (eds).

Hamilton, D. et al. (eds) (2005), *Protecting the Homeland: European Approaches to Societal Security – Implications For The United States*, Center for Transatlantic Relations (Washington D.C.: The Paul H. Nitze School of Advanced International Studies).

Kerttunen, M. et al. (eds) (2005), *EU Battlegroups – Theory and Development in the Light of Finnish – Swedish Co-operation*, 2(30) – Department of Strategic Studies (Helsinki: Hakapaino Oy).

Kuusisto, R. and Rantapelkonen, J. (eds) (2005), *Struggling to Understand Information War*, 2(1) – Department of Tactics and Operations Arts, 2(15); Department of Leadership and Management Studies (Helsinki: Hakapaino Oy).

Maanpuolustuskorkeakoulu (2005), *Tietoja maanpuolustuksesta 2006* [Information on Total Defence 2006] (Helsinki: Edita Prima Oy).

Martelius, J. and Sallinen, A. (2006), *Societal Security Bridging Hard and Soft Security*, OSCE Review no. 2/2006.

Matlary, J. H. and Østerud, Ø. (2005), *Mot et avnasjonalisert forsvar?* [Towards a De-nationalised Defence?] (Oslo: Abstrakt forlag AS).

Miettinen, P. J. (2006), *Kumppanuuksista puolustushallinnossa – katsaus kumppanuuden ulottuvuuksiin, tavoitteisiin ja keinoihin* [Strategic Partnerships in Defence Administration – A View on the Dimensions, Goals and Resources of Partnerships] [Huoltopäällikkö]. In Usvasalo et al. (eds).

Ministry of Defence (2004), Mahdollisen sotilaallisen liittoutumisen vaikutukset *Suomen puolustusjärjestelmän kehittämiselle ja puolustushallinnolle* [The Effects of Possible Military Alignment for Finnish Defence System and Defence Administration] (Helsinki: Ministry of Defence).

—— (2005), *Puolustusministeriön tulevaisuuskatsaus* [The Future Review of the Ministry of Defence] (Helsinki: Ministry of Defence).

—— (2006), *Securely into the Future*, Ministry of Defence Strategy 2025 (Helsinki: Ministry of Defence).

Solstrand, R. H. (2005), *Offentlig-Privat Partnerskap i det nye Forsvaret. Mot et avnasjonalisert forsvar?* [The Private-Public Partnership in the New Defence Forces – Towards a De-nationalised Defence?] in Matlary J.H., Østerud Ø. (eds).

Usvasalo, U., Saarinen, T. (eds) (2006), *Huoltopäällikkö* [Chief of Logistics] (Jyväskylä: Kirjapaino Oy)

Internet

Embassy of Finland in Latvia, History – The Finnish Jaeger Movement, <http://www.finland.lv/doc/en/embassy/jaeger.html>.

European Defence Agency, Birth of European Defence Equipment Market with Launch of Code of Conduct, <http://www.eda.europa.eu/news/2006-06-30-0.htm>.

Ministry of Defence, EU Battlegroups, <http://www.defmin.fi/index.phtml?l=en&s=90>.

—— International Defence Materiel Cooperation, <http://www.defmin.fi/index.phtml?l=en&s=151>.

—— Defence Materiel Industry And Industrial Participation, <http://www.defmin. fi/index.phtml?l=en&s=150>.

—— Defence Materiel Procurement, <http://www.defmin.fi/index.phtml?l=en&s=133>.

—— Division of Defence Spending, <http://www.defmin.fi/?l=en&s=120>.

—— The Strategic Partnership Initiative Of the Finnish Ministry of Defence, <http:// www.defmin.fi/index.phtml?l=en&s=177>.

Ministry of Foreign Affairs, Main outlines of Finnish history, <http://virtual.finland. fi/netcomm/news/showarticle.asp?intNWSAID=25909#gran>.

—— Main outlines of Finnish History, The Independet Republic, <http://virtual. finland.fi/netcomm/news/showarticle.asp?intNWSAID=25909#inde>.

—— Main outlines of Finnish History, The Impossible Happened Thrice, <http:// virtual.finland.fi/netcomm/news/showarticle.asp?intNWSAID=25906>.

The Finnish Defence Forces, Puolustushallinnon kumppanuusohjelma [The Partnership Program of the Defence Administration], <http://tietokannat.mil.fi/ kumppanuusohjelma/>.

—— Security and freedom of choice, <http://www.mil.fi/perustietoa/esittely/historia/ index_2_en.dsp;>.

—— Armed forces established during Civil War, <http://www.mil.fi/perustietoa/ esittely/historia/index_3_en.dsp>.

—— German leading the armed forces, <http://www.mil.fi/perustietoa/esittely/ historia/index_4_en.dsp>.

—— Aiming for territorial integrity, <http://www.mil.fi/perustietoa/esittely/historia/ index_6_en.dsp>.

—— Finland attacks, <http://www.mil.fi/perustietoa/esittely/historia/index_8_ en.dsp>.

—— After the war, <http://www.mil.fi/perustietoa/esittely/historia/index_9_en.dsp>.

—— From Defence Establishment to Defence Forces, <http://www.mil.fi/perustietoa/ esittely/historia/index_10_en.dsp>.

—— Operaatiot [Operations], <http://www.mil.fi/rauhanturvaaja/operaatiot/>.

Lectures and interviews

Kaskeala, J. Speech by the Chief of Defence at the opening ceremony of National Total Defence Course 178/06, 18 September 2006.

—— Speech by the Chief of Defence at the 50th Anniversary Celebration of Finnish Peacekeeping in Tampere, 4 December 2006.

Martelius, J., Director of Research, Research and Development Unit, Ministry of Defence of Finland. Personal interview, several occasions.

Miettinen, P. J. Lakimiesliiton koulutus [A Training Session for the National Lawyers Union], 12 September 2006.

—— Senior Adviser, Financial Unit, Ministry of Defence of Finland. Personal interview, 5 September 2006.

Salo, K. (2006), Adviser, International Division, Planning Department, Defence Command, Finland. Personal interview, 5 September 2006.

Santavuori, M. (2006), former Head of the European Crisis Management Branch, International Division, Defence Command. Personal interview, 8 December 2006.

Index